HAUNTED
LAKE MICHIGAN

by Frederick Stonehouse

Lake Superior Port Cities Inc.

First Edition: September 2006

LAKE SUPERIOR PORT CITIES INC.
P.O. Box 16417
Duluth, Minnesota 55816-0417 USA
1-888-BIG LAKE (888-244-5253)
www.lakesuperior.com
Publishers of *Lake Superior Magazine* and *Lake Superior Travel Guide*

5 4 3 2 1

Library of Congress Cataloging-in-Publication Data

Stonehouse, Frederick, 1948-
    Haunted Lake Michigan / by Frederick Stonehouse. – 1st ed.
        p. cm.
    Includes bibliographical references and index.
    Contents: Ghost ships – Cursed ships – Shipboard and underwater – Missing, presumed lost – Lighthouse ghosts – Lakeside spirits – We are not alone.
    ISBN 0-942235-72-X
    1. Ghosts – Michigan, Lake, Region. 2. Shipwrecks – Michigan, Lake. I. Title
BF 1472.U6S755 2006
133.109774 – dc22   2006049314

Printed in the United States of America

                Editors: Paul L. Hayden, Konnie LeMay, Robert Berg
        Book Design: Mathew Pawlak
        Cover Design: Joy Morgan Dey, Mathew Pawlak
Inside Illustrations: Joy Morgan Dey
                Printer: Sheridan Books, Chelsea, Michigan

This book is dedicated to
those who seek the magnificent
folklore of Lake Michigan.

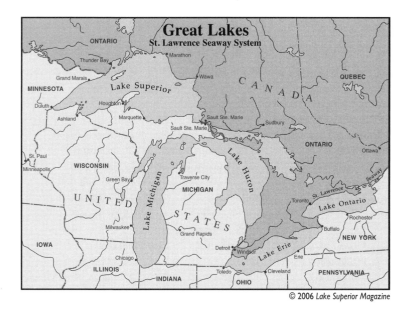

Lake Michigan Region

MICHIGAN

WISCONSIN

MICHIGAN

ILLINOIS

INDIANA

Illinois
1. Chicago
2. Evanston
3. Winnetka

Wisconsin
4. Kenosha
5. Milwaukee
6. Manitowoc
7. Two Rivers
8. Green Bay
9. Door Peninsula

10. Peshtigo
11. Chambers Island
12. Washington Island

Michigan
13. Menominee
14. St. Martin Island
15. Escanaba
16. Fayette
17. Gulliver
18. Beaver Island
19. Manitou Islands

20. Marion Island
21. Manistee
22. Ludington
23. Holland
24. Saugatuck
25. St. Joseph

Indiana
26. Michigan City
27. Indiana Sand Dunes
28. Gary

Contents

Great Lakes Regional Map. iii

Lake Michigan Region Map. iv

Introduction vi

Chapter 1 1
   SHIPBOARD AND UNDERWATER

Chapter 2 20
   GHOST SHIPS

Chapter 3 37
   CURSED SHIPS

Chapter 4 60
   MISSING, PRESUMED LOST

Chapter 5 68
   LIGHTHOUSE GHOSTS

Chapter 6 98
   LAKESIDE SPIRITS – MAINLAND

Chapter 7 142
   LAKESIDE SPIRITS – ISLANDS

Chapter 8 162
   MONSTERS – SEA, AIR & LAND

Chapter 9 174
   WE ARE NOT ALONE

Epilogue. 180

Endnotes 182

Bibliography. 188

Index 192

About the Author. 199

Introduction

I always loved ghost stories. Growing up on the New Jersey shore there were always tales of buried pirate treasure guarded by the ghosts of long dead buccaneers. According to legend the pirates always buried their treasure. It was part of the "Code of the Coast" so it had to be done. The pirate captain would lead the way to the secret location as two of the crew struggled along behind lugging a huge wooden chest bound with thick iron bands and filled with gold, silver and jewels. After the men dug a deep hole in an easily locatable site, one jumped to the bottom and the other carefully lowered the chest to him as the captain muttered his obligatory pirate curses about "shivering his timbers." Once the treasure was properly positioned the captain pulled two flintlock pistols from his leather belt. The first one roared and the pirate outside tumbled hard into the hole, a jagged puncture drilled through his forehead by a 68. caliber lead ball. Stepping up to the edge of the hole, the captain aimed and shot the second man. With both pirates laying dead over the chest the captain buried the treasure while singing, "Yo ho, ho and bottle of rum. 15 men on a dead man's chest, drink and the devil took the rest. Yo ho ho and a bottle of rum." The captain was now assured that only he knew the location of the loot. No swarthy son of a sea cow could double cross him now! According to the lore, burying at least one dead buccaneer with the treasure assured a ghost to guard it forever, or so goes pirate legend!

Lighthouses along the shore always had a ghost or two wandering around and phantom ships commonly cruised the coastal waters. Even yarns about beachcombing ghosts patrolling the lonely sands added to the stories making the Jersey shore a special place.

When I came to the Great Lakes, longer ago than I want to remember, I was amazed to find similar ghostly tales.

While I am a maritime historian, researching, teaching and recording the nautical history of the Great Lakes, I can't resist capturing a good ghost story when I find one. Every so often, I'll even go looking if the circumstance is right.

As a result of two earlier books I did, *Haunted Lakes, Great Lakes Ghost Stories, Superstitions and Sea Serpents* and a follow-on *Haunted Lakes II* (published by Lake Superior Port Cities), I am invariably asked if I believe in ghosts. I always answer that there are things that I feel we don't understand. I am also asked if I have ever seen a ghost. I dodge that question somewhat, but reading "Now What the Hell Was That?" in this book illustrates an example of my experience.

I am convinced that everyone who sails the lakes has a tale of something they experienced they can't explain, whether it is a light that shouldn't be there, the faint outline of a ship where the radar says there isn't anything or even a shadowy figure standing by the bow rail. Perhaps there is something special about being on the big water that energizes the imagination, or makes the mind sharper, better able to "see" things. I don't know, but I am certain there are things out there we don't understand.

It seems that in the process of every book I have written I discovered something I didn't expect. In *Haunted Lake Michigan* it was the haunted submarines. That there is one World War II submarine on Lake Michigan is surprising. That there are three is nothing short of amazing. And that all have ghost stories associated with them further stretches the imagination.

Are these Lake Michigan stories all documented and investigated by qualified investigators? Not by a long shot. That said, paranormal researchers have looked at or documented many of the occurrences of supernatural acts and continue to do so.

Others tales in *Haunted Lake Michigan* are folklore, tales told and retold from generation to generation. Still others are of more recent origin, unexplained mysteries that defy rational explanation. But all are true in the sense that someone experienced them.

I hope you enjoy reading *Haunted Lake Michigan*.

Frederick Stonehouse

CHAPTER 1

Shipboard & Underwater

If houses can be haunted, why not ships? Just as the spirits of previous residents still stalk the halls of homes, specters of sailors who have long "crossed the bar" still sail the lakes.

The schooner *Augusta*, of *Lady Elgin* infamy, later renamed the *Colonel Cook* in an unsuccessful effort to escape her tragic past, was reportedly haunted. One old-timer, who signed on the vessel before realizing who she was, claimed that every trip she lost a crewman overboard or injured one in another way.[1] Others remembered that she always had trouble getting crews. Sailors claimed that restless ghosts from the *Lady Elgin* constantly plagued her. During the dark night watches, the lifeless eyes of motionless silent corpses were said to stare vacantly from the foredeck at her living crew. By any account, the *Augusta* was not a happy ship. Sailors avoided her whenever possible and left as soon as they could find another berth. It is one thing to share the forecastle with a fellow who snores, but "living" with one who doesn't even breathe is too much.

Can the dead converse with the living? Can the desire to pass a last message overcome the last barrier between life and death? A particularly chilling ghost story that appeared in the December 15, 1899, issue of the Manistique, Michigan, *Courier* indicates it can happen. "Thanksgiving will ever remain a sad anniversary for the family of Captain W. H. Hargrove, of 897 Trumbull Avenue. Wednesday brought to their home the body of the only son, Benjamin L. Hargrove, who on Tuesday last fell 70 feet from the mast of the steambarge *Ira H. Owen*, at Erie, Pa., and died four hours after he struck the deck.

"A few nights before, the father, who is captain and owner of the schooner *John Kelderhouse*, was passing through the Straits of Mackinac, when through the darkness he suddenly saw a big barge bearing down on him. It was out of its proper course, but straightened in time to avert an accident. The two boats passed very close to one another and Captain Hargrove was standing at the rail in no amiable mood, when a voice sang out from the other ship.

"Hullow, father, where are you going?" Captain Hargrove recognized his son's voice.

"Chicago," he answered. And then, "How are you boy?"

"I'm all right," came the reply. "Are you?"

"Yes."

"Goodbye father. Take care of yourself."

"You do the same. Good-bye."

"The son had recognized his father's ship in the distance and bore down on her to exchange greetings.

"When Captain Hargrove arrived at Chicago he found awaiting a telegram announcing his son's death.

"The ill-fated young man, who was 27, was to have been married within a few weeks to a young lady of Belleville, Ontario. He had sent her money to make some purchases for the little home that was to have been theirs, and she was about to carry out his instructions when the news of his death came. The young man was formally a resident of Belleville and was a member of the Belleville lodge F and A."[2]

At 10:30 Monday night, November 29, 1897, a small tendril of black smoke curled skyward from the wooden steamer *Nahant*'s cargo hold. The steamer, moored to the Chicago, Northwestern Ore Dock Number 4 in Escanaba, Michigan, had already received half her iron ore cargo. The rest would be loaded the following morning. At the base of the billowing smoke column red flames licked hungrily at the dry wood of the old steamer. Unnoticed by the crew the fire escalated quickly. Apparently most of the men were enjoying the "delights" on Thomas Street, Escanaba's infamous and very hospitable red light district. Before anyone realized the danger, the flames were out of control and no action by the few crewmen remaining aboard could in the least contain it. Desperately, they ran for their lives, jumping from the ship to the temporary safety of the wooden dock. Despite their fast retreat, several men were burned, one severely enough to require hospitalization. Two of the crew, fireman Peter Bernstein and

deckhand Harold Miller, didn't get off in time. They were burned alive, cremated in the funeral pyre of the old *Nahant.*[3]

The flames soon spread from the *Nahant* to the wood ore dock, destroying the greater part of the structure despite the best efforts of the Escanaba Fire Department. Subzero temperatures certainly hampered the firefighters. Had the wind been north or northwest, all of the complex of ore docks, coal docks hoist and stockpiles, plus a large part of the Third and Fourth wards, could have burned to cinders. Many locals not directly affected by the fire considered the conflagration to be "indescribably grand" and the entire city turned out to watch in awe. It was nearly as much fun as the 4th of July fireworks. Regardless of the spectacle, the loss of the ore dock alone cost the Chicago Northwestern Railroad an estimated $250,000 to replace.

The following day, after the fire had burned itself out, the captain of the steamer and the Escanaba fire chief searched the smoking wreck for the remains of the two missing men. All they discovered was a small fragment of bone. Everything else was gone, obliterated in the hellish heat. Later the harbor tug *Delta* pushed the still floating steamer away from the remains of the ore dock and onto a nearby beach near today's municipal pier. She was not insured and was a loss of $30,000. In the 1940s, the wreck was removed to an area just north of Sand Point.

The bulk freighter *Nahant*, a frequent visitor to Escanaba, was built in 1873 at Springwell's yard at Clark Street in Detroit. She measured 251 feet long, 35 feet in beam and 16.2 feet in depth. Her original capacity was 909 tons. In 1880, she was sold to Milwaukee interests and rebuilt, increasing her capacity to 2,000 tons. As typical for the time, she had three masts capable of carrying sail to assist her if the wind was right. Her primarily power was a single cylinder, low-pressure steam engine.

The remains of the *Nahant* lay quietly along the shore until March 9, 1898. Late that night an upstanding Escanaba citizen was rounding the corner of Ludington Street and Smith Court when he was startled to see something "dancing" on the black hulk of the steamer. More curious than scared, the man carefully crept through the lumber piles of the I. Stephenson Company Mill toward the blackened hull. In the cold light of a full moon, he saw a "perfect apparition" standing on the wreck. For a short moment the ghost stood motionless, a sad look on its ghastly white face. Then it erupted with "demonlike laughter." In a flash, it catapulted to a distant part of the dead hulk and then vanished.

Although understandably shaken by what he had witnessed, the observer drew his overcoat tighter around his neck and huddled down deeper in the rough shelter of a lumber pile. He wanted to see if the mysterious spirit would return. In less than half an hour, the same or another ghost appeared in the wreckage. With shovel in hand, the silent specter went through the motions of digging. For two long minutes it continued with its unholy task, then it unexpectedly flew off toward the ore docks, waving the shovel wildly. A hideous, shrill scream of a poor soul suffering unbearable pain echoed over the docks. This was more than the man could take and he beat a hasty retreat.[4]

Were the two ghosts that of the dead *Nahant* crewmen? Was the first the watchman and the second the coal passer? Was there anything there at all or just the delusion of a wandering drunk?

Our paradigm is that we "expect" to see ghosts in the surface world – in our houses, old hotels, and graveyards or along lonely lakeshores. But if we accept the idea of ghosts, there is no reason to believe that they are confined to the surface of the planet. There is increasing anecdotal evidence they also inhabit the underwater world.

Numerous ships have sunk on the lakes with great loss of life. Scuba divers explore many of them and search for those still "missing." It isn't uncommon for divers to lose their lives while exploring wrecks. It can be dangerous business. In some instances divers perished in the open water, either from equipment failure or physiological problems. Others met their end after being trapped deep within the wreck, unable to find their way out. Desperately they searched for an exit until they emptied their air tanks, finally facing a ghastly and lonely death.

If there is any truth to the belief that spirits are often the result of violent death and that such spirits haunt the site of their demise, then these death ships should logically be home to spirits of both their drowned crews as well as lost divers. Their spirits are being held hostage by the wreck.

My experience is that real Great Lakes wreck divers usually have two common characteristics. They have little imagination in that they are not given to easy flights of fancy. Diving on the hulk of a long dead shipwreck is spooky enough. The water is cold and usually dark and deep. Visibility can be very limited, sometimes measured in inches. The divers also tend to be "macho," in that they admit to little bothering them and prefer to just work through problems. Blown dry suit seals or balky regulators, are no reason to end a dive. Neither is a small "bending" of bottom time. The macho characteristic is not exclusive to the male of the species. Female wreck divers also exhibit "macho" characteristics. No matter the sex, few real wreck divers will ever admit to feeling "uneasy" on a wreck or to getting "spooked."

But some divers will, when properly "loosened-up" with a libation or two (or six), claim that when diving some wrecks on which people lost their lives, they feel an overwhelming "presence" of not being alone, of someone or something else being with them. It is not necessarily a threatening sensation and can be somewhat comforting. Nonetheless, it is there. The reader must understand that real wreck divers generally dive alone. They may have started the dive with a buddy, but inevitably somewhere along the way, they separate (by design or accident).

It is not unusual to "hear" things on a wreck, a deep groaning or almost moaning or rumbling sound coming from everywhere and yet nowhere. When moving slowly though interior compartments every sound is magnified. Escaping air from a regulator doubtless causes sound. But not all of it. Some divers claim that if they stay very quiet in a wreck and just listen very hard, they can "hear" the faint, indistinct voices of people talking. It is never clear enough to discern words, but nonetheless is still there.

One of the earliest underwater ghost tales involves the wooden propeller *Westmoreland*, lost in Lake Michigan's infamous Manitou Passage on December 7, 1854. The narrow passage runs between the Michigan mainland and South and North Manitou Islands. It is a long-established shortcut for ships running between Chicago and the Straits of Mackinac. The big steamer was bound for Mackinac Island with a cargo of winter supplies, including a large amount of liquor and, as legend claims, $100,000 in gold. Ravaged by a terrible storm, the vessel became top-heavy with ice and foundered somewhere in the passage, taking 17 passengers and crew down with her.

Because of the rumored gold aboard, she became a much sought-after wreck by divers through the years. Reportedly she has been located several times, but the discovery has never been admitted or proven. There are divers who stand on top of the Sleeping Bear Dunes and look out into the Passage, muttering to themselves about finding the old *Westmoreland*.

There is a wonderful tale that soon after the loss, salvagers, who promptly put a hard-hat diver down on her, found the wreck. He reported the vessel sitting upright and relatively undamaged. Working his way into one of the cabins he discovered half a dozen lumberjacks still seated around the table playing cards. The stack of coins was piled high in the center of the table and each man's grubstake was still in front of him. Several of the jacks clutched cards in their hoary hands. Evidently the men were damned if the storm would stop their poker game. They would play to the end and let the devil take them if he wanted to. The diver closed the door and left, never finding the gold cargo.

There could be more truth to the hard-hat story than not. There is a story that the engines of the *Westmoreland* were recovered in 1874 and taken to Chicago. This, of course, means divers were on the wreck to make the recovery. Did they find any gold? If so, did they tell anyone? Are they the source of the card-playing ghosts tale?[5]

In the early evening of October 14, 1954, about four miles off Milwaukee, Wisconsin, in Lake Michigan, the 258-foot Dutch freighter *Prins Willem II* collided with the barge *Sinclair No.12* pulled by the tug *Sinclair Chicago*. The resulting crash tore a huge 20-foot-by-8-foot hole in the freighter. It was a fatal wound. The *Prins Willem II* continued on for two more miles before sinking bow first. Her well-trained crew of 30 safely escaped in lifeboats without injury.

The *Prins Willem II*'s infamous reputation is not the result of her collision loss, but rather the number of divers killed exploring her decaying carcass. To my knowledge, more divers have been killed investigating her than any other Great Lakes wreck. The first died in 1985, the second in 1989, the third in 1992 and the fourth in 1997. Certainly there have been numerous near misses, too. She has proven herself to be a very deadly encounter for the unwary.

The following story was related to me a couple of years ago over a few beers at a dive show. Whether it is true or false is unknown. In that regard, diving stories can be a lot like fishing stories. But the diver who related it was most earnest and believable.

"Man, that one scares me! It did the first time I dove it and it still does! It's a hell of a dive, lots of stuff to look at and explore, but after my last dive I don't think I'm going back. Look, I haven't told this to anyone before and I don't want my name used, but the last time was really weird. The second I hit her at about 40 feet I started to hear voices. I couldn't be sure what they were, it was kind of muffled like someone's talking and you can't quite make out what they are saying. Visibility was pretty good, 10 feet or so, and I looked at my buddy, but he looked all right so I gave him the 'OK' sign and we headed back for the engine room. There's lots of good stuff there, especially tools. All the way back the voices kept fading in and out. But I still couldn't make out any words. We started down into the engine room and it got black fast. There isn't a lot of light anyway. We both switched our lights on and kept moving down. I was leading, my buddy swimming behind me. The whole wreck is knocked over on a 45-degree angle so it is disorienting, but not too bad. By the time I got to the engine room I had lost my buddy. He must have stopped to look at something. Since we both had been on the *Willy* many times, I figured he would meet me in a few minutes. I was still hearing the voices, but still couldn't make them out. When I finally reached the engine room door, I gave a last look back for my buddy, didn't see him anywhere and I went on in.

"I was poking around in a corner when I had this feeling that I wasn't alone. I could feel someone else. I figured it was my missing buddy, so I turned around, but no one was there. Everything is black in there, so I easily would have seen his light. I swung my light around and still there was nothing. Then I saw it. Just above the engine was a diver just kind of floating there. It wasn't my buddy. I don't know who it was. I didn't see another boat when we tied up. The voices suddenly became louder and very clear, 'Get out, get out!' The diver I was looking at was not solid either. My light went right through him. I have never seen a ghost and up to now thought it was all BS. Well it isn't! The diver started to move, slowly finning his way past the engine and right through the wall and out of the engine room. I said, 'S__t, I'm out of here.' As I was swimming up the companionway toward the deck, I saw another ghost diver looking around a cabin door. I kept going. Once I reached the main deck I thought I saw another moving to my left. Now I was really rattled, right on the edge of panic. My buddy was waiting at the anchor line. I calmed down a bit then. When we got back to the boat, I asked where he had been. He said he stopped for a minute on the way to the engine room to look at something. When he turned back to continue, he briefly saw a diver heading up and around the corner. Thinking it was me and something was wrong, he followed, but lost him in the gloom. When he got to the deck he continued on to the anchor line figuring that he would meet me there whatever happened. Other than that, he had seen nothing. I didn't tell him what I saw!"[6]

Can it be that the souls of the lost sailors are still with the wreck and that it is their strong presence divers feel? Haunted houses frequently give this "presence" feeling to visitors. Why can't a sunken ship do the same to divers? The evidence seems to point to this inescapable possibility.

Many old sailors, especially on "dark and stormy nights," were always worried when they sailed past areas where other crews perished by shipwreck. Lake Michigan areas like the Straits of Mackinac, Manitou Passage and Death's Door Passage on the Door Peninsula were especially feared. Not only did some sailors claim to hear their death screams, but claimed the ghosts called out to them by name. Others remembered yarns of the ghosts actually climbing aboard their ships. These very sad spirits moved silently to their regular stations where they slowly went about normal duties as if they were still living. Before long, they would either vanish, or just climb noiselessly over the side, returning sorrowfully to their watery tombs. This type of haunting, especially, was feared on vessels that had lost crew during a previous accident and later were salvaged and returned to service. Superstitious sailors claimed that the dead crew always returned to their old ship. This phenomenon is not unique to the lakes and was most often reported by fishermen working the North Atlantic's Grand Banks. This was also particularly true of sailors from Cornwall in England where the belief has long been held. And many Cornishmen crewed ships on the lakes.

Ghostly happenings aboard ships are not just a thing of the past. They still occur today.

For a number of years I did periodic trips aboard several Great Lakes cruise ships as an onboard lecturer. My job was to introduce the passengers to the wonderful history of the Inland Seas. The pay was acceptable and since I believe the good Lord doesn't subtract any time spent "fooling around in boats" from your allotted time on earth, it is time well invested. As I am uncertain how the particular transportation line will react to these stories, I will not identify it. These are not experiences I had but rather were reported to me by both passengers and crew.

In one of the cabins, I think it was 54B, guests and stewardesses were startled to occasionally see the bunk depress as if someone just sat down on it. Passengers usually were very good-natured about it while housekeeping staff sometimes refused to be in the room with the door shut. As long as the door remained open, they would make up the bunks and clean as the job required but, as one put it to me, "it is just really creepy. It isn't like I feel threatened or anything, but I know someone is always watching me."

Passengers in adjacent cabins will also complain about the loud noises from the cabin. Raucous voices, slamming doors and dresser drawers, a loud radio, all cause passengers to grumble to the purser who in turn will "complain" to the "occupants." The purser will never tell the passengers that the cabin is empty. Who or whatever is in the cabin will be quiet for the remainder of the trip and usually not "act up" for several weeks. If the cabin is occupied by paying passengers, there are no complaints of strange doings other than perhaps the depressing bed.

Another cabin had a toilet that occasionally flushed itself. These were not normal porcelain johns but rather a special shipboard design that required a very strong step on a foot pedal to activate. It was impossible for them to accidentally flush. So who, or what, was flushing the john?

One stewardess on another ship reported that when she turned up from making a bunk, she saw a figure standing at the foot of the bed. It was indistinct and misty-like but definitely that of an elderly man. It didn't move but stayed stiff like a statue. After a few seconds it just faded into nothing. She refused to enter the cabin again, which caused a problem for the purser to rearrange the cleaning duties. Finally another stewardess agreed to take the room. She never mentioned any additional sightings, but always finished very, very quickly and always with the cabin door open.

The purser had her own strange experiences. Her cabin is located directly off her small office about amidships forward. Having to go through the office to reach it really makes it the most private cabin on the ship. On several occasions she entered her cabin only to discover all of her shelved material, including books, files, work boxes and clothing, scattered over the floor. The time from when she left to when she returned was only several minutes and the cabin was locked. The seas were perfectly calm and there was no rational explanation for the "trashing" of the cabin. If this wasn't eerie enough, at least twice she awoke in the middle of the night to see a shadowy gray figure standing over the bed looking down at her. When she yelled at it, it faded away. She wasn't afraid of what was happening, only mad that whatever it was didn't leave her in peace.

On another ship in the line the television and videotape player in the crew quarters lounge had the unearthly habit of turning on by themselves. While one could be explained by an electrical fault, both doing it was inexplicable.[7]

The fleet submarine USS *Cobia* (SS-245) is a featured attraction at the Wisconsin Maritime Museum in Manitowoc, Wisconsin. The submarine is moored in the river directly behind the museum and connected to it with carefully planned walkways to facilitate visitor access. Thousands of visitors a year crawl through the World War II diesel submarine on guided tours. Expert escorts provide colorful commentary on the actions of this historic warship. None of the visitors ever suspect that it has a ghost, thought to be the spirit of the only crewman killed aboard during her Pacific war patrols. Losing a single man was relatively rare. It was usually the loss of the submarine and entire crew, normally eight officers and 72 men.

During her six war patrols the USS *Cobia* sank 13 Japanese ships, accounting for more than 18,000 tons of enemy shipping. *Cobia* also earned four Battle Stars. She didn't just ravage shipping, but, when the need arose, rescued downed American pilots. The boat also rescued two Japanese from a raft on which they had been adrift for 40 days. Intelligence duties were an important function of the American submarine force and *Cobia* performed this mission, too, landing teams on the east coast of Java.

Virtually the entire submarine is open to visitors, including the torpedo rooms, wardroom, crew's quarters and engine rooms. It is one thing to see a submarine in the movies, but to actually go aboard a veteran U.S. combat submarine is a tremendous experience. Periodically the submarine's engines are again fired up and *Cobia* truly comes back to life.

The 312-foot *Cobia* was launched on November 28, 1943, by the Electric Boat Company in Groton, Connecticut. After appropriate trials and crew training she departed from Pearl Harbor on her first war patrol on June 26, 1944. *Cobia* proved a vital part of the fleet and an effective combat vessel. Her fourth war patrol brought her into the Java Sea where she made a surface attack on two Japanese armed transports called "sea trucks." Small shallow draft transports like the sea trucks were very difficult for a submerged attack, thus going in on the surface with deck guns blazing was the only option. During the ensuing firefight, 19-year-old Ralph Clark Houston, a 20 mm gun loader, was hit by machine gun fire and killed.

When the war ended she was placed into reserve only to be reactivated in 1951 for the Korean War. Deactivated again two years later, she was struck from the Navy Register in 1970 and towed to Manitowoc as an international memorial to submariners. Since declared a National Historic Landmark, she is on the National Register of Historic Places. *Cobia* has special significance to Wisconsin. The GATO class submarine is reflective of the 28 submarines built in Manitowoc during World War II.

Apparently Ralph Houston is still on the *Cobia* or perhaps the spirit of another since-deceased crewman who deeply loved "his boat." By long Navy tradition, a sub is always called a "boat." For want of a better name, however, the ghost is just called "Ralphie." His actions are those of a prankster and have no malicious intent. Regardless of motivation, his ghostly antics can be disconcerting to people not prepared for them.

The museum runs a very active overnight education program on *Cobia*. It gives people the once-in-a-lifetime opportunity to experience a first-hand taste of what it was like to sail aboard a World War II submarine. Participants receive a guided tour as well as partake in various educational experiences related to submarine operations and have access to some non-public areas. Many of Ralphie's activities focus on the overnight program.

The submarine is essentially a long series of compartments, a visitor passing from one to get to the next and so on. Part of the job of an overnight museum guide is to make a final walk-through to assure everything is ready for the night. In one instance, as the guide walked through the boat, a light bulb exploded in each compartment as she reached it.

Other overnight guides talk about hearing footsteps in the officer's wardroom or connecting passageway. The wardroom is a very small dining area set aside for the ship's officers. When everyone is asleep, the boat is dead quiet. Sometimes the curtains move as if a person were moving through them. Since there is no wind below deck, rational explanations are hard to conjure up. Guides have also reported a feeling of an eerie presence or of being watched, that they were not alone regardless of what logic told them. Just because they couldn't see anyone didn't mean no one was there.

In another instance, a tour guide opening the boat for the day discovered that all the benches in the crew mess were pushed off to the side, so he straightened them out so visitors could sit down. He finished checking the boat over then went up to the museum to gather his first tour. No one else was on the boat in his absence. The museum does an excellent job of providing security on the *Cobia*. When he returned with his group, the benches he so carefully rearranged just minutes before were all pushed back to one side. Was Ralphie planning to mop the deck?

One night, a former guide and a museum staffer were in the museum around 3 a.m. or so standing around the tour guide kiosk and talking. They chatted for about half an hour or more when they heard some noise down the hall near the front desk. Jokingly, the former guide yelled, "Ralphie, get back on the boat." A few minutes later the motion detection lights above the front display came on. A few seconds later, the concourse doors leading to the submarine made noise as if someone were going through them. Rattled, the pair went back aboard the boat to be around living people.[8]

Perhaps Ralphie feels a duty to remain on watch, to man *Cobia* as he did during the dark and dangerous days of World War II?

World War II ended on September 2, 1945, when the last remnants of the broken Japanese Empire surrendered to the Allies on the deck of the battleship USS *Missouri*. While all of the Pacific Theater Allies did their part, China, Australia, Britain and the United States providing the greatest effort, it was American forces that truly battered the Japanese into submission.

Army and Marine ground forces stormed ashore on island after island, rooting out stubborn enemy defenders, clearing the way for air bases needed for heavy bombers. Each aircraft carried heavy loads of well-deserved death and destruction bound for the Empire's home islands. Fast far-ranging aircraft carrier battle groups cruised the Pacific supporting amphibious assaults and seeking out and destroying the Japanese fleet. The Americans "remembered Pearl Harbor," the "Bataan Death March" and a hundred other atrocities.

Deep beneath the sea were the submarines, silent and deadly, stalking elusive Japanese shipping. The submarines were also the first American warships to strike back at the enemy. In the dark and desperate days following the sneak attack on Pearl Harbor, they were the only offensive weapons we had. The American subs struck again and again, waves of torpedoes slamming into the hulls of enemy vessels sending ship after ship to the bottom. When they ran out of "fish," it was "Battle Surface" and the crews used the deck guns to destroy the hated Japanese. The submariners fought until there were no targets left and enemy ships were swept from the sea. The subs destroyed more than 600,000 tons of enemy naval vessels and more than 5 million tons of their merchant shipping. All this was achieved with a force never numbering more than 2 percent of the military personnel engaged in the war.

The battle beneath the sea was a difficult fight. Fifty-two American subs and 3,617 crew didn't return. They are still on patrol, their rusted hulks and lifeless crews resting forever deep in the dark abyss.

The USS *Silversides,* officially SS236, was one of the submarine force that fought from the beginning of the war to the end. *Silversides* was launched at the Mare Island Navy Yard, California, on August 25, 1941, and commissioned on December 15, 1942, only eight days after Pearl Harbor. A fleet type sub of the GATO class, she was 312 feet long and carried a crew of eight officers and 72 men. At the end of the war her final armament included 24 torpedoes (six tubes forward and four aft), a four-inch deck gun, a 20 mm Orelikon gun and a 40 mm BoFors. In civilian parlance, she was "armed to the teeth." She could hit a top speed on the surface of 21 knots with her four powerful 1,535 horsepower Fairbanks Morse diesels and 10 knots submerged on batteries. She could also stay submerged for 48 hours, but her speed dropped to a slow two knots. Maximum depth was 300 feet with a test maximum of 425 feet. With a nominal 12,000-mile range and duration of 75 days, she was ideally fitted for the Pacific War.

Silversides is credited with sinking 30 Japanese ships and damaging another 14, ranking third highest among all World War II American submarines in ships sunk, totaling 90,080 tons. She has a Presidential Unit Citation in recognition for four war patrols and 12 Combat Insignia Battle Stars. She completed a total of 14 war patrols.

She is famous, too, for something that had nothing to do with sinking ships. During one patrol a crewman became desperately ill with an acute gangrenous appendix. There was no doctor aboard, only a pharmacist mate, and the appendix needed to come out immediately. The pharmacist mate rose to the occasion. The captain brought the boat down to a smooth cruise depth and held her quiet. The patient was laid out on the wardroom table, makeshift instruments were found or cobbled together, and with the medical book open and a volunteer surgical team, he performed the 4^1/$_2$ hour operation successfully. Six days later the patient was back on duty. The operation later was appended by Hollywood and used in the movie "Destination Tokyo."

Her first war patrol took her to the southern coast of Japan, right into the teeth of the dragon. America was clearly going to bring the war right to the Japanese. Her first enemy target was an armed trawler, a vessel specializing in anti-submarine warfare. Because it was too small for a torpedo, the captain decided to attack on the surface. Sounding "Battle Surface," the sub broke free of the waves and her crew tumbled out on deck to man the guns. Soon they were blazing away at the trawler, which quickly began to fire back. Unfortunately enemy machine gun bullets hit Torpedoman Third Class Mike Harbin, killing him instantly. In retaliation, the crew riddled the trawler with shellfire until she burned and sank. Torpedoman Harbin was the first and only casualty *Silversides* would suffer during the entire war. Once *Silversides* cleared the area, Torpedoman Harbin was ceremoniously buried at sea. Today a bronze plaque is permanently affixed to the deck at the exact spot Harbin was killed.

On the same patrol, *Silversides* torpedoed a Japanese submarine, although a sinking wasn't officially confirmed. A few days later she became the only American warship to attack enemy vessels while flying a Japanese flag. Sighting two enemy cargo vessels, *Silversides* moved in for a torpedo attack. During her approach she went through some fishing nets, the end of which were marked by Japanese flags on buoys. The flag buoys fouled on the periscope, so as she drove in for the kill, she "flew" Japanese flags! The result was one freighter sunk and one damaged. Other war patrols brought her to the Marianas, Carolines, Bismark, Solomon Islands and Guadalcanal.

Following the war she was decommissioned at New London, Connecticut, and assigned into reserve. In October 1947, she was placed in service as a Navy Reserve training ship and stationed at Chicago. She was reclassified as an auxiliary submarine in November 1962 and struck from the Navy Vessel Register in 1969. She remained at Navy Pier as a memorial but continued to fall victim to neglect. In 1987, she was towed across the lake to Muskegon, Michigan, becoming the star of the Great Lakes Naval and Maritime Museum. *Silversides* was granted National Historic Landmark status in 1986.

Like her sister *Cobia* in Manitowoc, Wisconsin, *Silversides* tells the story not only of World War II submarine combat in the Pacific, but also serves as a memorial to the "Greatest Generation." Also like *Cobia, Silversides* runs an active and successful overnight program. It is one experience to tour her by day, but to bunk in her overnight as her crew did provides an entirely new understanding of sailing in a submarine.

Silversides and *Cobia* have another similarity. Both have a resident ghost. Apparently the spirit of the lone sailor killed on each boat continues to be on patrol. On *Silversides,* Torpedoman Mike Harbin is said to haunt the boat to assure things are always kept shipshape. He is particularly active during the overnight programs. Although usually very friendly, he can become angry if disrespect is

15

shown to the submarine. Guests are startled sometimes by the sound of a hatch closing, but when checked, all are still locked open. Lights left on are found off. A cup of coffee placed on a table in the mess will be found on another table. Sometimes footsteps are heard in another compartment, but, of course, no one is there. Guides know it is just Mike – still on his endless patrol.[9]

She is a forbidding vision, a deadly warship ready to take to seas once more, to wreak deadly havoc among the Atlantic convoys. Bathed in powerful spotlights, each inch of her steel hull reflects her lethal purpose. She was built to kill and was supremely effective at it.

Today she is on display at Chicago's Museum of Science and Industry, a memorial to the thousands of sailors whose cemetery is the vastness of the wild sea. The *U-505* is remarkable. Containing nearly 200 artifacts, including a once top secret Enigma code machine, torpedo, historic film footage, interviews with the crew and captors and various special effects, the exhibit immerses the visitor in the heroic Battle of the Atlantic.

The story of the *U-505* is one of the most remarkable tales to emerge from World War II. Technically a Type IXC submarine, she was built by Deutsche Werft in Hamburg in 1940. Commissioned into the German Navy on August 26, 1941, she served until captured by the United States Navy on June 4, 1944. At 252 feet in length she is far smaller than contemporary U.S. fleet submarines like the *Cobia* at the Wisconsin Maritime Museum in Manitowoc. Although her diesel engines gave her a surface speed of 18 knots, underwater on batteries it dropped to eight knots. During the height of the war she was part of the force of German submarines that almost drove Allied shipping from the Atlantic.

Her fame, however, is based on her capture. The very idea of boarding and capturing an enemy submarine is, at first blush, ludicrous. But Admiral Daniel V. Gallery of the U.S. Navy thought differently. Famous for always "thinking out of the box" before the term was popular and often ruffling the feathers of a very straight-laced and "by the book" Navy, Gallery realized the intelligence bonanza that an intact German submarine could give the Allies. Gallery was also famous for saying, "regulations are only for people who can't figure out a better way to do something." If anyone could figure out how to do it, it was Dan Gallery.

As Commander of Task Group 22.3, a U-boat hunter-killer unit made up of a jeep aircraft carrier and numerous destroyers,

Gallery was in position to put his idea into operation. Working with his staff and commanders, he soon had a plan put together and rehearsed. Instead of trying to immediately sink the next U-boat that they forced to the surface with heavy weapons, they would "encourage" the German crew to abandon ship with machine gun fire, then rush a salvage team aboard.

Their opportunity came with the *U-505*. After they worked the submarine over with depth charges and her captain blew her to the surface to avoid being destroyed, Gallery put the plan into action. The German crew quickly set the scuttling charges designed to sink the sub with explosives, opened the seacocks to flood the ship and abandoned her. To their horror, the Americans rushed over to the sub in a whaleboat, boarded her and quickly disarmed the explosives. A damage control team found and closed the seacocks and rigged a towline. Within days the *U-505* was safe in Bermuda and her secrets were revealed to the Allies. She was the first enemy man-of-war captured by the American Navy since the War of 1812.

In 1954, the submarine was brought to Chicago and has been on exhibit ever since. An estimated 24 million people have visited her. The old warrior is easily the most popular exhibit in the Museum.

Apparently one of her old crewmen is still aboard the *U-505* and he is a very disturbed soul. The life of a submariner at any time is highly stressful. A single error in operation can mean death for the entire crew. In war it's even worse. While human error is still lurking in the background, it is compounded by enemy action. Every ship and plane must be treated as an enemy and nearly all were. Should the submarine be sighted by an aircraft or sharp-eyed lookout on a ship, all hell would be loosed against her. Depth charges fell like rain drops as did aerial bombs. Armor-piecing shells spewed downward from strafing airplanes. The constant pinging of sonar warned the submarine crew that the enemy was probing the depths for them. When the pinging increased in volume it was clear the ship was closing in for the kill. The depth charges were worst of all. Exploding with a thundering power, they shook the submarine from stem to stern, smashing light bulbs and twisting high pressure pipes until the joints failed, allowing powerful streams of water into the compartments. The air soon turned foul, a barely breathable mixture of diesel, sweat and a near lethal level of carbon dioxide. The crew's only hope for salvation was for the submarine to run as quietly as possible, to make the least possible amount of noise and try to slink away into cold depths unnoticed by the attackers.

The toll of lost U-boats was staggering. By the end of the war, only one in four German submariners survived the conflict. But they never quit. They never broke. Until the last day of the war, the U-boats continued to go to sea, in a desperate effort to keep up the uneven fight.

Some German submariners understandably broke under the pressure. Some even committed suicide. Only one German captain ever did so, Peter Zschech, commander of the *U-505*. Doubtless it is his tortured soul that is condemned to spend all eternity aboard the command he forsook.

The *U-505* was in the midst of a terrible depth charging when Zschech started to act strange. The crew was desperately waiting for orders, but he said and did nothing, just stood by quietly in the control room. No one ever heard the shot. When he slumped to the deck it was assumed he had hit his head in the violent shaking of the submarine during the attack. Only when a petty officer noticed a large pool of blood forming under him was he examined. Then the bullet hole in the center of his head was seen. Zschech had shot himself with his revolver. Still alive, he was carried to his bunk where he writhed in agony. In an act of mercy, two crewmen held his pillow over his head until he stopped moving.

Several hours later, the *U-505* having evaded the Allied destroyer attack, Zschech was sewed up in a hammock with a heavy weight at his feet. When the executive officer was sure that the horizon was clear of the enemy, he surfaced the submarine. The captain's body was carried to the open bridge and dropped over the side without ceremony. There was no time for the time-honored funeral at sea traditions. With Zschech gone, the executive officer ordered full speed to leave the area as quickly as possible.

The crew felt no sympathy for Zschech. They were angry and felt betrayed. They needed the captain and for him to commit suicide in the midst of battle was the ultimate treachery. Why didn't he have the decency to do it back in Lorient at the base instead of when all their lives depended on him?

Afterwards, many of the crew would not enter the captain's old cabin. Neither would the executive officer move in as was his privilege. He, too, felt Zschech was still there. His act of treachery prevented him from ever achieving the escape he wanted.

Zschech was not the captain on the *U-505*'s final patrol. But his ghost never left her. It is said a brave man dies only once but a coward dies a thousand deaths. This was the trap Zschech was caught in. Like the ancient mariner, he was doomed for eternity.

Fast forward to 1954 and the *U-505*'s arrival at Chicago. Extensive renovation was needed to prepare the submarine for public display. It was during the overhaul that several workmen noticed a shadowy figure moving about the submarine. Never clearly seen, the figure was always just at the edge of vision. There were at least two exceptions, however. Once a workman arrived a bit early and as he was climbing up into the conning tower he looked up to see a figure stooped over looking through the periscope. The figure was solid and wearing dark green leather jacket and trousers. A white officer's cap was tipped back on his head and his face was covered with a short beard. The figure turned toward the workman and glared at him as if to say, "Get out of here! You have no right to be here!" The workman quickly dropped down the ladder and ran out of the submarine. When the rest of the work crew arrived, they searched the submarine but found no one.

Shortly after the current renovation, one of the workmen entered the captain's cabin to do some final touch-up painting. Having the uncomfortable feeling of being watched, he slowly turned around only to see the image of a man lying in the bunk with a bullet hole in his forehead. The man's face was twisted in agony while blood welled up the hole and onto the bed.

Some visitors, perhaps those more sensitive to the "other world," report a feeling of extreme uneasiness aboard. Something isn't right. Zschech is still aboard, trapped in a coward's hell from which he can't escape.[10]

CHAPTER 2

Ghost Ships

Ghost ships continue to be part of the fabric of Great Lakes legend and lore. There are stories of persistent ghost ships like the *Bannockburn* and *Chicora*, seen again and again by lake sailors down through the years. Tales of these vessels and others are told in the original *Haunted Lakes*. However, there are many more yarns of phantom ships and the crews that man them.

The oldest ghost ship on the lakes is the *Griffon*. More than one old "salt" reported her phantom shape gliding through a storm-whipped northern Lake Michigan. The fact that the vessel disappeared with all hands and has yet to be found only adds fuel to this earliest of the lake's "Flying Dutchmen."

The *Flying Dutchman* is one of the most endearing legends of the sea. The tale of the *Flying Dutchman* trying to round the Cape of Good Hope against strong winds and never succeeding, then trying to make Cape Horn and failing there, too, has been the most persistent maritime ghost story for more than 300 years. The cursed spectral ship sailing back and forth on its endless voyage, its ancient white-hair crew crying for help while hauling at her sail, inspired Samuel Taylor Coleridge to write his classic "The Rime of the Ancient Mariner," to name but one famous literary work involving her. The real *Flying Dutchman* is supposed to have set sail in 1660.

The small 45-ton barque *Griffon* was built in 1679 near Cayuga Creek in Lake Erie at the direction of the famous French explorer and fur trader Rene Cavalier Sieur De La Salle. It was named for a mythical creature with an eagle's head, wings and a lion's body. He intended to use her for combined fur trading and voyages of discovery. She left on her first trip on August 7, 1679, with 32 men aboard bound for Lake Michigan's Green Bay. There she loaded a rich cargo of furs and with a crew of six sailed for Niagara on September 18. La Salle and the remainder of the men continued south along the west shore of the lake by canoe. The *Griffon* never reached Niagara or any other place yet known to man. She and her crew just "went missing."

Various stories have surfaced explaining her disappearance, but none can be proven. Some claim a party of American Indians saw her sheltering from a storm in northern Lake Michigan. Warned by the Indians to wait out the blow, her impatient and quarrelsome pilot, "Luke the Dane," was said to have laughed at their "heathen fears." Without a second thought he sailed off into a still rough lake never to be seen again.

Over the intervening centuries many stories regarding her fate have surfaced. One tale said the crew mutinied and tried to make off with her valuable fur cargo. Others said that Indians boarded her and massacred the crew or that the vessel subsequently perished in the storm. The wreck has been reportedly discovered at locations as varied as Russell Island on the tip of the Bruce Peninsula, Meldrum Bay on Manitoulin Island and Lake Michigan's Door Peninsula and Beaver Island. Perhaps the most intriguing claim was the Manitoulin Island one in which shortly before the turn of the 20th century the lightkeeper declared to have found five or six skeletons in a cave. One was especially large and the Danish pilot was known to have been a very big man. Old French coins and brass buttons added authenticity to the find. At the time the importance and relationship to the *Griffon* wasn't realized. When it finally was, all the important artifacts had been lost.

For some time, however, the keeper kept some of the bones, including ribs, arm bones, shinbones and pieces of vertebrae, in a burlap sack. He eagerly displayed them all for interested tourists and it was common for him to even give bones away as souvenirs. The assistant keeper carried one of the skulls on the bow of his fishing boat for years until a storm finally knocked it off.

Reportedly an old-fashioned gold watch chain found hanging from a tree led to the discovery of the nearly hidden cave. A matching watch was discovered alongside one of the skeletons.

Regardless of how she met her end, generations of old sailors periodically reported seeing the *Griffon*, "coasting along the north end of Lake Michigan with all sails set." When they tried to approach the strange apparition, it just disappeared.[1]

Death's Door Passage, or "Porte des Morts," as the early French explorers called it, is a notorious ship trap. A narrow channel beset by reefs and strong currents, it cuts directly through the Door Peninsula and is the quickest path from Green Bay into Lake Michigan. Although the full total may never be known, hundreds of vessels have wrecked on its deadly reefs. In one 1880 gale alone, 30 ships wrecked in the area.

As might be expected, there are numerous tales of phantom ships still running through the deadly gauntlet of reef and shoal. Lighthouse keepers, fishermen, sailors and landsmen have seen these "Flying Dutchmen." All were amazed at the wonderful sight these old wind-wagons presented, blasting along through the gray seas with all sails set, only to vanish in a twinkling.

A classic sighting happened in the 1940s. A small cabin cruiser with two couples aboard was running through the passage eastward for Gills Rock when it hit rough water. The couples had intended to make the trip during daylight but had delayed too long, and then mounting winds and waves slowed them down so night overtook the boat before reaching Gills Rock. The moon was full so visibility was very good.

The small boat periodically went from trough to crest as large waves passed beneath. One minute they were deep in the water unable to see anything, the next high enough to see for miles. While perched momentarily on one of the crests, the occupants were startled to see lights from a boat dead ahead. Their first thought was that it was the Washington Island ferry, but at the next crest they realized it had three masts and all sails were set. The big schooner seemed to be heading toward Gills Rock, too. When the boat again climbed to the top of crest a moment later, the schooner was gone. There was nothing there but an empty horizon. What had happened to the phantom ship?[2]

Some people believe that ghosts can be the result of actions unfinished, that the spirit is trying to complete the job interrupted by death. If so, the strange sightings of the old sidewheeler *Alpena* can be, to a fashion at least, explained.

The 197-foot, 653-ton *Alpena* was built in 1867 at Marine City, Michigan, by Thomas Arnold. Owned at the time of loss by the Goodrich Steamship Company, she had recently been rebuilt and was considered in prime condition. A massive single cylinder vertical beam engine with a long 11-foot stroke drove her 24-foot diameter paddlewheels. The massive walking beam was visible amidships just aft of the stack. Although she served a variety of ports, she usually ran the Muskegon-Grand Haven-Chicago route. Her captain was Nelson W. Napier, an experienced and well-respected mariner. He was considered the best captain in the fleet and highly popular with passengers and shippers. He knew all the regular passengers by name and kept to schedule, which made shippers happy. The lakes ran deep in his blood. Two uncles also were masters on the sweetwater seas.

At 10 p.m., October 15, 1880, the *Alpena* steamed proudly out into a calm Lake Michigan. Behind her the lights of Grand Haven winked in the dark. Ahead was Chicago. Indian Summer weather, including temperatures in the 60-70-degree range, promised a quick and comfortable passage. Three hours later, the *Alpena* passed close aboard her fleet-mate the *Muskegon*, bound to Grand Haven from Chicago, and exchanged whistle signals. The weather continued excellent and both vessels steamed on their way; the *Muskegon* to the east shore and the *Alpena* to another world.

At 3 a.m., all hell broke loose. The temperatures plummeted to 33 degrees. The wind screamed down from the north with the fury of a thousand shrieking banshees. Mountainous seas smashed into the staunch vessel, each sending a shudder through the wooden hull. It's assumed Captain Napier kept trying to fight his way through to Chicago. He didn't make it. What really happened to the *Alpena* isn't known. The wreck has never been located. It's conjectured that she was knocked over on her beam ends, floated for a while and then sank to the bottom of the lake. The fierceness of the storm, which later became known as the "*Alpena* Storm," was devastating. Approximately 94 vessels were damaged or wrecked and at least 118 people perished. An estimated 70-80 souls went down with the *Alpena*. Passenger lists were unreliable and the true number will never be known.

Although the hull and machinery rests somewhere deep on the floor of the lake, old-time sailors claimed that the *Alpena* is still trying to finish her trip. In sailor hangouts on both sides of the lake, in engine rooms, forecastles and pilothouses, men told tales of still seeing the lost *Alpena*. On foggy days her dim outline was seen plowing through the waves, in a hopeless effort to reach the windy city. Dead men manned her pilothouse and fed her boiler fires. Ghostly passengers played cards in the salon and looked mournfully for the glimmer of Chicago's lights. If the men listened carefully, the clanking racket of her rocking beam engine could just be heard above the waves.[3]

Occasionally crew members on the Lake Michigan car ferries reportedly sighted the ghostly image of the long lost steamer *Chicora*. Each time the ghost ship was picked up a few miles off the bow only to quickly disappear, although the image lasted long enough for the men to point it out to each other. Afterwards, the crews were always ready for a "hell of a blow."[4]

The *Chicora* was built in 1892 for the Graham and Morton Transportation Company. The wooden steamer was 217 feet long and 1,122 gross tons. Her 1,300 horsepower engine powered her along at a fast 17 mph. Designed especially to run passengers and freight between Milwaukee, Wisconsin, and St. Joseph, Michigan, she was well fitted out with luxurious accommodations and public rooms. Ornately decorated with heavy drapes and rich wood paneling, she was very popular with the traveling public. Commercial shippers also found her dependable and fast and consequently she was given considerable business. By any measure, she was a well-found vessel, with many years of life built in her.

In the fall of 1894 the *Chicora* laid up for the winter in St. Joseph. Typically traffic lessened during the winter and the big steamer wasn't needed. But the harvest that year was abundant and a surplus of flour had built up in Milwaukee needing transportation to the railhead at St. Joseph. To meet this demand, the steamer

came out of lay-up and with a 23-man scratch crew, ran over to
Milwaukee. Forty-two-year-old Edward G. Stines, her regular
master and a 25-year veteran of the lakes, commanded her. William
J. Russell of Benton Harbor, the normal second mate, was too ill to
make the trip. His place was taken by Bennie Stines, the captain's
son.[5] Captain Stines was sick the morning they sailed from
Milwaukee. Earlier he had consulted a physician who advised him
not to make the journey. Captain Stines was inclined to agree with
him, but inexplicably at the last moment, he changed his mind. He
decided he had to take his boat and crew on the final trip.

Insurance was unavailable because of the lateness of the season,
so the *Chicora* ran without it. The high freight rates would cover
the risk. The *Chicora* was especially built for running in the ice.
Although sailing during midwinter was always risky, little real
apprehension was felt.[6]

In the predawn darkness of Monday, January 21, 1895, the
Chicora steamed out of Milwaukee bound for St. Joseph. Deep in
her hold were 40 carloads of barreled flour. Shortly after leaving, a

powerful storm swept down, whipping the lake into a frothing sea of demented fury. Torrents of rain lashed the *Chicora*, followed by thick snow squalls. The wind shrieked at 60-70 mph, piling the lake into 20-foot-plus waves. Between morning and night the temperature fell 40 degrees. For two full days the storm blew unabated.

When the *Chicora* didn't reach St. Joseph as expected, little concern was initially felt. Local marine men thought she probably just returned to Milwaukee or sheltered in another port. But the *Chicora* wasn't anywhere, at least not in any port on Lake Michigan.

Wreckage was first discovered on the beach near Grand Haven, 35 miles north of St. Joseph. Consisting of hull sections and part of the upper bulwarks, it was jammed in the ice about a mile offshore. Later searches in the same area found furniture, deck railing, curtains, hull planking, barreled flour and both spars. The beaches were carefully swept by 200 searchers, while the steamers *City of Ludington*, *Petosky*, *Nyack* and tug *Crosby* cruised the offshore waters. Despite their diligence, the searchers didn't locate a single body. There was a story, however, years later that a cloth cap with a G & M on it was found on the beach with a skeleton hand still grasping it.[7]

There are those who believe that the *Chicora* was cursed by a duck and it was all the fault of Joseph F. Pearl, a local St. Joseph druggist and a friend of James R. Clark, the temporary clerk. A piece in the *Milwaukee Journal* of January 24, 1895, elaborated the details. "Joseph Pearl took with him on the trip to Milwaukee a gun which he shot a duck that was in the act of alighting on the boat in mid-lake. The appearance of the duck in such a place and the fact that it had been shot, awakened a superstitious dread that spread among the crew. The incident preyed upon the captain's mind and he constantly referred to it as an evil omen while the *Chicora* was loading for the return trip."[8]

There were also two reported "bottle" messages from the *Chicora*, both discovered in the spring of 1895. The first stated, "All is lost. Could see land if not snowed and blowed. Engine give out, drifting to shore in ice. Captain and clerk are swept off. We have a hard time of it. 10:15 o'clock." The second note was found sealed in a glass preserving jar. "*Chicora* engines broke. Drifted into trough of sea. We have lost all hope. She has gone to pieces. Good bye, McClure, Engineer."

What actually happened to the *Chicora* is unknown. The wreck remains one of Lake Michigan's fleet of the missing, only to reappear as a "ghost ship" of the lakes, at least according to the old time car ferry sailors.

The White Lake area of Lake Michigan has its own ghost ship, the schooner *Ella Ellenwood*. During the dark and brooding nights when the mists roll heavy over Lake Michigan, the ghostly image of the lumber schooner *Ella Ellenwood* is said to periodically return to the waters just offshore of White Lake. The 157-ton, 106-foot schooner was built in East Saginaw in 1870 and home-ported out of White Lake for many years. On October 1, 1901, she ran hard up on Fox Point, just north of Milwaukee, during a roaring gale. The crew safely made shore in the yawl, but savage fall storms battered the old wind wagon to kindling. However, the schooner would not end her association with White Lake quite so easily. In a strange effort to finish her trip, her name board was discovered the following spring floating in the White Lake Channel. She had come home at last.

The old schooner is remembered locally to this day. A replica of her is mounted on top of the "world's largest weather vane" at the White Lake causeway.[9]

Like the famous *Mary Celeste* of salt-water fame whose discovery sailing merrily along between the Azores and Portugal in 1872 without a soul aboard led to the wildest of speculation, the lakes also had instances of strangely disappearing crews.

When the schooner *William Sanderson* drifted ashore at Empire, Michigan, Lake Michigan on November 26, 1874, there wasn't a soul aboard. All the crew had vanished ... somewhere! The schooner had left Chicago the week before bound for Oswego with 19,500 bushels of wheat. Whether the crew was driven off by storm, with perhaps the schooner thrown on her beam ends, forcing the men to leave her, or just panicked and took to the boats, was the hot topic in maritime circles. The answer was unknown. What was known was that the *William Sanderson* was on the beach without her crew.[10]

The 518-ton schooner *Ellen Spry* was another vessel with a disappearing crew. The schooner was found after a November 1886 blow in mid-Lake Michigan without a soul aboard. Several vessels sighted her in this condition before she finally drifted ashore at Point Betsie. But where was the crew?

When the steamer *Eastland* capsized in the Chicago River on Saturday morning, July 24, 1915, with the loss of an estimated 844 lives, it was the greatest maritime disaster in the Great Lakes. The

day was supposed to be the annual Western Electric Company picnic in Michigan City, Indiana. To transport the 7,500 employees, friends and family members, the company chartered four steamers, the *Eastland, Theodore Roosevelt, Missouri* and *City of South Haven.* All the ships were moored in the Chicago River between the Clark Street and LaSalle Street bridges. Since the *Eastland* and the *Theodore Roosevelt* were the newest ships, most employees were eager to travel aboard them instead of the other steamers.

The *Eastland* was built in 1903 for passenger and freight hauling across Lake Michigan between Chicago and South Haven, Michigan. Later she cruised between Cleveland and Cedar Point, Ohio. For the 1915 season she was owned by the St. Joseph-Chicago Line. Always known as a fast ship, she also had a well-known tendency to roll and some mariners considered her unstable.

At 6:40 a.m. passengers began to board the *Eastland.* Almost immediately she began to list to starboard, toward the dock. Doubtless this was due to the crush of passengers rushing aboard to secure the best viewing locations for the trip down the river. Most of the passengers had not yet spread out throughout the ship. Nevertheless, the chief engineer was able to flood the port ballast tanks to straighten her out. At 6:51 a.m. she was again level.

Two minutes later the *Eastland* lurched 10 degrees to port, which caused the engineer to fill her starboard tanks to level her

28

again. At 7:10 a.m. she resumed her port list, causing the engineer to pump out her port tanks in an effort to balance her but not before she had reached a 15-degree list. Eventually the engineer was able to briefly level her before lurching to a 20-degree port list. At this point water began to flood through the lower port side view ports, many of which were reportedly open. At 7:28 a.m. the list reached 45 degrees. Now everyone recognized the real danger, but it was too late to take remedial action. The big steamer gently continued to roll to port, snapping her mooring lines, eventually ending up with her starboard side out of the water. Lucky passengers found themselves standing on the steel hull. Many others were thrashing desperately in the river while others were trapped inside.

An observer remembers the horrible scene. " I shall never be able to forget what I saw. People were struggling in the water, clustered so thickly that they literally covered the surface of the river. A few were swimming; the rest were floundering about, some clinging to a life raft that had floated free, others clutching at anything that they could reach at – bits of wood, at each other, grabbing each other, pulling each other down and screaming! The screaming was the most horrible of all!"

Local boats in the river came as fast as possible to help the victims. People ashore threw planks, wood crates and anything else that would float into the water. Some men jumped in and dragged drowning people to safety.

Hundreds of men, women and children also were hopelessly trapped in the hull. The view ports were too small for any of the people trapped inside to escape through so crews from rescue boats worked frantically cutting holes through the steel hull to let people out to safety. People caught inside screamed in terror adding to the confusion. Cutting the holes was a slow process and by the time the cutting torches burned through the hull, many had drowned. Some rescuers entered the hull in a frantic effort to pull victims out. One man was especially brave, making several trips into the interior hell of the dead ship, but the horrible death scene finally unhinged his mind. For days afterward rescuers worked at the grisly task of hauling bodies out of the hull and fishing them from the river.

An immediate problem was what to do with the dead. They had to be stored somewhere until each could be identified by friends or family and proper arrangements for final disposition made. Identification of the bodies was sometimes difficult when no one knew the dead. Numerous locations were used. One of the larger ones was the Second Regiment Armory on Washington Boulevard.

When all of the victims were counted, 844 people were dead, 841 passengers, two crewmen and one rescuer. Entire families were wiped out. It is little known that more passengers were killed on the *Eastland* (841) than were killed on the *Titanic* (694). The total for the *Titanic* of 1,532 was reached only when the crew was included.

Why exactly the *Eastland* capsized has never been answered to complete satisfaction. It is clear that she was top heavy and had a reputation as being a crank ship. By design her 265-foot length and 38.2-foot beam would have caused stability problems, which to certain extent could have been corrected by altering the water ballast. However there were other factors. Prior to the 1915 season, two inches of concrete was poured over her decks to keep the wood planking from rotting. This added to her top heaviness. Passengers preferred to ride on her upper decks for the better view, which further increased the stability problems. In a way the *Titanic* also contributed to the loss of the *Eastland*. After *Titanic's* loss in 1912, there was a frantic rush to add sufficient lifeboats to passenger vessels to assure all passengers could be provided with a seat in a lifeboat. The heavy lifeboats of course were added to her upper decks, further decreasing stability. The ship's capacity had also recently been increased from 2,000 to 2,500 passengers. All of these factors ultimately played into the disaster.

The official cause of loss was found by the civil courts to be the engineer failing to fill the water ballast tanks correctly. Of course, the courts determining the cause of a maritime loss is in itself absurd. Instead of a detailed investigation by a competent maritime expert without the impress of cheap politics and know-nothing civil lawyers and judges, Chicago got a legal circus complete with elected clowns.

The *Eastland* was refloated on August 14, 1915, and for years was a cursed ship. No one wanted a ship with her unsavory past. Eventually she was acquired by the U.S. government for use as a Navy training ship. The hull was cut down and she was rebuilt as the U.S.S. *Wilmette*. For 31 years she trained naval recruits. In 1948 she was finally scrapped in Chicago.

The previous is fact. What follows is something else, perhaps even "spiritual."

One historian claimed that the *Eastland* was always a hoodoo ship, things always went wrong on her. Shortly after launching, she failed to meet her design specifications and modifications were needed. She also had a propensity for breaking down at the height of the season.

Throughout her career there were rumors of being unsafe. At one point her owners reputedly offered a reward of $5,000 to anyone who could prove she was unsafe. No one ever took them up on the offer, but even to make it showed how desperate they were to defuse the issue.

In the months and years after the disaster, there were claims that pedestrians walking the area between the Clark and LaSalle Street bridges, the place where she capsized, heard cries of terror near the riverbank. On bright sunny mornings other people reported hearing a sudden splash, followed by hundreds of screaming voices. When they looked, there were no ripples, just the smooth undisturbed surface.

If there is any truth to the old sailor's tale that those areas of the lakes that suffered great calamities remain haunted by the spirits of the dead, then indeed this small stretch of the Chicago River is indeed filled with ghosts.

Two of the buildings pressed into service as temporary morgues were the old Reid Murdock building, now the traffic court, and the building that houses the Oprah Winfrey Studio. The tale goes that workers and visitors in both buildings have reported unusual occurrences and sensations. Sometimes it's a cold spot, or the soft sound of quiet weeping echoing in an empty room. Psychics claim that the overall impression of death and mourning is pervasive. See Chapter 6 for more details of this haunting.

Most ghost ship tales involve ships from the past. Not so this remarkable account. As is common in such stories, no one will quite come forward and swear to its veracity, but enough of it rings true to well bear repeating. True or not, let the reader be the judge. Just remember, there are some very strange and unexplained things that happen on the lakes, especially when surrounded by an impenetrable fog.

Several years ago the Coast Guard station at St. Joseph, Michigan, heard a radio call from a small sailboat lost somewhere in the fog, asking for assistance. The boat's navigational instruments had failed and the engine refused to run. Coast Guard replies to the boat went unanswered. Evidently the boat could transmit but not receive. Eventually the Coast Guard was able to get enough of a rough fix on its position by radio direction finder to allow them to send out a patrol boat. After a time the Coast Guard boat located the sailboat, determined that all aboard were safe and towed it to safety at St. Joseph. Aboard were two couples. To the Coast

Guardsmen's observation, none of the sailboat's crew had been drinking, were on drugs or were otherwise anything but weekend sailors out for a cruise. They were bound out of Chicago when the unearthly fog overtook them.

It was only later when the sailboat crew stopped at the station to fill out the inevitable report that they inquired, "What about the other sailboat?" The Coast Guardsmen replied that they had seen no other boat. Their radar had shown only the one sailboat. The 24-mile search range showed no other targets. This statement rattled the sailboaters. According to them shortly after they realized the seriousness of their situation, lost in the blinding fog without any navigational instruments, a broken radio and engine, another sailboat suddenly loomed out of the gray mist, stopping close alongside. The crew aboard the new vessel calmed them down and took them in tow for St. Joseph. On the way, both crews spoke of fogs and storms long past and adventures yet to come, the typical talk of summer sailors. Just before the Coast Guard boat arrived the second sailboat dropped the towline and silently slipped into the thick fog. Shouted questions from the first boat went unanswered.

None of the Coast Guard boat crew could explain the unknown boat, except for one old hand who remembered another about 10 years before. But she had disappeared with all hands leaving not a trace to explain her fate. As sailors in the old days used to say, she just "sailed into a crack in the lake." Was there a connection, somehow a boat from the past helping one from the present? In this instance the ghost ship didn't warn of danger. Instead, it kept a ship and crew out of it.[11]

There is a tale, supposedly related by the mate of a downbound schooner running the Manitou Passage at the turn of the previous century. The passage, often called the "dreaded Manitou," is a shortcut for vessels bound from and to the Straits of Mackinac and southern Lake Michigan ports. The channel is narrow and twisting, especially at the northern end, and dangerous for a careless mariner. There are different versions of the tale, depending on who the teller is, but in general it goes something like this.

"It was early fall and normally a period of reliable winds but instead of driving along under all canvas, the schooner lay becalmed, drifting aimlessly on the still lake. Not a breath of air rippled the oily surface. She was also utterly alone. Not another craft could be seen in the approaching twilight. Other than the gently lapping waves against the hull, the silence was deafening

"The captain's name was Smyth and he hailed from Kincardine, Ontario, a breeding ground for many good lake sailors. Glancing around with his glasses, he was attracted to a grey fog forming several hundred yards to the west. The vapor appeared to be boiling and after a short time slowly formed into a smoke-belching steamer, or at least that's what she looked like."

Now where the hell did she come from? Surely she must have been lost in the distant mist. Regardless of the captain's speculation the stranger was heading straight for the schooner and judging by the white froth at her bow, coming fast.

"Quickly the captain ordered the old hand-cranked fog whistle blown, but the steamer paid no heed. She continued on, her sharp bow aimed dead at the schooner's amidships. The crew frantically waved and yelled in a desperate effort to warn her off, but on she came. The captain and crew stared at the approaching steamer in terrified disbelief. They noticed three things. First, the closer the steamer came the colder it got. When they first sighted her, the air was pleasantly warm. Now it was downright cold and getting colder as the steamer bore down on them. They also noticed that there was no one aboard her, at least no one they could see. The wheel seemed to be unmanned, with no lookout at the bow and no one about the deck. Finally, it was as if the steamer was part cloud. Wisps of grey vapor seemed to swirl around her. Even as she drove on through the lake, tendrils of fog hung onto the strange steamer.

"Mesmerized by the appalling scene unfolding before them, not a single man thought to run for the lifeboat. Instead, all stood transfixed at the rail, watching impending death. The bow kept coming and coming. Collision was unavoidable. But nothing happened. Not a dozen yards away the steamer just vanished into nothing as if it were never there.

"Before the schooner's crew had much time to think over what happened, a fresh breeze from the southwest sprung up and the captain ordered a course for Grays Reef and out of the Manitou Passage. For a time the tale of the extraordinary encounter made the rounds in the sailor saloons, but most who heard it blew it off, just another tall tale from a schooner's crew trying to convert a good story into a round of drinks. But there were those old-timers who silently nodded their heads. They had experiences on the lake, too, that couldn't be explained."

This is a story I can attest to. It happened to me. Certainly the reader should make his own judgment regarding what I experienced and may in fact be able to offer an explanation that hasn't occurred to me.

It has been my habit for the last five years or so to work for a few weeks every summer as a lecturer for different Great Lakes cruises. The line and vessel involved are immaterial to what I experienced and since I am unsure how the company will react to connecting the tale to their ship, I will err on the side of caution and not name it. The cruise typically departed Chicago and stopped at numerous ports including Holland, Manistee, Beaver Island, Mackinac Island, Sturgeon Bay and Milwaukee before returning to Chicago. It was a great trip and passengers enjoyed it immensely.

The port call at St. James on Beaver Island was always my favorite. It is the opposite of the fudge-mad, thundering herds of tourists mobbing Mackinac Island. Quiet and laid back, it's where folks go to step back from the maddening crowd. Unlike the infamous Mackinac Island, visitors don't have to be careful where they step either.[12] Beaver Island is famous as the home of the only "king" in the United States, one James Jesse Strang, a Mormon leader who had himself "crowned" in 1850. Strang's reign was short-lived, being shot down, murdered by several followers in 1856 as the result of a spat involving a woman's bloomers. The island abounds in haunts, many dating from the Mormon period.

The ship usually arrived at the Beaver Island dock shortly after midnight, which allowed enough time for the crew to have a quiet beer at the renowned Shamrock Bar. Since the turn of the last century the Shamrock has been the epicenter of the island's social and cultural scene.

About 11:30 p.m. we were running up the east shore of the island with the entrance to Paradise Bay and St. James dead ahead perhaps a mile or so. The entrance buoys were clearly visible and the welcoming flash of St. James Light proved that we were right on track. Although it was night, visibility was excellent with a full moon and bright stars. The weather on the trip had been beautiful and this night was continuing the trend.

I was in the pilothouse with the captain. We were the only people there. We were discussing the details of our imminent arrival at the dock. Both pilothouse radars were on, painting clear visions of the island and navigation buoys.

I noticed a target on the port radar moving out of the bay and turning towards us. It looked like it would pass just off our port side. It was very fast moving, perhaps 25 miles an hour, and showed no lights of any kind. It was also tracking on the starboard radar.

The radars were of different manufacture and set for different ranges. I called the captain's attention to the target and we both studied it for a while as well as trying to spot it visually. The night was so clear that not seeing it was unthinkable. We never saw it, either with the naked eye or binoculars.

In short order the target sped out of the bay, made a right turn towards us and passed about 50 yards off our port side until reaching a point about 50 yards behind the vessel and vanishing. We never saw a thing. No lights. No wake. No boat. It was only visible on the two radars. Once it disappeared, the captain and I just looked at one another, shrugged at one another and continued on to St. James. It was just another mystery of the lake. We both had sailed enough to understand that there are some things we don't understand.

Several years later I was at a fund-raiser for a hometown theater group. As part of an outing on a local lighthouse island, I told a few ghost stories to entertain everyone. I included the Beaver Island incident, since it illustrated that there still are things out there in the dark that we don't understand, despite our technology.

When the event was wrapping down, a woman of long acquaintance came up and provided an interesting interpretation of what the captain and I witnessed. I change her name to protect the innocent but the key parts of her story are accurate. Her explanation went something like this. "When John (her husband) and I were younger we always spent our summers on Beaver Island. John's family was old islander so it was a chance to visit family and get away from things for a while. Anyway, I remember when we were in the Shamrock Bar one night and three Indian boys were in there drinking and got really drunk. Sometime before midnight they decided to go out and haul their fishing nets. Instead of using the tug, for some reason they jumped into a speedboat one of them had and went tearing out of the harbor. The boys made the turn to the east and ran smack into the big steel buoy, killing them all! What you saw was the recreation of that terrible accident."

Her story amazed me for a couple of reasons. First, it fit what the captain and I had witnessed perfectly. The timing, location and activity all meshed. Second, I had always considered her to be as solid a member of the local community as possible. For her to relate such a tale was completely out of character. She would not be inventing anything.

The incident also fits the historic mold of haunted areas of the lakes, places where, under the correct conditions, shipwrecks would "re-create" themselves, occur again and again as if part of a broken CD track. More typically, such re-creations were confined to areas of higher shipwreck concentration like the Straits of Mackinac, Death's Door, Manitou Passage Long Point. But certainly if we suspend the "known" limits of science, which is critical for the entire consideration of the supernatural, then it does make sense.[13]

CHAPTER 3

Cursed Ships

The old sailors on fresh water and salt water believed that some vessels were "bad luck boats," cursed to have misfortune dog their careers. If they could at all avoid it, they refused to ship on a "hoodoo ship." Sometimes these ships were also called "black cats" and comments such as, "I only stayed two weeks on that black cat," were common.[1]

One old Lake Michigan salt remembered that his father purchased a wrecked schooner on which crewmen died. After being salvaged and returned to service, the father always had great trouble getting a crew. Sailors considered her to be bad luck and usually refused to ship on her.[2]

On reflection, the loss of the schooner *George F. Whitney* in Lake Michigan in 1872 was seemingly preordained. First, she wrecked on Sugar Island in 1871 while bound from Buffalo to Chicago. After being recovered the following spring, she was rebuilt, but on her next trip went ashore at Vermilion. Again she was hauled off and repaired. The next trip out she disappeared with all eight hands on Lake Michigan. At the time, she was bound from Chicago for Buffalo with a cargo of corn. Before leaving the windy city, Captain Wellington Carpenter inexplicably flew all of his flags upside down, including the national ensign (U.S. flag). Although he told local marine men that it was merely an invitation for tugs to bring him down the river, they shook their heads in bewilderment over such strange antics. Surely he had tempted the gods and they responded![3]

An infamous Lake Michigan hoodoo was the two-masted schooner *Augusta*, of *Lady Elgin* fame. Built in Oswego in 1855, she was 126 feet in length and 357 tons. On the evening of September 8, 1860, while sailing in a thunderstorm-tossed lake, the *Augusta* rammed the 252-foot sidewheel passenger steamer *Lady Elgin* square amidships. Known as the "Lady of the Lakes," the *Lady Elgin* was named for the wife of the Governor-General of Canada, Lord Elgin. The accident occurred 10 miles off Winnetka, Illinois. The *Augusta* was downbound for Chicago with lumber and the *Lady Elgin* upbound for Milwaukee from Chicago. Reportedly the captain of the *Augusta* saw the *Lady Elgin* in plenty of time to steer clear and gave the command to "hard up," but the schooner refused to respond to the wheel. It was as if she had a will of her own. In the confusing minutes immediately following the crash, the captain of the *Augusta*, Nelse Malott, asked the big steamer whether he should stand by in case help was needed. Unaware of the terrible extent of his damage, the captain of the *Lady Elgin* told him to continue for Chicago. It wasn't until she reached the city that Malott found out the steamer had sunk with the loss of an estimated 300 lives. Survivors later claimed that the *Augusta* showed no lights, a charge Malott vehemently denied. Local papers claimed that more than 1,000 children were, mostly in Milwaukee's German wards, orphaned when the steamer sank.[4]

There is another version of the collision. The *Lady Elgin* was said to be delaying her entry into Milwaukee to avoid landing until a series of midnight thunderstorms had passed. To accomplish this, she was circling slowly, supposedly with her wheel lashed and unattended. Twice the steamer crossed the bow of the *Augusta*, each time forcing the schooner to jibe to avoid collision. Thunder squalls were rolling over the lake and each jibe caused the *Augusta* crew to fall out of their bunks and battle her stiff and unwieldy sails. The steamer passed so close, her dance music, "Listen to the Mockingbird," could clearly by heard by the schoonermen and her bright oil lamps cast shadows across the decks. Perhaps the *Lady Elgin* never saw the small *Augusta*, but the schooner's crew had cause to curse the steamer's thoughtless actions. As a sailing vessel, the *Augusta* did have the right of way, a right the *Lady Elgin* was blithely ignoring. The third time she cut the *Augusta* was the charm, or more correctly, the curse. Again unseen until the last moment, the big steamer came pounding out of a squall and the schooner was unable to jibe in time to avoid hitting her, the schooner's bow ripping deep into her side forward of the paddle

box. Seemingly oblivious to the collision, the *Lady Elgin* continued on her way. The schooner was left bobbing in her wake, the disgruntled crew battling wind-whipped sails while the strains of the "Mockingbird" swirled about their ears.[5]

Narratives claim that even before her fateful collision with the *Lady Elgin*, the *Augusta* was known as a bad luck boat. Afterwards she was considered truly cursed. The *Augusta* ran the lakes for the rest of the year, finally wintering in Detroit.

Trying to hide her role in the disaster, the following spring her hull was painted black and she was renamed the *Colonel Cook*. Her unsavory reputation always was there, festering just below the surface. For example, in April 1861 she sailed to Milwaukee with lumber. After unloading, she took aboard 16,000 bushels of grain for Buffalo. Before she left, however, local citizens learned that she was in port and soon an angry mob was ready to burn the cursed boat, the killer of so many good Milwaukee men. The owners quickly sent her down the lakes and through the Welland Canal to the Atlantic. After trading for a time on the East Coast, the schooner was sold in New York.[6]

Years later the *Augusta* (as *Colonel Cook*) returned to the lakes, but never lost her cursed reputation. People always remembered! Once when locking through the Soo, a captain on another schooner looked at her and instantly recognized her as the *Augusta*. When he asked her master if he knew what ship she was, the man replied that they had just found out and that they all had their bags packed in case of emergency.[7]

The old *Augusta* went through a large number of changes in ownership and accidents. Getting crews was very difficult. Sailors continued to claim that the spirits of those she killed on the *Lady Elgin* haunted her. The night deck watch said they "saw things … lights that went round and round and were never there." Sailors in the forecastle "heard clawing, scratching and scrapings of dead men's fingers on the planking outside." The owners laughed and said it was only "rats and rotgut," but sailors knew different. They knew the terrible deed the *Augusta* had done. Many thought for certain she would be the coffin of her crew.[8] On September 23, 1894, she stranded with a stone cargo and went to pieces near Euclid, Ohio, on Lake Erie. The Life-Savers brought the crew off without loss. It was the ship the lake wanted, not the men; at least not these men. Whether the accident was connected with the *Augusta* curse certainly can't be proved, but there are those who "knew."

There was also a second *Augusta* on the lakes. Built at St. Catherines in 1872 for the timber trade, she was 137 feet and 372 tons. On December 1, 1900, she wrecked at Port Credit, becoming a total loss. Giving a ship the name of a wrecked ship was never good, especially one with a reputation as tainted as the *Augusta*.

The *Augusta* was also the second vessel named *Colonel Cook*. The first was a 327-ton American schooner that left Detroit in 1858 for Liverpool with a cargo of staves only to wreck in the St. Lawrence River. Again, giving the ship the name of a wrecked vessel was not a good idea.

Nelse Malott, her master at the time of the collision with the *Lady Elgin*, was by all accounts a fine and conscientious seaman who would struggle with the *Augusta* for the rest of his life. In 1861, the year following the *Lady Elgin* disaster, Bissell and Davidson, owners of the *Augusta*, gave him command of the bark *Ravenna*. He made many lake trips with her, including several across the Atlantic to London. Doubtless being off the lakes was a good thing. In early 1864, he was given the bark *Mojave*, considered the flagship of the company fleet. On September 8, 1864, Captain Malott, his ship and crew of 10 disappeared in mid-Lake Michigan, reportedly very near to the spot the *Lady Elgin* perished. At the time, the weather was fine and no explanation for the loss was discovered, although it was surmised that a "white squall" was the culprit. It was, however, four years to the day that the *Augusta* sank the *Lady Elgin*. It also was said that almost to a man, the crew of the *Mojave* was the same that was on the *Augusta*. This was a crew the lake did want![9]

There is even a more macabre twist. Stories spread that a vigilante posse from Milwaukee caught up with Malott and his men and lynched them, then stuffed their bodies in the *Mojave* and sunk it in deep water to both hide the crime and make a rough retribution for the *Lady Elgin*.

Well before the *Augusta* punched a hole in her, the *Lady Elgin* also was considered a cursed vessel. When launched at Buffalo in 1851, she had the engines and boilers from the old slave ship *Cleopatra*, an ocean slaver confiscated by the U.S. Navy.[10] Reusing gear from a wreck was never good, but from a former slaver was worse. She also had two major "accidents." In August 1854 she struck an uncharted reef six miles south of Manitowoc. Luckily, she was able to back off and struggle back to Manitowoc without injury to any of the 300 passengers aboard.[11] A fire in 1857 destroyed much of her hurricane deck and heavily damaged a number of staterooms.[12]

A lakes vessel infamous for killing two complete crews was the 100-foot, 132-ton two-masted schooner *Rosa Belle*. Built in Milwaukee in 1863, in 1875 she was found by a Lake Michigan car ferry floating upside down in mid-lake. Her entire crew of 10 was missing. Towed into port and righted, she soon returned to service. On October 20, 1911, the *Rosa Belle* was found by a Grand Trunk car ferry again floating hull up. The stern was missing, which implied a collision, but the other vessel could not be identified. None had reported a collision or showed up with unexplained damage. As before, her entire crew of 10 to 28 had again disappeared. They had just gone "through the door."[13] Since the House of David, a fanatical religious cult based in Benton Harbor, Michigan, used her to service their High Island colony and owned the *Rosa Belle*, her loss had mysterious and perhaps even religious overtones.

When the 136-foot schooner *Fleetwing* went ashore at the dreaded Death's Door, at the tip of Wisconsin's Door Peninsula, in September 1867 becoming a total loss, she was just a cog in a line of hoodoo ships carrying the cursed name. In December 1866, the first *Fleetwing*, a large and graceful schooner-yacht, raced with two other vessels across the Atlantic as part of a $10,000 challenge match. The other two came through safely. The *Fleetwing* didn't. In mid-ocean, a rouge wave swept into her cockpit and washed six men overboard to a cold and lonely death. In 1863, the 108-foot schooner *Fleetwing* was built on the American side of Lake Ontario.

She was still nearly new when a sudden squall knocked her over, drowning the captain's wife, 5-year-old son and the cook. Since she was without cargo, the *Fleetwing* floated and was eventually salvaged. The wife's body was found trapped in a lower bunk in the cabin and that of the son eventually washed ashore at Salmon Point. He still wore the little blue sailor suit his mother had lovingly made for him. The old cook's body was found near Whitby lying forlornly on the sandy beach. One hand continued to grip his old butcher knife. Repaired and returned to service, the *Fleetwing* always carried with her the stigma of death. In April 1893, she was bound for Kingston with Oswego coal. The weather was bitterly cold and by now the old schooner was thickly coated with glistening ice. It was also night and as black as there ever was. When the short-handed crew fought to take in a steel-stiff sail, one of them lost his footing and slid overboard. Although the yawl was quickly launched, the unfortunate man was gone into the dark forever. He left a young wife to mourn alone. The maritime community knew that the *Fleetwing* was just a "bad" ship.

The small, 60-ton wooden ferry *Fleetwing* burned and sank in Conneaut harbor in 1920. In theory, *Fleetwing* was a wonderful name for a vessel. In practice it was cursed.[14]

Comparatively modern vessels also earned hoodoo status. The whaleback steamer *Henry W. Cort* is a case in point. Built in 1892 by the American Shipbuilding Company in Superior, Wisconsin, the 320-foot vessel earned her distinction as the result of numerous mishaps, several on Lake Michigan.

On December 17, 1917, she was rammed by the steamer *Midvale* and sunk in 30 feet of water 4½ miles from the Colchester Light in Lake Erie. When salvers finally located her on April 24, 1918, she was 4 miles from the point of collision. Evidently she had no desire to be found, for the lifeless hull had drifted along the bottom with 7 feet of water over her. It took a year's worth of work, four attempts and a large amount of money before she was finally raised on September 22, 1918. In 1927, she was converted into a crane-equipped freighter. A year later she ripped her bottom out, again near Colchester Light. In 1933, she went on another reef, sinking to her decks. Again salvage costs in both instances were considerable. The following year the *Cort* rammed and sunk a fish tug in Muskegon, Michigan, harbor with the loss of two lives.

The end for the unlucky ship came on November 30, 1934, when a 60 mph gale drove her into the rubble breakwater at Muskegon. The mountainous waves broke the unlucky *Cort* in two, spelling the end of an infamous Lake Michigan hoodoo. The Coast Cutter *Escanaba* saved the 23-man crew, although one Coast Guardsman lost his life during the rescue.[15]

The *Pere Marquette 16* was an infamous Lake Michigan railroad ferry hoodoo. Originally christened the *Shenango No. 2*, she was built by the Craig Shipbuilding Company in Toledo in 1895. The wood steamer was 282 feet in length and had three propellers, two aft and one forward.

Throughout her career she showed an amazing propensity for getting into trouble again and again. Early on, she was in ice difficulty on Lake Erie. On October 20, 1898, she was entering Milwaukee during the very early morning hours when she inexplicably stopped responding to the helm. The captain frantically signaled the engine room, but nothing happened. Finally, he frantically rang full astern to the engine room, it was misunderstood and the engines shifted to full ahead, sending the steamer crashing into a partially completed grain elevator, damaging herself and the elevator.

On December 18, 1899, after being sold and renamed *Muskegon*, she departed Milwaukee with a full cargo of 26 railroad cars. Caught in the open lake by a storm, she was blown into the trough of the waves and punished badly, eventually barely struggling back to Milwaukee.

A bare two months later, February 23, 1900, she again left Milwaukee in good weather only to be overtaken by a roaring norther in mid-lake. Heavy seas broke her rudder quadrant. Unable to steer, she was again blown into the trough of the waves. This time the heavy rolling knocking several cars from their tracks, ripping off the chains securing them in place. The loose railcars created havoc, smashing into other cars as well as ship's bulwarks. After a desperate effort, the crew chained the rudder amidships and the captain was able to bring her into safety at Racine by using her engines to steer.

The following May the *Muskegon* collided in the fog with the scow *Silver Lake* off Manitowoc. Cut in two, the scow sank with the loss of one life. In 1906, the steamer was renamed *Pere Marquette 16*.

On the night of December 21, 1901, she ran hard up on a sand bar attempting to enter Ludington, Michigan, in a storm. The waves soon broke her back, snapping several steam pipes, which seriously burned three of the engine room crew. Pile driver-force waves drove her against the north pier, sinking the badly damaged steamer in 16 feet of water. One of the injured men died before the

Life-Savers were able to rescue them. After a heavy repair bill she returned again to service.

Beginning in 1906 she ran into a string of accidents. On November 22 she went aground at Peshtigo, Wisconsin, suffering minor damage. She collided with a scow in the Sturgeon Bay Canal on May 26, 1907. In another collision off Kewaunee on June 21, 1907, she damaged the old schooner *Rosebud*. On September 20, 1907, she struck the city dock at Waukegan. The next month she was disabled off the city, requiring an expensive tow to Chicago.

Her end as a ferry came on November 20, 1907. Running south on Lake Michigan she was struck by a powerful north gale and, after fighting the mountainous seas, was eventually forced into the wave trough. Two of the cars broke loose and crashed around the car deck, shattering several steam lines and knocking out the engines. The captain dropped her anchors, trying to ride out the blow. Repeatedly hammered by the waves, the pitching and rolling of the ship caused more cars to jump loose, nearly destroying the car deck. As in the February 23, 1900, accident, only the desperate work of the crew brought the engines back on line and allowed her to safely limp into Milwaukee in near sinking condition. The repairs needed to put the old wooden steamer back in order were too extensive and she was laid up until she could be sold off, but who would want a jinxed ship?

The answer was the Hammerhill Paper Company, purchasing her in 1918 and cutting her down to a steam barge. Renamed *Harriet B.*, her end came on May 3, 1922, when the big 504-foot steel steamer *Quincy A. Shaw* smashed into her in the fog off Two Harbors, Minnesota. Within 20 minutes the old ferry dove for the bottom, a hoodoo to the last.[16]

Another hoodoo car ferry was the *Ann Arbor No. 4*. Built by the Globe Iron Works in Cleveland in 1906, the 269-foot ferry was an important part of the Ann Arbor Railroad-cross-Lake Michigan link. She suffered misfortune after misfortune in a career as troubled as the *Pere Marquette 16*. Some claimed that she had an accident for every year she sailed. Major misadventures included: Running ashore at Point Au Barques, Lake Michigan, on January 24, 1909. Believing his vessel was hard aground, the captain hiked over the ice to shore to wire for a tug. However, once he had trekked out of sight, the wind shifted and the ferry blew free. Imagine his surprise when he returned to discover his boat gone.

While loading railcars in Manistique on October 14, 1909, she suddenly capsized. There was no apparent reason for the flip. It took more than a month to right her and salvage costs were considerable.

She ripped off bottom plates on October 14, 1911, while running through the Door Peninsula's Rock Island Passage. Strangely the channel was always deep enough before. What happened now? Repairs took a month.

On February 12, 1912, she grounded and was badly damaged a mile north of Manitowoc while trying to enter the harbor. At the time, she was under the command of the first mate, since the captain was attending his brother's wedding. Because it was an utterly normal run, without any strange storms or mechanical problems, the accident was inexplicable.

She went aground November 18, 1913, on Green Island in Green Bay, during a stiff northeast gale. Damages were slight.

Her worst accident occurred in February 1923 on her Frankfort-Kewaunee run. She started in calm seas and light snow but within half an hour an 80 mph storm slammed into her. Temperatures plummeted to 20 degrees below zero and heavy ice formed everywhere. While battling through the heaving seas, part of her railcar cargo broke loose. Eventually the battering cars knocked the stern sea gate off, opening her up to potential flooding. In a remarkable feat of seamanship, the captain swung her back around for Frankfort. He nearly made it back to port. At 7 a.m. on February 14, almost without steerageway, he tried to enter the harbor, but since his stern was flooded and drawing about five feet more than normal, she struck bottom, shearing off her starboard wheel and rudderstock. When the next wave brought her up, she hit the south pier. The dying car ferry slowly swung toward the north until she ended up broadside to the pier. After great difficulty the Coast Guard rescued the crew by breeches buoy. Following extensive repairs she returned to service.

November 28, 1924, saw her aground off Kewaunee, but with little damage. Grounding again off Kewaunee on February 13, 1925, damage was extensive enough to require a trip to the dry dock.

In 1937, she was sold to the Michigan State Ferries and renamed the *City of Cheboygan*. After converting her railcar deck for autos, she carried traffic over the Straits of Mackinac for 21 years until the bridge opened in 1958. No longer needed by the state, she was sold and converted to a fish processing plant and finally scrapped in 1974. It is fascinating that, as the *Ann Arbor No. 4,* she was considered a hoodoo, but as the *City of Cheboygan* she experienced no problems. In her case a name change brought good luck instead of bad.[17]

It was common in the early days of sail and steam that when a vessel experienced a spell of bad weather, or if things were not going well, crew members tried to fasten blame on another crewman, " ... that SOB is a Jonah, we had nothing but bad luck since he got on. ..."[18] Cross-eyed or "swivel-eyed" sailors were also considered Jonahs. It was said that a wheelsman couldn't steer straight if a cross-eyed person, crew or passenger, were aboard.[19] Some also thought a cross-eyed wheelsman brought head winds and at a minimum tempted fate.[20]

When the schooner *M.J. Cummings* went ashore near Milwaukee in 1894, there was a considerable amount of "I told you so," since one of her crew was a reported Jonah. Many of his previous vessels had burned, capsized, wrecked or foundered.[21] Why a captain would have such a sailor aboard is strange indeed. Why take the chance?

If one chooses to believe in such things, a strong case could be made that the steamer *Anna C. Minch* was a cursed vessel. Launched in 1903 by the American Shipbuilding Company, she was named for the daughter of a Great Lakes ship owner.

Throughout a career every freighter goes through any number of bumps and scrapes, the price of working the hard lakes trade. But right from the start, the *Minch* had more accidents than expected and superstitious sailors considered her a hoodoo.

In the years between April 1907 and December 1925, she was involved in six serious collisions with other vessels and an equal number with piers and docks. You could argue that collision with another ship was the fault of the other ship, but hitting an inanimate object like a dock certainly was only the fault of the ship. The *Minch* grounded three times and was damaged by ice once. In 1925, she stranded on Fox Point Shoals, 15 miles south of Port Washington, Wisconsin, on Lake Michigan. Enough was enough, and in 1926 she was sold to the Western Navigation Company of Fort William, Ontario. Under her new colors she ran mostly in the Canadian grain trade. However, her mishaps continued.

The end for the unlucky ship came during the infamous 1940 Armistice Day storm. For reasons still unknown, she foundered with all 24 hands off Pentwater, Michigan, Lake Michigan. When divers found the wreck in 40 feet of water, they discovered a large hole in the bow, the heavy steel smashed in by some great force.

For many years it was believed that the *Minch* had collided with the steamer *William B. Davock*, also lost in the same area with all hands during the storm. But when the *Davock* was finally found in 1972, she had no evidence of a collision. So what had struck the cursed *Minch*, finally taking her to the grave? Did she find a dock to hit in the middle of Lake Michigan?[22]

The U.S. Revenue Cutter *Tuscarora* apparently figured in solving but not explaining another lake mystery. The *Tuscarora* 's normal cruising grounds were lakes Michigan and Superior. Built in Richmond, Virginia, in 1902, the 178-foot steamer spent most of her early career based out of Milwaukee. Her crew consisted of seven officers and 58 enlisted men. The majority of her time seems to have been spent transporting dignitaries and assisting at various yacht races and civic celebrations. Often the duty was referred to as "showing the flag." Like the Great Lakes commercial fleet, she laid-up in the fall and most of the crew were discharged until spring when she was placed back on duty and the crew was hired back. With the coming of "Mr. Wilson's War" (World War I), she and her crew were transferred to the Navy on April 6, 1917. It was while under Navy control that she made her stop at Traverse City. On September 18 she was sent out of the lakes for duty on the East Coast. She returned in 1920, remaining until 1925 when she returned to the Atlantic to assist in prohibition patrols. The *Tuscarora* was decommissioned in 1936.

In a small article in the *Grand Traverse Herald*, on June 12, 1899, mention was made of the annual "boiling of the bay" phenomenon. It seems that the previous day, a patch of water in the bay, opposite the present day power plant in West Bay, literally boiled. After a short period of "boiling," a great geyser of water bolted upward then collapsed back. Shortly afterward, everything quieted back down to a flat calm.

Three years later, a local fisherman drowned in the same area. Some speculated that it might have been connected to the boiling phenomenon. In 1910, the newspaper noted that an excursion boat had become caught in the boil but none of its two-dozen passengers were injured.

The strange boiling water was apparently common enough that everyone knew about it. Generally, it just wasn't newsworthy, so it was only infrequently reported. Still, no one ever recorded the cause of the phenomenon.

Then the government got involved in the mystery. The *Tuscarora* anchored off the Grand Rapids and Indiana Railroad dock precisely where the water periodically boiled. Supposedly the

Tuscarora was in town to tow away a seized tug. The captain of the cutter, B.L. Reed, told a newspaper editor that he would only be in the city for a couple of days. When pressed for details, he gave evasive answers. Intrigued, the newspaper arranged to have men keep an eye on the steamer and her secretive captain. During the dark of the second night, a remarkable sight rewarded their vigilance. The stern of the steamer bustled with activity and in short order two hard-hat divers were dressed, a working stage rigged and the two divers went into the water. The divers were only underwater a short time before they were brought back to the surface and onto the steamer's stern. Nothing could be seen of what they had done or recovered. The *Tuscarora* quickly hauled anchor and departed Traverse City without help of the tug.

The water never boiled again. What had caused the strange boiling? And what did the *Tuscarora* do to stop it? Was this a 1917 version of the infamous Roswell, New Mexico, UFO incident?[23]

Among UFO supporters it is believed, as an article of faith, that in July1947 a flying saucer crashed in the desert near Roswell, New Mexico. The Air Force immediately sealed off the site and recovered the bodies of four to five space aliens, and then covered up the entire incident, denying it ever happened.

Another case of a strange underwater disturbance happened on Lake Michigan, at Sylvan Beach in Muskegon, Michigan, on May 2, 1902. The *Detroit Free Press* of May 5 reported the story. "Bennett & Schnorbach, of this city, who have the contract for raising the private launch, *Amelia*, wrecked at Sylvan Beach, say they have a hard job ahead of them. The *Amelia* now stands perfectly upright, only about 6 feet of its bow being above the surface of the lake. There is now nearly 25 feet of water alongside the boat, and it is 53 feet in length, over 20 feet of its stern is buried in the sand at the bottom of the lake.

"This singular disaster, which occurred last Thursday, was caused by a mysterious subsidence of the bottom of the lake, which phenomenon was accompanied by such a precipitous rush of water as to uptilt the *Amelia* and bury its stern in the bottom of the lake. Whether this occurrence was due to a sudden caving in of a subterranean channel, or an equally mysterious sloughing off of the shore into deeper water is unknown and will doubtless remain forever an unsolved riddle. At any event, where there was formerly shallow water from 3 to 4 feet in depth there is now 18 to 25 feet of water. A portion of the shore 250 feet long and 50 feet back from the water's edge was submerged at the same time. This unusual disaster occurred a short distance south of the Sylvan Beach dock.

"The *Amelia* was sheltered in a boathouse which was built last season at a cost of $1,000, about 100 feet out from the shore. It is elegantly appointed, had a roomy cabin, and cost nearly $6,000. It is the property of F. D. Russell, of New York City, who owns a cottage and has spent several seasons at Sylvan Beach. The Russells, however, intend to spend the coming summer on the Hudson, and Ives Russell, their son, was at Sylvan Beach at the time, looking after the work of preparing the boat for reshipment to New York.

"So far as is known, the *Amelia* is uninjured except by the damage caused by the water to the engine and interior. It is possible, however, that the piles on which the boathouse rested, in rising to the surface, may have struck the yacht with sufficient force to break a hole in her. The boathouse itself was badly wrecked and had to be cut away from the yacht and floated to a place of safety. The chief difficulty in floating the boat that now presents itself is the fact that 20 feet of its stern are buried in the sand at the bottom of the lake. A strain could not possibly be brought to bear in lifting the boat out without breaking it in two until the sand was worked away from her stern by means of steam jets or a sand sucker."[24]

So what triggered the strange bottom collapse? Native Americans long believed that the Great Lakes were interconnected by rivers running deep under the bottom. Could one of the subterranean passages have caved in?

The cardinal rule of the sea is to always help fellow mariners in distress. Not to do so is to be cursed by the gods. The *Vernon* episode is an excellent example of this old unwritten law of the sea.

The steamer *Vernon* was launched on August 16, 1886, at the Chicago Drydock Company. A crowd estimated at 5,000 people watched as the new Booth Fishing Company vessel slid into the water. With a length of 177 feet, beam of 26 feet and draft of 18 feet, she wasn't the biggest steamer, but she promised to be among the fastest. Two 6-foot-diameter Scotch boilers fed her powerful 565-horsepower engine. If the designers were correct, she would be one of the fastest ships on the lakes. She was named for Vernon Booth, the son of the owner of the company. Local papers claimed that no expense was spared to outfit her to first class status, including her 18 passenger cabins and well-appointed lounge.[25]

But the naval architects erred badly. She was fast indeed, but the long narrow hull and deep draft made her unstable when

loaded with a full cargo. Not only was she unstable, she drew 3 feet more water than intended, which meant that she couldn't get into the small ports as her owner intended.[26]

While the amount of water she drew could be easily and safely tested, her seaworthiness couldn't. Experienced captains took one look at the long narrow hull and high superstructure and claimed that she was an accident waiting to happen. One good storm and she would be over on her beam-ends. Other sailors, however, took the opposite view, claiming she would do just fine.[27]

Her sea trials were a disaster. Booth invited a number of friends and guests aboard for the occasion and provided an elaborate buffet complete with musicians and liquid libations. After required onboard speeches, the order was given to go to full speed, which proved to be a miserable 12 miles per hour. The engineers, hull designers and machinery company all glowered at each other, but the *Vernon* went no faster. In simple terms she was a seagoing pig! Not only was she slow, but she was also unstable.[28]

The question of what to do with the *Vernon* became moot when the steamer *A. Booth* sank on Lake Superior off Grand Portage, Minnesota. A replacement vessel was needed immediately and the new *Vernon* was tapped for the job. As expected, she proved a poor replacement for the *Booth* and the following year was chartered to pull ore barges from Lake Superior to Cleveland, an unglamorous assignment for a ship launched with such high expectations. It was a simple job and true to form she screwed it up, wandering out of the channel and pulling the barges onto a reef near the Soo.[29]

When the Northern Michigan Line (NML) steamer *Champlain* burned with the loss of 22 lives in Lake Michigan off Charlevoix, Michigan, in June 1887, another golden opportunity for success was handed to the *Vernon*. The NML needed a replacement vessel quickly and Booth provided the *Vernon* under a charter arrangement. Ominously three of the men who escaped the *Champlain* fire signed on to the *Vernon*.[30] Did they bring bad luck with them?

The last run for the *Vernon* started on October 20, 1887. She made a routine trip from Chicago to Cheboygan with brief stops at Manitowoc, Sutton's Bay, Northport and St. Ignace, dropping off and picking up passengers and freight at each port. On October 26, she pulled out of Cheboygan on the return run. She briefly stopped at Mackinaw City, then went on to St. James on Beaver Island, Leland, Glen Haven and Frankfort before heading across the lake for Chicago on the night of October 28.

Around 10 p.m. a northeast gale blew up. After a time the winds shifted to dead north and huge waves, now rolling down the entire fetch of the lake, slammed into the *Vernon*. The steamer battled on, but she was overmatched. Soon the engine room was flooded and without power, she was forced into the trough of the waves. Sometime between 3 a.m. and 4 a.m., Saturday, October 29, she foundered somewhere east of Rawley Point, Wisconsin, taking an estimated 44 to 50 people to their deaths. The exact number will never be known since who got on and who got off at her various stops was not recorded. The true tragedy is that even after the *Vernon* sank, some people could have been saved had not other vessels ignored her survivors.[31]

Slowly the horrible truth came out. After the schooner *Joseph Paige* arrived in Milwaukee Saturday night, her captain reported seeing people clinging to wreckage, but he failed to pick them up. The steambarge *Superior*, captained by Moran, reported sighting several rafts with survivors signaling for help but didn't stop, either. He also saw people in the water wearing life jackets. A yawl boat with a woman and two men signaling frantically for assistance was ignored, too. The schooner *Blazing Star* apparently came through the same wreckage field and also didn't bother to stop, survivors or no survivors. The schooner *William Home* discovered floating bodies and a live survivor hanging on to the pilothouse, but followed the heartless lead of her sisters and sailed blithely on without stopping. The attitude clearly was "survivors be damned."

All of the vessels had some kind of a pathetic excuse for not stopping. The *Paige* claimed that her sails were torn from the gales and she couldn't be maneuvered. The captain of the steamer *Superior* maintained that his rudder was disabled. The masters of the *Blazing Star* and *William Home* said that it was just too rough. If lake conditions were too bad for the vessels to save anyone, imagine how bad it was clinging to a piece of wreckage!

Even worse, all the vessels sailed past Manitowoc to reach Milwaukee but never bothered to report the wreckage or survivors to anyone at Manitowoc. Had they taken the time to report the survivors, the local U.S. Life-Saving Service could have attempted rescue. The lifesaving crew didn't even learn of the disaster until the *Milwaukee Sentinel* contacted them regarding it. Even when the NML learned of the rescue, they made no effort to send out tugs or other craft to search for survivors or even recover bodies.

What is known of the wreck is largely the result of the single survivor, Axel Stone, a 23-year-old Swedish immigrant. He was found on a raft by the schooner *S.B. Pomeroy* eight miles east of Sheboygan, Wisconsin. Stone's testimony was damning, claiming that the *Vernon* was grossly overloaded, the cargo of pig iron, fish, staves, apples, potatoes and general merchandise packed so tightly that all the passageways were jammed with it. The freight also prevented the closure of some of the gangway hatches. Once the storm hit, the *Vernon* was a dead duck. Water poured into the overloaded boat, far more than the pumps could ever handle. The mate pleaded with Captain Thrope to return to the shelter of the Manitou Islands, but the old man refused, preferring to tough it out. Earlier, when she was running through the Straits of Mackinac, Stone said that he overheard the second mate accosting the captain to "sober up." Thrope told him to "go to hell" and continued to nip at his hip flask. About 3 a.m. the inevitable happened: the steamer went over on her beam ends and was forced into the trough of the waves. When she dove for the bottom, Stone managed to reach a raft where the schooner found him the following day.

Regardless of the poor design of the *Vernon*, her overloaded condition and even accusations of drunkenness on the part of the captain, the inexplicable part of the disaster was the refusal of not one ship, or two, or three but four to make any effort at all to rescue the survivors. Such callous behavior flies against every tradition of the sea. The lake gods didn't forget such treachery. The lakes later destroyed every ship. None lived to honorable retirement.

An inquest held in Two Rivers, Wisconsin, where many of the bodies eventually came ashore, damned the captains of every one of the vessels who refused to rescue the survivors. The panel couldn't understand how none of the ships, in consideration of their supposed inability to rescue the victims, at least didn't stop at Manitowoc and report the wreck and desperate survivors. In part the report stated, " ... we hold these captains deserving of the execration of all brave sailors, and the reproach of human men everywhere."[32]

All of the vessels that ignored the victims were shipwreck victims themselves.

The schooner *Joseph Paige* was downbound with ore in tow of the steamer *H.B. Tuttle* in eastern Lake Superior when a powerful northwest gale roared down on her. The crashing seas soon broke her towing hawser and drove the helpless *Paige* onto a sandbar off Vermilion. Luckily, the courageous Life-Saving Service crew was equal to the challenge, unlike the *Paige*'s opportunity a decade earlier. Launching their surfboat into the teeth of the breakers, the crew reached the schooner and brought the crew of eight men and a woman cook to safety.[33]

The schooner *Blazing Star* lasted less than a month after the shameful *Vernon* performance, going ashore in a gale and breaking up on Fisherman Shoal, near Washington Island, just north of the *Vernon* wreck site.[34]

The *William Home* foundered with all six hands in a storm off Seul Choix Lighthouse in northern Lake Michigan on September 25, 1894.[35]

The steamer *Superior* stranded and broke up off Gull Island, near Beaver Island, in northern Lake Michigan on August 28, 1898. One crewman perished.[36]

It is indeed a remarkable coincidence. Four ships ignore the oldest tradition of the sea – rescuing fellow sailors in distress – and all in turn perish in the same manner. Clearly the lake gods were wreaking their vengeance.

Scuba divers discovered the *Vernon* in 1969. The wreck rests in 200 feet of deep, dark and cold Lake Michigan water. Their examination proved Stone's allegations of overloading to be correct.

There is the strange and unexplained tale of the small 117-foot schooner *Miranda*. The schooner was discovered drifting and waterlogged off Michigan City by another vessel. When the crew boarded her they found that her yawl was still on the davits but apparently no crew aboard. Discovering the cabin door locked and bolted from the inside, the men forced it. Inside they discovered the drowned bodies of an old man and 17-year-old boy sloshing to and fro in the flooded cabin. A third crewman was missing. What had happened to the schooner? Where was the crew? And what happened to the man and boy? There were questions, but no answers.[37] The *Miranda* was returned to service and later wrecked on Port Austin Reef, Lake Huron.[38]

Hoodoo ships are classically defined as bad luck boats, vessels that are dogged by things going wrong. Sometimes they start their careers that way. Other times it is the result of a "change in life." Captain Reuben A. Johnson and the *Highway 16* is a great example of a change in mid-course for the worse.

Johnson was born in Ludington, Michigan, in 1894 and gained extraordinary experience on the *Pere Marquette* car ferries, working them for 20 years, 15 as a captain. In 1935, he moved to the Wisconsin-Michigan Steamship Company as a mate. In 1949, he became captain of the fleet's *Highway 16*, a converted 328-foot World War II LST (Landing Ship Tank) used as a carrier of new cars from the auto plants in Michigan to Milwaukee.

For the four years Johnson ran the ship, she had a perfect record, arriving on time and without an accident to ship, cargo, docks or other vessels. While the achievement certainly reflected his careful attention to detail and safety, it can be argued that it was also due to the "spirit of the boat." It "knew" the captain and responded to his touch and personality.

Disaster struck on April 21, 1953, when Captain Johnson dropped dead of a heart attack in his home. While a devastating loss to his loved ones, it was also reflected in the operation of the boat. Running under a new captain, the ship was suddenly plagued by mishaps. Where Captain Johnson handled the *Highway 16* with a deft and careful hand, never causing an accident, the new man drove her on regardless of the circumstance. Damage followed in her wake. Small craft were smashed and broken left and right. Critics claimed that she never slowed entering Muskegon Harbor and her lookouts were blind to danger. For example on July 5, 1959, she collided with the yacht *K-D-Bob*, killing six innocent boaters. But there were many examples of other damages, too. It was almost as though the ship knew Johnson was no longer in the pilothouse and now she could do whatever she wanted![39]

54

Lightning, volatile fuel and a ship can be a deadly combination as ably demonstrated by the small tanker *Altamha* on July 13, 1929. The small 189-foot steamer was loaded with a full cargo of 8,000 gallons of oil and had just pulled away from her Muskegon, Michigan, dock when the unimaginable happened: a bolt of lightning struck her.

The results were catastrophic. The cargo immediately ignited and exploded, sending burning oil out in a huge arc around the ship. The 10-man crew dove for safety as best they could, some leaping into the harbor, others jumping for the still-close dock. One man suffered internal injuries from hitting the dock as well as burns over 70 percent of his body. Most had at least some burns. The *Altamha* blazed to the waterline becoming a total loss.

Later, one of the mates, named Harvey, commented ominously that it was the fourth ship he had been on that was struck by lightning. One can only wonder two things. First, if the rest of the crew knew they were sailing with such a hoodoo? And second, why Harvey thought he should take his lightning-prone career in an oil tanker, of all ships?[40]

The infamous brigantine *Helfenstein* was one of the worst bad-luck ships on the lakes, but perhaps least well known of the cursed fleet. Built in Milwaukee in 1847, her entire career seems to have been spent careening wildly from one accident to another. The *Detroit Free Press* estimated that she and her crews suffered through about 40 various scrapes and was commanded by nearly double that number of captains. Good ships do not "churn" masters.

Her first disaster occurred on Lake Michigan on July 4, 1852, when she became disabled in a gale, lost both anchors and ended up on the beach at Milwaukee. Quick work got her off the sand and she continued to Chicago, but sank in the windy city with a loss of $3,600. In October, she smacked a pier, receiving additional damage. Four years later she lost part of her deck load of cut slate on the lake, dropped her foreyard, damaging herself, and collided with the steamer *Omar Pasha* when entering Chicago. That November she inexplicably lost a man overboard, and a few years later a mate went over the side, too. August 1866 saw her ashore at Harrisville on Lake Huron. In June 1871, she sank in Marquette after loading an ore cargo. These are just some of her long list of "accidents." Marine men claimed that by 1874 few of her masters were still living. Ill fortune must have dogged them, too. In June of that year she was finally cut down from a brig to a lowly tow barge, but her terrible record of accident and mayhem continued.[41]

The admonition against starting a season on a Friday was as strong on Lake Michigan as any of the Great Lakes. In May 1895, the steamer *Kalamazoo* was set to leave South Haven with an excursion party on a Friday when her crew rebelled, refusing to depart on such an unlucky day. The captain, who evidently agreed with the crew or at least didn't want to "buck" them, delayed sailing until quarter past midnight.[42]

The single most important event in the life of a ship, regardless of purpose or size, is her launching. Nothing can be allowed to mar the occasion. Everything must be perfect. The prelaunch speeches, smashing the bottle of spirits on the bow with a strong and steady swing, christening her in a loud clear voice and, of course, she must slide easily down the well-greased ways to meet her new element. For a ship to "stick" on the ways is a terrible calamity. But that is exactly what the *Material Service* did.

The motorized barge *Material Service* was built by the Smith Dock Company at Sturgeon Bay, Wisconsin. Construction started during the summer of 1928 and she was ready to launch on March 6, 1929.

The 240-foot-long, 40-foot-beam steel barge was a one-of-a-kind vessel designed to handle bulk sand or gravel in the most efficient manner possible. With her hold divided into eight compartments and an internal conveyor and boom system, she could unload directly at construction sites. Most important, since she was intended to run the Chicago River system, her design held to a maximum height of 14.5 feet to allow unfettered passage under the many bridges.

Regardless of her design, when the bottle was smashed on her bow and the yard workers knocked out the blocks keeping her on the ways, she refused to move. It seemed like she was welded to the structure. The builders were greatly embarrassed as were the owners. This was a terrible omen. For a day prior, Sturgeon Bay was lashed by a strong spring snowstorm and evidently the barge literally froze on the ways. After several hours of frantic chopping of ice, the barge reluctantly splashed into Sturgeon Bay. Doubtless the old timers, veterans of hundreds of launches, must have shook their heads knowingly. Certainly nothing good would come of the cursed barge.

Regardless of such an ignoble beginning, the barge went along her career with only the expected number of bumps and scrapes. Delivering construction material was neither glamorous nor especially dangerous. It was just plain old work.

This work-a-day existence ended on November 30, 1930, while moving through the Chicago Sanitary and Ship Canal. Without warning, a powerful fireball blew out of the engine room and exploded into the galley, crew quarters and wheelhouse. Seven crew were injured, including the captain, two seriously. One, the woman cook, died as a result of the blast.

Investigation showed that it wasn't a mechanical failure but clearly the result of a bomb. A Cook County Sheriff's investigator concluded that the explosive was nitroglycerin. Why someone bombed the barge was never determined, but considering the various mob wars going on in Chicago, it isn't hard to build a scenario around political corruption, missed payoffs and the like. The exact reason for the bombing remains a mystery.

After repair, the barge bumped along her mundane life until July 28, 1936. Around 11:30 p.m. she cleared the Chicago River and turned south on Lake Michigan bound for the Calumet River. She was deeply laden with a full cargo of sand. Although running on the lake could be more risky than taking an inland route, it was much faster than getting caught in the typical delays of the Cal-Sag Canal. Besides, the weather on the open lake looked fine for a quick trip. Ominously the captain did not close his deck hatches. After a while a small chop kicked up, but certainly nothing for the crew to be excited about. All went along apparently fine until about 1 a.m. when an engineer noticed a large amount of water in the bilges. Soon the small chop got larger and the wheelsman detected that she was getting sluggish to handle, not responding well to the rudder. The water flooding in was more than the pumps could throw out. Before the mate in the wheelhouse could sound an alarm, the barge rolled to the left and dove for the bottom of Lake Michigan. Of the 22 crew aboard, 15 were killed in the tragedy.

When the news of the sinking flashed out over the lakes, old-timers in Sturgeon Bay just nodded in agreement. What other end could there be for a ship cursed at birth. Imagine, though, their thoughts when one of her life preservers drifted ashore at Sturgeon Bay nearly a year later.[43]

It is said that human siblings have a relationship beyond the physical, a connection of spirit that can't be broken without repercussions. The same is sometimes true for sister ships.

The steamers *Andaste* and *Choctaw* were both built by the Cleveland Shipbuilding Company on the banks of the Cuyahoga River in 1892. Their unique design often has been described as a "semi-whaleback," straight-back steel freighters similar to a whaleback but with straight sides and a conventional bow. Both were 266 feet long with 900 horsepower engines and a capacity of 3,000 tons of ore.

They plied the Lake Superior iron trade, running between northern ore docks and southern steel mills without incident until the parent company went bankrupt in 1898 and soon after were acquired by the Cleveland Cliffs Iron Company.

The *Choctaw* "died" on July 12, 1915, when she was rammed in a Lake Huron fog by the Canadian steamer *Wacondah*, falling to the bottom of the lake 275 feet down.

The *Andaste* continued on without her sister. During the winter of 1920-21, the Great Lakes Engineering Works cut 20 feet out of her midsection to bring her to 246 feet, allowing her to trade through the small Welland Canal. 1925 saw her sold to the Leatham D. Smith Company of Sturgeon Bay, Wisconsin, and converted into a sand sucker. Part of the conversion involved mounting large derricks on the deck giving her the capability of unloading at a multitude of small ports, but ominously making her more top heavy, too. Although efficient in their work, sand suckers were never known for their seaworthiness.

The *Andaste* operated without incident until September 9, 1929. She loaded gravel at Ferrysburg, Michigan, just upriver from Grand Haven, and cleared the light shortly after 9 p.m. bound for Chicago. It was all routine. She had made the run four times a week and was due in Chicago the following night. About an hour after leaving, a strong northwest wind came up which soon increased to a gale. Still, no special fears were felt for the *Andaste*. Fall gales were common and ships were expected to sail through them as a matter of routine. When she didn't arrive on time, no concern was raised. She was, after all, an old ship, so certainly Captain Albert L. Anderson must have just throttled back and rode out the blow. She didn't have a radio, so Anderson had no way of advising those on shore of his plans. When another day passed and she didn't show up, the alarm was finally raised. Aircraft from the Naval Air Station at Chicago, Coast Guard vessels, commercial ships and private craft all looked for the missing steamer and crew.

Soon wreckage was discovered on Michigan beaches from

Grand Haven to Castle Park, just south of Holland. Eventually the bodies of 14 of the 25 men aboard washed ashore. Only 11 wore life jackets.

The question of how and why the ship sank is unanswered. Since 11 men had life jackets on it is clear that they knew she was in trouble and took the time to prepare. Perhaps she slowly flooded through an unsecured hatch or just went over on her beam ends and dove for the bottom without warning. We may never know the answer, even if the wreck is eventually found.

An inquest in Holland concluded that the ship was in good condition and there was no discernable reason for the loss. The *Andaste* remains missing to this day. Some marine men speculate that she sank 25-30 miles out. Other witnesses on land stated that the whistle of a steamer close by awakened them inshore near Port Sheldon and that's where she perished. When all speculation was over, there was no doubt that she joined Lake Michigan's fleet of the missing, just another unexplained loss on Lake Michigan.

While there are no answers to where and how she perished, there is no doubt that she followed her sister.[44]

CHAPTER 4

Missing, Presumed Lost

What is it about the Great Lakes that causes so many ships and planes to be swallowed up? Is it the sudden and severe storms, deficient seamanship or airmanship, just bad luck or something else ... something we do not yet understand? While all the Great Lakes have their share of these types of mysteries, Lake Michigan seems to have more than her "fair share."

It wasn't always the loss of an entire ship or plane. Sometimes only a single person turned up "lost." But the mystery remained. What happened? The disappearance of Captain George R. Donner on April 28-29, 1937, is a case in point.

Donner was the captain of the steamer *O.M. McFarland* as she was working her way through northern Lake Michigan bound for Port Washington, Wisconsin, with a coal cargo when the veil of inexplicable mystery dropped over her. The steamer left Erie, Pennsylvania, a few days before and it was a difficult early season run. Ice was still on the lakes and constant attention was needed to dodge around the floes. Fifty-eight years old, Donner was an experienced master who "knew the ropes." Running his ship in early spring ice was "old hat" to him.

At 10:15 p.m., Donner told his second mate that he was going below for while but to call him as soon as they were off Port Washington. He estimated that it would take three hours or so. Donner mentioned that he wanted a couple of hours rest, an entirely natural need for any captain feeling the weight of his job. His cabin was just aft of the pilothouse and for some minutes the mate and wheelsman heard him rustling around, perhaps finishing some paperwork needed on arrival.

When the steamer was three hours off Port Washington, the mate dutifully went to the captain's cabin and knocked on the wooden door. There was no answer. He knocked again, but still there was no reply. When he tried the door it was locked. Still thinking that Donner was sleeping very soundly, the mate got the master key and opened the door only to find the cabin empty. Thinking that the captain slipped out to the galley for a late snack before coming back on duty, the mate went below and checked, but the two firemen finishing their meal in the galley hadn't seen him. Now deeply concerned, the officers performed a complete search of the ship but failed to find the captain. He had utterly and completely vanished.

The disappearance was all the more remarkable since he was too big to slip out the cabin's two portholes and the only door led to the companionway in which no one saw the captain between the time he went to the cabin and was discovered missing.

Other ships were asked to keep watch for Donner on the thought that he may have somehow fallen overboard. Coastal communities were also warned in case his body came ashore. His human remains were never found. What ever happened to Captain Donner is still unexplained.[1]

A more modern example of the missing captain syndrome is that of Captain Frederich Helling of the salty *Serius*. The 579-foot freighter, registered in the Cayman Islands under the typical "flag of convenience," was sailing from Chicago to Duluth in October 1987 when her captain stepped into another world.[2]

The *Serius* off-loaded a cargo of cheap foreign steel at Chicago then turned north for the Soo and eventually Duluth and a load of grain. About 2 a.m. on October 21 the captain laid out a course taking his ship up the Manitou Passage, an area fraught with dangers and shipwreck. Shallow reefs line both sides of the shipping lane and at the north end care must be taken to keep to the narrow channel. The 48-year-old West German master made sure that all was well on the ship, then went off to his cabin for the night, promising to return to the bridge at 8 a.m. He would never be seen again.

When he didn't show up on the bridge, the officers went to his cabin to see if he overslept, unheard of for the experienced master. When there was no answer to their knocking, the door was opened showing an empty cabin. A complete search of the ship found no trace of him. With no other recourse, at 11 a.m. they called the Coast Guard and a search rapidly initiated.

Three 44-foot Coast Guard motor lifeboats soon joined a Coast Guard helicopter scrambled from the Traverse City, Michigan, air station. An immediate radio message notified all boats in the area, large and small, to keep a sharp watch for the missing man. All told, the search covered 900 square miles of water and found exactly nothing. Zip, zero, nil, zilch, nothing at all, not a single clue pointing to the captain ever hitting the water.

The Detroit office of the FBI and Grand Rapids, Michigan, U.S. attorney general launched investigations. There were 35 men on the ship. Someone must have seen something. And, of course, there was always the clear possibility of foul play. Did a crewman have a grudge against the captain, one serious enough to commit murder? Every member of the crew was interviewed and every lead followed up, but all to no avail.

The investigators didn't see the captain as a likely suicide. He left no note, had no known problems and was eager to see his wife and children again.

So what happened? Did he walk off the ship, stepping into empty air before hitting the cold lake? Did a crewman take advantage of the dark night and lonely lake to knock him on the head, throw a couple of links of heavy chain about him to assure the body went to, and stayed, on the bottom, then push him off into the water? Could he have just slipped in to the unknown?

The mystery has never been solved.[3]

Strange and unexplained disappearances are not anomalies from the past. Fast-forward to October 8, 1999, when a small 20-foot boat named *Atlantis* was discovered going in circles in the lake eight miles east of Whitefish Bay, near Port Washington, Wisconsin. The boat's owner and apparent sole occupant was one Sean O'Brien, a scuba diver and advertising salesman for the *Milwaukee Journal* newspaper.

When the Coast Guard boarded the boat, they found no evidence of foul play, no evidence of survival gear or a single clue to what happened. The marine radio was working and running lights were on, indicating that he left Milwaukee in either darkness or fog. Earlier, the lake was covered in an early morning fog. There were no apparent mechanical problems and everything seemed in working order. There was no diving gear in the boat. The water was not unduly "rough."

O'Brien was supposed to leave Milwaukee around 11:30 p.m. after a John Mellencamp concert and arrive at Port Washington the following morning to have his boat hauled out for the season.

When he didn't show up, the panic button was pushed and the search started.

A massive search by the Coast Guard, Coast Guard Auxiliary and Milwaukee Police and Fire Department boats, assisted by two helicopters and an airplane, covered 200 square miles of water but failed to find a single trace of O'Brien.

So another human being joins the long list of the missing on Lake Michigan.[4]

In August 2001 the small boat *North Wind* issued a mayday when she was three miles west of St. Joseph, Michigan, at the southeast corner of Lake Michigan. The call gave the impression that she was apparently taking on water. The Coast Guard lost contact with her before determining the number of people aboard or other particulars. Heavy fog also hindered the search. Regardless of a search, no trace was ever found. The *North Wind* was gone.

Aircraft also vanished over Lake Michigan. Northwest Airlines Flight 2501 departed New York City bound for Seattle, Washington, with an intermediate stop in Minneapolis, Minnesota, on June 23, 1950. Well before the days of jet travel, the old but reliable four-engine DC 4 carried a crew of three and 55 passengers. The pilot in command was 35-year-old Robert C. Lind of Hopkins, Minnesota. He had been with Northwest since 1941. His copilot was 35-year-old Verne F. Wolfe of Minneapolis. He had nearly as much time with the airline as Lind. Stewardess Bonnie Ann Feldman, 25 years old, watched over the passengers, who consisted of 27 women, 22 men and six children.

By any standard, the DC-4 was a good airplane. Originally conceived as a long-range airliner for United Airlines, later models, designated the C-54, saw extensive service in the U.S. Army Air Corps during World War II. An early prototype was sold to Japan in 1939 for domestic airline use. The Japanese reported it lost in an accident, but in reality it was disassembled and used as the model for a new military long-range bomber program that never reached production. C-54s made nearly 80,000 Atlantic crossings during the war with only three losses. The first Presidential aircraft, the *Sacred Cow*, was a C-54. Following demobilization, many were declared surplus and sold for civilian use. Demand was so high for this very reliable aircraft that the assembly line reopened.

Over Battle Creek, Michigan, the captain called air traffic control at 11:51 p.m. (local) and updated his planned arrival over

Milwaukee to 11:37 p.m.(local). He was cruising at 3,500 feet. Since thunderstorms were dancing over Lake Michigan, he turned to a northwesterly heading to dodge around them, running between South Haven and Ludington, Michigan. At 12:13 a.m., Lind called traffic control again and requested permission to drop to 2,500 feet. The request was denied since other traffic was in the area. Flight 2501 was never heard from again. Whatever happened was quick, leaving no time for a radio call. It was the worst aviation disaster in the world up to that date.

The airline kept good tabs on the flight. When it failed to report in at Milwaukee, they notified New York, Minneapolis and Chicago that the flight was missing. All Civil Aeronautics Administration radio stations tried to contact it without success. The airline notified air-sea rescue to stand by. The flight was officially presumed lost at 5:30 a.m. when the fuel would have been expended. At first crack of dawn the search began.

Coast Guard, Naval and State Police units from Illinois, Wisconsin, Indiana and Michigan all went to work. At 6:30 p.m. Coast Guard Cutter *Woodbine* located an oil slick, aircraft debris and logbook floating off the Michigan shore northwest of Benton Harbor. Two other Coast Guard Cutters, *Woodrush* and *Hollyhock,* and the Coast Guard icebreaker *Mackinaw* joined in the effort. Additional debris was recovered, including seat cushions, clothing, blankets, luggage and parts of bodies. Captain Bowman of the *Mackinaw* told the press that, "tiny pieces keep floating to the surface all through the area." Among airplane parts, his crew recovered human parts including hands and ears. The Coast Guard ships spent several weeks chasing wreckage and "parts" up the Michigan shore. So much came ashore near South Haven that the city closed South Beach for nine days following the disaster because of the "parts" washing upon the beach. All in all, it was precious little from a four-engine airliner with 58 souls aboard.

The Coast Guard dragged grapples in an effort to find enough wreckage to put Navy divers down. On the 28th, two divers were lowered to the bottom, 150 feet below, and spent half an hour searching for wreckage. The mud was two feet deep and visibility a bare foot. They found nothing.

Several witnesses near the tiny village of Glenn, Michigan, claim to have seen the plane shortly after midnight. One claimed it cruised low over the area about 12:15 a.m. He heard the motors "plunk" and then saw a "queer flash of light." Other stories were similar.

Regardless of the smorgasbord of small bits and pieces of plane and people, a detailed examination by the federal authorities failed to determine the cause of the disaster. It is officially listed as "unknown." Did she suffer a midair explosion? Perhaps a storm cell was powerful enough to drive her into the lake, especially since she was cruising at comparatively low altitude. Or did something go wrong with the engines and Captain Lind attempted a failed water landing? Could it have been something else?

There is a UFO connection to the disaster. Reportedly two Whitefish Bay, Wisconsin, policemen sighted a large object with an eerie red glow hovering in the sky above the lake to the southeast, on a direct course to Ludington. They watched it for 10 minutes before it just disappeared. Ominously they first sighted it at 2 a.m. on June 24, precisely when the Coast Guard started the search and two hours after the airliner's last radio call. This was the height of the national UFO fever. Was there a connection?

The crash continues to fascinate researchers. In May 2005, it was announced that Michigan Shipwreck Research Associates, working with the National Underwater Maritime Agency (a.k.a. Clive Cussler, the well known novelist), would search for the missing airliner. Apparently the missing plane remained missing.

So what happened to the NW 2501? To this day it remains a mystery of the lake.[5]

Other aircraft have vanished over Lake Michigan, too. On July 3, 1998, a privately owned Czech-built L-39 Albatross jet once used to train Soviet Air Force pilots disappeared after leaving an air show at the National Cherry Festival in Traverse City, Michigan. When the jet dropped off radar, a search was started. Two Coast Guard helicopters and two military cargo planes scoured the water for 25 miles northwest of Traverse City, but nothing significant was found. It was simply swallowed by the lake.[6]

Local people often develop strange explanations for such inexplicable losses. Folks around Menominee, Michigan, blame the infamous "Menominee Triangle." The triangle is said to lay off Ingallston, about five or six miles off shore between Menominee and Chambers Island, seven miles or so northeast of the Menominee shoreline. Claims are made that compasses swing erratically and radios don't work there. A commercial fisherman claimed his GPS and chart plotter also often failed in the area. A resident of the area claimed that he knew of at least six or seven planes that went down in the area over the last 20 years. Occasionally fishing vessels will drag pieces of one up from the bottom, but the mystery still remains about why they were lost to begin with. Reputedly ships lost in the area have never been found.[7]

On February 3, 1992, a Beechcraft was inbound over Lake Michigan for Benton Harbor airport when it suddenly dropped off the radar screen. The Coast Guard rapidly responded with a helicopter, which discovered an oil sheen and three aircraft tires with pieces of landing gear floating in the water. More than a month later the body of the passenger washed ashore and eight days later that of the pilot was discovered on the beach. Autopsies revealed that both men drowned. The aircraft is still missing and the cause of the crash is officially listed as "undetermined."[8]

There are more theories about where ole Jimmy Hoffa finally ended up than you can shake a stick at. Some people claim he was buried in the concrete foundation of New Jersey's Meadowlands football stadium, which was under construction when he disappeared. Others conjecture that he was pushed through a wood chipper and fertilized a farmer's field somewhere. And certainly there is always the idea of just being fed a bullet to the head and dropped in a local landfill. What is clear is that there is absolutely no genuine evidence supporting any of the theories, including one maintaining that space aliens from Mars abducted him to help organize a workers union on the red planet.

What is known is that the 62-year-old former Teamsters president vanished from the parking lot of a suburban Detroit restaurant in 1975. For a man with connections at various times to the mafia, White House and perhaps, as some maintain, CIA, any theory, regardless of how bizarre, is thought possible. There were charges that he may have been involved in an aborted assassination of Fidel Castro and perhaps even that of President Kennedy. My point here is that if ever there was a man with weird possibilities swirling around him, it was Jimmy Hoffa.

So what is the connection with the Lake Michigan paranormal? What if after Hoffa got "popped" by a mob killer his body was sealed into a 55-gallon steel drum and taken by truck to a small harbor on the west coast of Michigan. Jimmy wasn't considered missing for a while, so there was no reason that an innocent barrel on an innocent truck would draw any attention. Saugatuck, South Haven or even Holland is an easy day's drive from metro Detroit. Whether it was a mob or CIA hit, either group would have access to a small cruiser. The Jimmy-filled drum is taken out to a deep hole in Lake Michigan and dumped overboard. Punching a couple of holes in the drum assures a quick sinking and prevents an untimely "rising." The beautiful part of it all is that there is no body. Unlike an on-land disposal, the evidence is virtually gone forever. Even if they knew where to look, the effort and expense would be extraordinary, far greater than could be expended on a mere tip from someone. Lake Erie is closer to Detroit, but the water is too shallow. Lake Michigan is the better choice.

So my guess is somewhere on the bottom of Lake Michigan, likely in the southern third, is the barrel-entombed remains of Jimmy Hoffa, just another "went missing" story of the lakes.

CHAPTER 5

Lighthouse Ghosts

I am convinced that every lighthouse is haunted. It is only a question of asking the right person the right question the right way at the right time to get the right answer. And once the dam is broken, the stories flow uninterrupted.

Chambers Island, Wisconsin, first settled in 1857 and 2,900 acres in size, soon hosted a population of 250 people. Principal occupations in the early days included shipbuilding, lumbering and fishing. The lighthouse was built in 1868. An important aid for guiding vessels through Green Bay's west passage, the tower stood 68 feet above the water and had a nominal range of 16 miles. In 1961, the Coast Guard relocated the light from the old stone tower to a new 60-foot steel tower, placing the beacon 97 feet above the water.[1]

Although it may date back many years, the ghost of Chambers Island Light first came to notice in the Spring of 1976 when the present caretaker, Joel Blahnik, arrived to take up his duties. At the time, the old lighthouse was in tough shape, having been abandoned for more than 20 years. Every building needs human habitation. Left lifeless, deterioration is rapid. Lighthouses are no different. Tremendous effort would be needed to bring the facility to the standard envisioned for a planned 40-acre Gibraltar Town Park and museum.

The first night he spent in the light, Blahnik awoke to a loud, "BOOM, BOOM, BOOM," the heavy foot falls of someone coming down the spiral staircase from the lamp room. At the time,

Blahnik was camped out in the old bedroom on the main floor. He tried to wake his 9-year-old son so he, too, could hear the strange noise, but the youngster simply rolled over, telling his father not to bother him and to go back to sleep. Listening closely, Blahnik plainly heard the heavy footsteps of the mysterious intruder. They clumped down the hallway, through the living room, down the steps into the kitchen and continued on to the outside grounds. The kitchen door closed behind with a very distinctive "click."

For the next 10 years the spirit always appeared the first night Blahnik arrived to open the light in the spring. It was never seen, but clearly heard. The pattern was always the same, down the stairs, through the house and out the kitchen door.

The ghost seemed to have a sensitive soul. If others visiting the light expressed a disbelief in his existence, the ghost was sure to wake the doubters during the night. The unbelievers were startled into consciousness by loud footsteps and an overwhelming sense of unearthly presence. Something was with them. Something was there, in the room, although they couldn't distinguish what it was. Unbelievers quietly became believers.

The spirit was always friendly and at times even playful. During the summer of 1979 it behaved much as a poltergeist. Various tools and other minor items disappeared only later to be discovered in other unlikely locations. For example, when Blahnik and his father were working on a window, a screwdriver placed on the sill "went missing." Later it was found under a pillow in the bedroom. Nothing bad ever happened, however. It was just a series of jokes and gags.

The haunting unexpectedly ended in 1987. The spiritual director from a local Catholic retreat took a group of nuns on a tour of the lighthouse and grounds. After he repeated the tale of the supernatural activities at the light, one of the sisters became very concerned. Walking briskly to the southwest side of the building, she placed her hands firmly against the old brick tower wall and prayed intensely for the spirit's release from its earthly bounds. After a minute or so she stopped and came back to the group. Whatever she said was apparently effective. The ghost has not been heard from since.

Although there was no real evidence of who the spirit was, Blahnik thought it was likely that of the first keeper, Lewis Williams. His 22-year tenure was the longest of any of the island's keepers, long enough to sire 11 children while tending faithfully to the beacon in the tower.

Before the light was built, Lewis Williams operated a sawmill at the northwest point of the island. The water was deep close inshore and schooners were able to come right up the beach to load. When Congress decided in 1866 to construct a third class lighthouse on the island, it was Williams who, for the sum of $250, sold the property to the government. His salary as keeper was $450 a year. He tried several times to have his wife appointed assistant keeper, but without success. The government must have reasoned that with 11 children, she was too busy to help with the light.[2]

Some spirits are explained, or at least people think there is a logical explanation, supernatural or otherwise. The mystery of the creaking stairs at Grand Traverse light, at the tip of Michigan's beautiful Leelanau Peninsula, has no rational reason, at least none that anyone has related.

Doug McCormick, a longtime Coast Guard veteran and son of James McCormick, an early Grand Traverse lightkeeper, vividly remembers hearing the eerie creaking stairway often. The effect was always startling, just as if a living person were climbing them. The stairs in question led from the ground floor to the second floor where the bedrooms were located. Try as he may, he could never catch the "creaker." Every time he heard the mysterious footsteps, he flew out of his bedroom and into the hall, but it was always empty. Whatever was causing the sound had disappeared. Was it the spirit of an earlier resident still making its way through the house, or just the settling of the building? He never found it.[3]

The only keeper recorded as dying in the lighthouse was Dr. Henry Schetterly, 1862-1873. Is he still on watch, still checking his light?

The Grand Traverse light, an important aid for vessels sailing through the dangerous Manitou Passage, was ordered constructed by President Millard Fillmore in 1850 and was in operation by 1852. The old tower was demolished in 1858 and a new lighthouse built on higher ground nearby. It is claimed that Mormons from Beaver Island raided the lighthouse a couple of times in an effort to steal the lens for use at Beaver Island. The Coast Guard abandoned the original light tower in 1972 and the beacon was transferred to a skeletal steel tower.[4] Today it is a wonderful lighthouse museum.

St. Martin Island, Michigan, sits roughly halfway between Wisconsin's Door Peninsula and Michigan's Garden Peninsula. Slightly smaller than 200 acres, the island is mostly rock bound.

The light tower proper is six-sided, composed of six steel posts latticed together. The height from base to lamp room is 57 feet. The original Fourth Order Fresnel lens had a range of 24 miles. A brick keeper's building is nearby.

The ghost on St. Martin Island is supposed to be that of the lightkeeper, still searching for his lost children. As was the custom, the keeper's children attended school at nearby Washington Island, 10 miles to the southwest. Every day they rowed to class in the morning and back again at dismissal, weather permitting. One terrible day when they were coming home and about halfway across, the children were caught in a vicious squall and they and their boat disappeared. Heartbroken, the old keeper desperately searched the shore looking for his missing offspring. His efforts were in vain. Their bodies were never recovered. Today, some say that when the nights are dark and stormy, and the north wind blows down from an arctic hell, the faint green glow of the keeper's lantern can still be seen as he wanders along the island's desolate shore, ever searching.[5]

There is another version to this ghost story. It seems that one storm-blown night the keeper failed to properly trim his wicks and the beam winked out. Without the trusty light to guide her, a schooner struck hard on an outlying shoal. Waves soon began to batter the helpless ship to pieces. The crew counted their chances for survival as nil. Turned around in the black night and pummeled by the wild seas, they lost all sense of direction. Missing the steady gleam from the light, they didn't even know which way the shore was. Surely their end was at hand.

Suddenly, a small thin beam of green light pierced the darkness. While it shimmered like an old handheld kerosene lantern, wobbling and flickering in the cold wind, it burned true. Eagerly, the desperate men jumped into the cold lake and struggled for the dim but very welcome light.

When they finally stumbled ashore, the mysterious light was not waiting on the beach for them, but instead bobbed off in the distance. Anxiously the crewmen walked toward it, past an old cemetery and up a twisting path through thick and forbidding forest. It always seemed to "float" somewhere just ahead of them. Blusters of wind tore at their wet and frigid bodies and driving rain pelted them. All the while, the bedraggled crew followed the strange flickering glow. Finally they stumbled into a small clearing. Ahead was the partially open door to the keeper's house, a warm and welcoming light leaking out into the forbidding night. When they entered, a brightly burning green-lensed lantern was sitting on the table. It was the same beacon that had guided them to safety. Exploring further, the crew discovered the keeper lying stone cold dead on his bed. His oilskins hung from a nearby wall peg. They were dry to the touch. No one else was on the island. If the keeper hadn't carried the lantern out into the storm to guide them, who did?

The old tale continues that the official report only stated that the keeper died in the act of saving the crew. No mention was made of the strange green light. The crew, though, knew the truth. There was no doubt in their minds that it was a dead man who saved them. A dead man and his light had led them to safety.

In the following years, others reported seeing the unearthly green light. The ghostly lantern continued to search for shipwrecked crews to lead to safety on a dangerous shore.[6]

Not all lighthouse ghost stories are natural. Some were simply created because it seemed like there should be one. After all, every old lighthouse ought to have a good ghost story. A case in point is Escanaba's Sand Point Light. The fascination is that while it may have started as a "made-up" story, it seems to have "come alive" and now explains many unusual happenings.

The 1¹/₂ story light was built in 1867 at a cost of $11,000. Located at the tip of a sand spit, the light was intended to guide ships safely into the growing iron port of Escanaba. The first keeper was John Terry, but before the light became operational, he died of consumption. His wife, Mary, was appointed keeper in his place.

Friday, March 4, 1886, a devastating fire swept the light. When the alarm finally was sounded in town at 1 a.m., flames had broken through the roof and the building was a roaring mass of fire. Ominously, when the local citizens arrived, nothing could be found of the lightkeeper, 69-year-old Mary Terry. An 18-year veteran of the light, she was highly regarded by the local community. Extremely methodical in her daily business, she was very careful in the discharge of her duties. To have a fire occur while Mary was keeper was considered unthinkable.

Mary was born in Dartmouth, Massachusetts. In 1845 she married Captain John Terry, a native of St. John's, Newfoundland. They arrived in Escanaba in 1863 where he was employed with the Chicago & Northwestern Railroad surveying and constructing a new rail line. The new line was coming down from Marquette to improve iron ore shipping. Marquette, on Lake Superior, was hostage to the Soo Locks as well as longer and more severe winters than Lake Michigan. Transporting ore from the Marquette mines to Escanaba improved shipping efficiency and more shipping translated into a lighthouse.

When daylight broke and the embers cooled enough for a search of the building, their worst fears were realized. The remains of what was thought to be Mary were found in the southeast corner of the house, in a room called the "oil room." There was little enough left, a part of her skull, a few bones and a small portion of her viscera were all that survived the charnel flames.

After closely examining all of the evidence, a coroner's jury reluctantly concluded that she came to her death from "causes and means unknown." They suspected that foul play was involved, but had no proof. Could it have been a botched robbery attempt? By rights, if the fire were accidental, Mary should have died in her bedroom, not in the oil room at the opposite end of the building. What if robbers broke in, were discovered by Mary, killed her and dragged the body to the oil room where they set a blaze to cover up the crime. Panicked, they fled without their loot. Since the body was in a room filled with oil, they may have assumed it would be utterly consumed by the blaze.

It was known that Mary Terry was frugal and had saved enough from her salary to purchase some property in the city. But in searching the charred structure, investigators found her money in the form of gold coins, exactly where they would have fallen from her cupboard. The searchers also thought that the door to the light may have been forced based on the location of the bolt. Since the money was still present as well as a packet of charred legal papers, they couldn't find a motive. Why murder her if all of her valuables were still in the light? None of this aligned with Mary Terry's well-known cool-headedness. The jury found it hard to accept that her death was accidental. Regardless of their suspicions, life went on. A new keeper was appointed, repairs made and the light continued to guide ships into Escanaba.

In the 1930s, due to various harbor improvements, including extensive dredging, the light ended up a quarter of a mile from the lake, too far to be effective. A crib light was built offshore to take its place and the old light was remodeled into living quarters for Coast Guard personnel. When the Coast Guard vacated the building in 1985, it was leased to the Delta County Historical Society for inclusion into their museum. After a tremendous amount of effort and money, the light was restored as a museum and dedicated in

1990. Visitors can still see where the smoke darkened the old bricks in the oil room and Mary's bedroom.

The only thing wrong with the new lighthouse museum was that it didn't have a ghost. So one was invented. Mr. Luther Barrnett, a longtime society member and chairman of the lighthouse restoration project, created the ghost of Mary Terry to go along with the restored facility. The tale has since become locally very well known, to the point where fact and fiction have merged. So is there a ghost or isn't there? In any case, now when unexplained lights are seen and strange noises heard, there is a ready explanation. It's just Mary making her rounds.[7]

The two women were working in the gift shop of the old lighthouse, putting books on the sales shelves, checking the cash box, doing the myriad of small things necessary to open for the tourists sure to visit during the day. Suddenly the woman nearest the door to the parlor looked up and sniffed the air. "Do you smell something burning? Boy, is it ever strong!" The other woman hurried out from behind the counter and into the parlor. "Yes, it's cigar smoke all right. It hasn't been this strong in a long time. I wonder if it means anything?" The other woman replied, "Oh, it's just the captain visiting. He will not be here long." This scene, or ones like it, has been enacted frequently at the Seul Choix Point Lighthouse, which is developing into one of the most haunted lights on the Great Lakes.

Seul Choix Point Lighthouse is located in Gulliver, Michigan, at the end of a small peninsula jutting into Lake Michigan known as Seul Choix Point (pronounced Sis Shwa). The light is about 60 miles west of the Straits of Mackinac. The name roughly translates to "only choice." It was the only harbor, however small, that the old French voyageurs found as a safe refuge along this long and open stretch of northern Lake Michigan shore.

Work on the lighthouse started in 1886 when Congress appropriated the money, but a series of delays, including rebuilding the tower, meant that the station did not open until September 1895. The 79-foot tower was originally fitted with a Third Order Fresnel lens. Today an aero beacon has replaced the old lens. A two-story brick-keeper's building is attached to the tower. A brick rear addition was added in 1925, which allowed the building to house the families of both the keeper and his assistant. A steam foghorn building, two oil houses and another assistant keeper's residence complete the principal structures on the grounds.

From 1895 until 1973, it continued as a manned light station, first by the old Lighthouse Service and, after 1939, by the new Coast Guard. Nothing much out of the ordinary happened there. Keepers and their families came and went, as did the inevitable inspectors. All seemed quiet and peaceful. There were no dangerous storms requiring heroic rescues by the keepers or unsolved murders. It was just a typical boring old lighthouse.

The Coast Guard automated the light in 1972 and station personnel left the following year. Since only Coast Guard personnel continued to maintain the actual tower and light, significant deterioration took place to the buildings. When the Gulliver Historical Society took over the structures in 1988, considerable repairs were needed. It was during this work that the society discovered that the lighthouse wasn't really empty. Someone was still there.

Inmates from Camp Manistique Prison under contract to the society did much of the initial restoration work, men paying their "debt to society" performed yard work, stripped old paint and applied new, refinished floors. On several occasions inmates refused to go upstairs, claiming they "felt the presence of something supernatural up there."

Some months afterward, a team of carpenters was hired to install floor tile in the kitchen and hallway. The work went along without interruption until it was nearly done. To finish the job, one worker came to the light alone on a bright and windless spring day. He let himself in, and then carefully locked the door behind. Although the light was still closed for the winter season, tourists sometimes would show up anyway. It was best to keep the doors locked and work uninterrupted.

He was kneeling on the floor in the parlor at the base of the stairs to the second floor. As he started to nail the subfloor, he heard the clear sound of someone walking in the upstairs hallway. When he stopped hammering, the footsteps stopped. When he started, they started back up again. At first he assumed he was hearing a weird echo from his hammering. Just to be sure no one was upstairs, he yelled, "Who's there?" Since he received no reply, he again checked the locked doors, assuring himself that he was alone, and then went back to work, continuing to hammer the sub floor. The sound of footsteps returned, again walking across the upstairs floor. He stopped work to listen, expecting the steps to stop too. They didn't. The heavy steps continued to march across the floor above, and then walk slowly down the stairs. He was shocked, quickly grabbing his tools and running from the lighthouse. He refused to come back alone to finish the job.

One of the most common ghostly manifestations at Seul Choix Point is the pungent, almost nauseating stench of cigar smoke. It is most common in the parlor around the base of the stairs, but also has been detected in the upstairs hall. One time, two visitors ran downstairs and into the gift shop to tell the tour guide that they were sure the lighthouse was on fire. There was a terrible smoky stench upstairs. Perhaps the wiring was burning or someone tossed a lit cigar into a bedroom. When the guide checked, everything was normal.

Just opposite the parlor is a dining room, which is a recreation of the dining room in the lighthouse at the turn of the 20th century. Working from an old photograph, the society strived hard to make it as exact as possible. Original china, stemware and silverware settings on an antique round oak table have become an

active spot for ghostly action. The round table was the only piece of furniture that was left in the lighthouse. It was discovered scattered in the basement. Was there reason why no one wanted it? And, why was it left in pieces? What was "wrong" with it? Silverware on the table has been known to "move." A curator will set it properly at night and the next morning it will be found reversed. When the silverware is discovered rearranged, it is often with the forks set upside down. This is an old English custom and Captain Townshend, an early keeper, whose ghost is suspected as being the principal haunt, was born in Bristol, England. Also in the parlor is an authentic family Bible. It is typically left open on a bookstand as part of the exhibit. One morning it was found closed. Since the pages are heavy paper and there is no draft, some other force must be at work. Was Captain Townshend closing a chapter of his life by closing the Bible?

In June 1997, a TV crew from Saginaw, Michigan, visited the lighthouse to do a documentary on its restoration. They were not there to focus on the ghosts. Regardless of what they wanted to do, the ghost dictated otherwise.

The TV crew was given a tour of the lighthouse by Marilyn Fischer, the president of the Gulliver Historical Society, and then taken out to the fog signal building where there are additional historical displays. Unknown to anyone else, for one of his shots the cameraman idly rearranged the stack of sheet music on the piano, switching the top music to "Blue Spanish Eyes." No one else knew of the change. When the group left the lighthouse, the doors were locked tightly. Even though it was early evening, tourists still visited the park grounds and since the tour guides were gone for the day, it was necessary to securely lock the building. After examining the foghorn building, the group returned to the lighthouse. Upon entering, the cameraman immediately asked who had been in the building. Marilyn Fischer replied that no one had. The man was insistent that someone must have been in the house. Fischer again replied that no one had been, that the guides were gone and she had the only keys. The man then explained about the changing sheet music. He had left, "Blue Spanish Eyes" on top and now it was, "For Whom the Bell Tolls." Obviously someone had come in and changed the music sheets. Fischer explained the illogic of it all. If the cameraman were the only person who knew about the music, then whether anyone came into the lighthouse or not was immaterial since only he knew about the music. The unanswered question was who did shift the music back? When the cameraman realized the implications of Fischer's statements, "his eyeballs got as big as saucers!" The sheet music changed position three times throughout the evening, as did the silverware on the round table.

Three members of the TV crew and a clairvoyant and his wife all slept that evening in their sleeping bags on the hard parlor floor. Five times during the night the crew smelled pungent cigar smoke. Each instance lasted for perhaps a minute. It was sickening enough that one of the members considered leaving for a motel.

The crew also observed and videotaped mysterious hologram-like images in an upstairs bedroom mirror. The mirror would suddenly cloud up with a boiling vapor effect, resolve itself into two faces and finally fade away into nothing. One of the faces seemed to transform itself into a skull-like image before disappearing. The second face had bushy eyebrows, mustache and beard, with a long nose.

The film crew left a video camera "on" all night aimed at the stairway in the hope of recording any supernatural activity.

Inexplicably the video portion failed, although the audio recorded a strange "whooshing" sound. There was no logical explanation for either since the camera worked fine all day, malfunctioning only when it was intended to photograph ghosts.

The next morning, one of the cameramen was setting up his gear in the upstairs bedroom when he flippantly remarked, "Okay, Mr. Ghost, let's stop playing games. Make your presence known." A harsh odor immediately overcame him, making him physically ill for the rest of the morning.

On another occasion, another videographer was shooting footage at the lighthouse for a historic documentary when he, too, experienced a spooky incident. He was outside at night looking inside through a window when he saw a dark shadowy figure walk across the hall by the parlor. A quick search revealed that no one was inside the locked lighthouse. Had he actually seen the ghost?

Marilyn Fischer has done extensive work in trying to determine just who the ghost may be. Her best estimate is that it is Captain Joseph Willy Townshend, the lightkeeper from 1902 to 1910. Born in England, he spent the first 16 years of his working life sailing salt water. After immigrating to the United States, he first entered a Presbyterian seminary but dropped out in less than a year. He worked on the Mackinac Island docks for a while, then as an engineer on a lightship. In 1901, he became keeper at Seul Choix Point. He seems to have the best connection to the supernatural activities. Captain Townshend died at the light at age 65 on August 10, 1910, and was buried in the Manistique cemetery. The local newspaper reported that "many visitors and friends came by boat to attend the funeral and his children came all the way from Marquette." It was said that he died a very painful death in an upstairs bedroom. The body was quickly embalmed in the basement of the lighthouse and prepared for burial. Placed in a rough cedar casket, he was laid out in the downstairs parlor for viewing. As custom, copper pennies were placed on the eyes to keep them shut. In those days, it was believed necessary to have the eyes closed when entering heaven as a means of showing respect. Likely, too, a rag soaked in soda water was also placed over the face to keep the skin from losing color. It would be removed just prior to viewing. Because of the distance his family had to travel, the body was kept in the parlor for a longer period than normal. A granddaughter, now in her 90s, remembers attending her grandfather's funeral while just a child. Her only memories were of watching a flickering oil lamp on top of a "lace-covered table and viewing the coffin with a white-haired man inside. He had bushy eyebrows, mustache and beard."

It is thought that the bedroom he died in is the one with the strange, boiling mirror. Is there a connection? Although little is known of his personality, it is understood that he was a heavy cigar smoker. Lighthouses can be romantic places and Seul Choix is no different. In 1995, the lighthouse hosted the first wedding since a keeper's son was married inside it in 1936, 63 years earlier. For the 1995 wedding, one of the family members went to the light to consider how best to place the myriad of flowers needed for decoration. While sitting in the parlor on a warm and still evening, the woman was struck by a sudden blast of cold air, followed by a sickening aroma of pungent cigar smoke. Undaunted by the experience, the woman looked through the house but found no one. Returning to the parlor, she again sat down and once again was hit by the cold air and nauseating smoke. Enough was enough. She quickly left, the flowers be damned!

Not long ago a woman new to the area drove to the lighthouse just to see what was there. She knew nothing of any ghosts, only that everyone in town talked about the great progress being made at the old lighthouse. After having a delightful tour, she pulled her car out of the parking lot and looked down the first paved walking path. At the end of it she saw an older man in a dark blue uniform with a bushy white beard. She briefly looked away down the road, then back to the path and he was gone. In such a brief time she didn't know where he could have gone. Later, she asked someone affiliated with the lighthouse about him. Did the society have a uniformed actor on the grounds, someone to impersonate an old keeper? When they replied, "No, you saw the ghost," the woman turned pale and said, "I will never go back to the lighthouse again!"

Another visitor was standing in the upstairs hallway in the middle of a hot summer day when she was hit by a blast of cold air. She thought it strange to find such cold air in the building and remarked about it to a tour guide. "Why did they have air conditioning only in the upstairs hallway? Was it to preserve antiques?" The guide just smiled. Was it the captain on the prowl?

A visitor walking around the grounds of the lighthouse reported briefly seeing a man with a white beard and dark suit looking out the upstairs window of the "mirror" bedroom. Who was it?

The ghost activity evidently predates the Gulliver Historical Society's acquisition of the property. One of the men who acted as a caretaker and lived in the lighthouse between the Coast Guard abandonment and society procurement of it reported that he and his family sometimes saw figures in the upstairs windows. Unexplained things happened in the house, too. Another man who was one of the last Coast Guard lightkeepers also claimed that there were ghosts in the house while he was there. He remembered particular problems cleaning the old Fresnel lens. He would carefully clean the lens until it was spotless only to return later and find fingerprints on it. He was alone at the time.

A clairvoyant visited the lighthouse before its recent ghostly reputation was widely known. The first time the man entered the house and walked upstairs, he ran back out saying, "I have to get out of here!" He started to hyperventilate. Apparently it was the result of the strong psychic energy within it. Several years later, when he finally went back in, he said, "Someone has died a terrible death," but it was "not a bad spirit." This has been taken as a reference to Captain Townshend's death. When the clairvoyant walked into the back display room, he detected a strong presence over the ceiling trapdoor in the hallway, implying that there was an entity in the attic. No one ever went up to see.

In June of 1997, Jack Edwards of *Great Lakes Cruiser* magazine led a team to the lighthouse to investigate the reported haunting. Making the connection between smelling cigar smoke and cigars, Jack positioned cigars in strategic places in the house. One was placed in an upstairs bedroom and another in the "mirror" bedroom. A third went on the corner post on the lower staircase and the last on the dining room table. The team then went to bed in sleeping bags on the parlor floor. The next morning the corner post cigar and dining room cigar were missing. Those upstairs were unmoved. The forks on the dining room table had also been repositioned. Where the cigars went was a mystery until several hours later when they were discovered in the breast pocket of lighthouse keeper Ronald Rosie's uniform. The uniform was displayed on a mannequin in the dining room next to the round oak table. As if to mark their location, the uniform cap was on backwards.[8]

For years the captain's mirror was unique for the appearance of the cloudy coalescing faces. But there is a second mirror across the hall. Known as the "bride's room," it features an exhibit of historic bridal gowns. A small antique mirror sits quietly on the dresser.

One of the curators was busy arranging a new display prior to opening when she noticed movement in the mirror. Looking closer, she was shocked to see it clouding up and the whiskered face of

Captain Townshend appearing. She quickly called her companion working in the downstairs gift shop to witness the incredible event. The pair watched it for several minutes before it faded away and the mirror cleared.[9]

In 2005, a group of paranormal investigators were working in the lighthouse and had established a high tech network of cameras, microphones, video and auto recorders and other gear to document the presence of spirits. Part of the investigation involved interviewing a psychic experienced in working in the building. Just as they were ready to start, the psychic jumped up, yelling "something" tapped him on his shoulder. When the investigators unleashed their portable cameras to record the episode, all their batteries were dead. Something had sucked the power down to zero.[10]

Inexplicable things continue to happen in the lighthouse. On one occasion the society president and a lighthouse writer were walking up to the exit to leave when the interior door to the vestibule inexplicably swung briskly open in front of them and the doorbell began to ring. The doorbell had been broken for months. All the other doors and windows were closed so there was no breeze that could have somehow swung the heavy door open. Did the ghost open the door to demonstrate it had "fixed" the bell, too? As the pair drew closer to the door, the second or outside door opened, too. Since it was already close to midnight, they quickly locked the door and left.[11]

The whole area around Seul Choix Point is rife with wandering spirits. Just down the road from the lighthouse is the old Indian graveyard. It was undisturbed until the present road into the station was built in the 1930s. Prior to then, the lake was the only highway. The new road cut directly through the cemetery, with little if any regard for the remains of those interned there. During and after construction, human bones littered the area.

Showing an appalling lack of respect for the dead, local pranksters often wired the bones into makeshift skeletons and hung their macabre creations from trees along the lighthouse road. On dark and windy nights the macabre rattle of ancient bones scared the wits out of many an innocent traveler.[12]

Just a few miles down the road to the lighthouse are several other haunted houses. The first two houses are side by side and less than 100 yards from an old commercial fishing harbor. One house is home to the ghost of an Indian woman who apparently had bad experiences in the house. Treated harshly by the original occupants, her spirit simply remained after death. Was it in revenge for the treatment in life or for another reason?

In one instance, a father and son were sitting around the kitchen table when the father noticed that the clock on the wall was broken again. Tired of the old clock's problems, he told his son to get rid of it, to take it into the swamp and throw it as far as he could. Later that day the son did exactly as he was told and was rewarded with a loud splash. Two days later the father, son and a neighbor were sitting around the same table when the father noticed the clock was still hanging on the wall. Irritated, the father asked his son why he didn't get rid of it as he was told? The son swore that he had thrown it into the swamp two days earlier. The neighbor left immediately, never to set foot in the house again.

In another instance, a young boy was returning from squirrel hunting when he looked up at an upstairs window of the house. Staring back at him was a young woman in a white, apparently floor-length dress. Years later he remembered her as the most beautiful woman he had ever seen. When he searched the house, it was empty. Who was the mysterious woman in the window? Why was she looking directly at him?

Two men and their children were sitting at the kitchen table on a hot and quiet summer day when the regulator in the unlit wood stove began to spin. Slowly at first, it increased speed until they could not follow the motion. Suddenly, the middle cast iron lid leaped into the air, turned over several times and nearly reached the ceiling before returning to the exact position it started from. The regulator slowly stopped moving.

A young bride and her husband were living in the house when another spooky incident occurred. Shortly after moving into the house the young couple were entertaining some overnight guests. The next morning the bride was in the kitchen when she heard a lot of movement and footsteps upstairs. Thinking that her house guests had finally woke up, she prepared a beautiful breakfast then leaned up the stairway and yelled, "Come and get it." No one came down! She called a second time without getting a reply. When she finally went upstairs to see what was keeping her guests, she found the rooms empty. Sometime later her husband and guests came home from a long walk on the beach. So who was upstairs? The newlyweds moved out soon after.

While exterior renovations were recently being done, there were examples of strange noises, breaking glass, footsteps and dreadful odors coming from inside. When checked, nothing was ever amiss. What was going on inside the old house?

It is said that during the renovations of this century-old house, a secret attic was discovered. Sealed within were old tins, trunks, fishing equipment, calendars from 1930-36, clothes and schoolbooks. It was like a time capsule. Why had the room been sealed shut?

Tearing up the old kitchen floor revealed a trap door leading to several mysterious below-level chambers. The walls were tongue-and-groove plank and the floors of sand. Part was evidently an old cold cellar used in the days before refrigeration to keep food fresh. Cans of preserved fish and berries were found dating from the 1920s. In one of the small chambers were discovered, buried in the sand, what were believed to be human bones from a young girl. The room was immediately closed back up and never spoken of. Was it a family secret best kept hidden? Were the bones connected with the strange happenings?

The same clairvoyant who visited the lighthouse also examined the haunted houses. He confirmed the presence of numerous spirits and said that one of the rooms in the north house was being used as a "guest room," that many spirits passed through it, staying only briefly. He explained that he felt nothing but happy spirits within.

On the same visit, the clairvoyant started to walk the grounds surrounding the houses. All of a sudden, he explained a shooting that took place on the shores of Lake Michigan in a grouping of tarpaper shacks. And he pointed out the spot where a dead body was found. What he was seeing was the famous "murder at Seul Choix Point" – the Pond-versus-Blanchard shooting that took place on June 18, 1859. Ironically, the date that the clairvoyant visited the area was exactly June 18, almost a century and a half later. Did a porthole in time briefly open to view this page from the past?

While building a pole barn nearby, a worker dug up a small hand-carved brass cross and two tin coffin plates. One was engraved with "Our Darling" and the other "Our Loved One." Scraping the ground a little deeper he found part of a girl's leather shoe, obviously handmade by a cobbler. He then stopped digging. Was there an old grave along the shore? Whose was it? Is it connected to the mysterious goings on? It was best to just move the barn and not disturb the dead.

Unknown spirits haunt the house next door, too. Once a man was sleeping in an upstairs bedroom when a voice shouting "son of a bitch" startled him. The man bolted upright and strained to hear more. Soft, subdued voices drifted up from downstairs, but were in a language he couldn't understand. Heavy footsteps echoed across the downstairs floor. Cabinet doors opened and slammed shut. The pet cat that lay by his side arched his back and hissed. Silently the man crept downstairs to find not a soul there. The rooms were empty of life. What was going on?

The two houses sit side by side on an old gravel road leading to the harbor. Once several people were eating at the kitchen table when they were startled to see a young woman in a long white flowing dress walking along the road from the beach and on past the houses toward the woods. What astonished them was that they all recognized her from old photographs, and she had been dead for half a century! When they ran outside she just vanished into thin air.

The third house is much newer but equally plagued by ghosts. The reason for the haunting could be its location, right on the old wagon trail along the lakeshore. The previous owner could sit in his easy chair watching TV and at the same time look down a hallway toward the bedrooms. Every so often he would see various-sized black figures moving across the hallway, actually passing "through" his walls and house. They never made a sound and seemed to travel in groups. He never said anything about these "travelers" to his wife. One day she sat in "his" chair and saw the baffling figures. After he confirmed seeing them, too, she insisted on moving out of the house.

Supposedly they were seeing "rock spirits," ghostly black shapes that would float over the rocks along the Lake Michigan shoreline. For two centuries local fishermen saw them when coming ashore from a long day with their nets. Priests were called in who said they were not evil and hung crosses and rosaries in the trees wherever the shapes were seen. It is thought that these rock spirits were simply continuing their ancient trek along the old trail. In this case they were going directly through a structure that wasn't there two hundred years ago. Do they represent a group of early travelers, perhaps a family that met death on the trail and today are simply trying to finish their interrupted journey?

I visited the lighthouse in October 1997 and was given an excellent tour and interview by Marilyn Fischer. While there, nothing supernatural happened. The cigars I had planted in different places failed to disappear, the silverware stayed in place and there was no pungent aroma of burning stogies. In short, everything was as it should be. It is my habit when interviewing people to use a microrecorder to capture their comments on tape. People talk faster than I can take notes and this assures me of a higher degree of accuracy. I recorded much of my interview with Marilyn Fischer on my microrecorder. When I got home I took the audiotape out of the machine, labeled it and filed it with all the material concerning Seul Choix Point Light. When I got down to writing the piece I would play the tape. In February 1998, I was ready to write. I did the initial draft based on my notes and other research material, then played the tape. The tape was good quality, with Marilyn's comments clear and understandable. There was also something more on the tape, a low moaning sound that made the hair on the back of my neck stand up. There was no such sound when I recorded the interview, but it's there now! I have no idea what caused it. It never happened before or since. However, considering the atmosphere I was recording in, it only fits right in, doesn't it?[13]

Waugoshance Shoal, 16 miles west of the Straits of Mackinac, marks an especially dangerous series of reefs and islands ranging seven or so miles out into Lake Michigan. The area is a graveyard of wrecks, the result of trying to navigate the treacherous run down the east side of Lake Michigan, between the Beaver Island group and mainland. A lightship first marked Waugoshance Shoal in 1832. 1851 saw the first lighthouse on the site with additional construction in 1870, 1883 and 1896. The tower stands 76 feet tall, with a 20-foot base diameter. The walls are fully $5^1/_2$ feet thick at the bottom, tapering to 2 feet at the top. Some early records suggest that Waugoshance may have had the first Fresnel lens used on the lakes. After White Shoal Light was erected in 1910, Waugoshance was abandoned two years later. Lake mariners often referred to it as "wobble shanks."

According to legend, there are two ghosts at the light. During the construction of the crib, a worker was apparently killed and his spirit is said to still haunt the light. When conditions are just right, the wind blowing hard and cold, his hideous cries are said to echo across the lonely shore. How precisely he met his death is unknown.

The second ghost is thought to be that of John Herman, a keeper from 1887 to 1900. He was known both as a man who thoroughly enjoyed the spirits of this world, especially the 100 proof bottled kind, as well as a tireless practical joker. Normally he did most of his hard drinking ashore when he was on leave, but on occasion he returned to the light still "potted." Apparently he once came back from leave, as sailors said, "Three sheets to the wind" and finding his assistant diligently working in the lamp room, locked him in as a prank. The assistant keeper called down for John to let him out but John, of course, refused. The assistant could only watch helplessly as the drunken keeper reeled back and forth as he tried to navigate down the narrow pier, eventually moving out of his view. Herman was never seen again. It is presumed he fell off the rocks and drowned.

Afterwards strange and unexplained things started happening at the light. Doors mysteriously opened and closed by themselves, napping keepers were rudely jolted awake when chairs were knocked out from under them sending the men crashing onto the floor. An unseen fireman also clandestinely shoveled coal into the firebox for the steam boiler. Bizarre things just happened. Keepers blamed such a plague of interference on their missing companion, who had apparently come back from wherever he went just to make their lives miserable. When Waugoshance light was finally abandoned in 1912, many felt that it was less that the new White Shoal light had made it redundant, than the Lighthouse Service got tired of dealing with the ghost. Perhaps they just said, "Good riddance!"[14]

Karen McDonnell is the director/curator of the White River Light Station Museum, a position she has held for a dozen years. She is straightforward and levelheaded. While a bit of a romantic, she also has the inquisitiveness of a scientist and questions what she sees and hears. She also cares deeply about the old light and cheerfully she does the many small jobs around the building to help make it a good home, not only for her family, but also for two friendly spirits. When Karen McDonnell first moved into the lighthouse, she had no inkling that actual other world spirits also occupied the building. The previous curator had only said that he had sensed "good spirits" in the old place.

As part of her curatorial duties, she researched the life of the first keeper, Captain William Robinson. An English immigrant, when he arrived at White River in the 1860s, he immediately realized the need for a functioning light to serve lake mariners. Until one finally was built, he took it as his personal responsibility to keep a welcoming beacon burning at the end of the old pier.

Congress recognized the need for a lighthouse in 1866 and authorized $10,000 for the project. However, it wasn't until 1870, when the White River Channel was cut from White Lake to Lake Michigan, that part of the money was spent for a small pier head light that was finished in 1871. The lighthouse itself was completed in 1875-76.

Robinson duly became the first keeper and served faithfully for 47 years. He and his wife, Sarah, raised 11 children in its friendly confines although two apparently died in childhood. According to local accounts, Sarah was a wonderful mother and very well respected in the community. When she died at a relatively young age, it was a hard blow for Captain Robinson and he clung even closer to "his" light.

The circumstances of Captain Robinson's retirement were related by Loretta Bush Pearson, daughter of the second keeper Captain William Bush, the eldest grandson of Captain Robinson, in an oral history conducted by Mrs. McDonnell. In 1919, at age 87, he finally was forced by the government to retire due to age, but was able to arrange to have his eldest grandson, Captain William Bush, named keeper in his stead. William Bush served 24 years as keeper until 1943. Old Captain Robinson continued, however, to do much of the work of tending to the light, claiming that his grandson, even though he was the keeper, wasn't yet ready. Slowed by age, he needed a cane to get around, but he still performed the duties much as he always had. Against government rules, he continued to live for a time in the building with his grandson. But regulations were clear. Only the keeper and his immediate family could live in the building. Captain Robinson would have to leave.

As the day came closer for his departure, he became frequently depressed. For nearly half a century his whole life was wrapped up in the light, especially after his wife's death. He had known nothing else. Finally, he told his grandson with great conviction, "I am not going to leave this building." He kept his word, at least with the living. The morning he was to vacate, he died. In compliance with his wishes, he was buried in the small cemetery just across the channel so he could be as close to "his" light as possible.

About a month after McDonnell finished her research on Captain Robinson, she heard the clear sound of someone walking upstairs on the second floor. Slow and a little hesitant, the halting steps were accompanied by an intermittent thud. Intuitively, McDonnell thought perhaps it was the old keeper. Although she had never really subscribed to and was skeptical about the idea of ghosts, she still had this "sense."

The strange upstairs pacing occurs on a frequent but irregular basis. In McDonnell's words, "The walking I hear is as if someone were checking. I have never felt fear, but I have never gone to the upper stairs when I have heard it. I feel it is a ritual and that I shouldn't disturb it. It's calming."

McDonnell is not the only person to experience Captain Robinson's prowling. During a trip away from the lighthouse, she left it in the care of a couple who agreed to house sit. Not wishing to scare them away before they even started, she mentioned nothing about the captain's walks. When she returned, however, her friend greeted her with the question, "Do you have some kind of ghost walking around upstairs?" Although a chill danced up McDonnell's spine, she kept a straight face and asked, "Why?" Her friend described identical experiences with the strange walking upstairs. While the spooky sounds didn't frighten the housesitter, they did make her very uneasy and uncomfortable.

McDonnell believes Captain Robinson appreciates the extra work she does at the light. When she finishes a project, she has a sense of being silently applauded, of being rewarded by the old keeper. The next time she hears the captain's walk, to her ear the step seems lighter and quicker, less heavy and elderly. It is as if the old keeper was brought back to a happier time so long ago.

What the captain's eerie walk means isn't known. McDonnell questions if it isn't him just checking on the children, walking down the hall, looking into each room and then slowly climbing the spiral iron stairs up to the lamp room for a final check of the light. It's a ritual his spirit continues beyond life.

Just below the lamp room, at the top of the spiral staircase, there is a window set deep into the octagonal tower wall. The wooden resting board for the weight pulley system is inset even with the window. McDonnell claims that people have experienced a strong "pull" or attraction at the window, that it is a very romantic place. From my experience it is also an extremely pleasant spot just to sit and think. It is indeed a perfect place for two people very much in love, as Captain Robinson and Sarah were, to sit and talk. Perhaps one on the windowsill and the other on the tower stairs opposite. Even for a man alone it's a wonderful place to sit and rest after climbing the tower and just enjoy a pipe while thinking of the day's events. Perhaps it was Captain Robinson's habit to stop at the window after checking on his sleeping children.

The more McDonnell found out about Captain Robinson, the more she wanted to know about Sarah. After all, behind every good man is a better woman. Being a lightkeeper's wife was especially arduous. Not only was she mother to the 11 children, but she also had to help with the lighthouse duties. When the keeper was sick, she also tended the light in his place while continuing all of her "normal" responsibilities.

After much work, McDonnell was able to locate several pictures of Sarah. She is particularly fond of a charcoal drawing that seems to have an unusual endearing presence about it. When she placed Sarah's photos on display, McDonnell felt that she had honored a very special lady, but wondered how Captain Robinson would feel about it. She didn't have a long wait to find out.

Upstairs, in what had been a children's room, was a large flat glass display case. The top of the case is a dust magnet and it has to be cleaned every other day. What happened next was decidedly unusual. In McDonnell's words, "A week after I got Sarah's photos up, the phone rang. I had the dust rag in my right hand. I put it on the corner of the glass and I ran downstairs thinking, 'I am going to open in 10 minutes and I don't want to have it on the case.' So I had a quick telephone conversation and ran back upstairs to finish. The case was dust-free! No windows were open and the rag was over on the other side of the case. That gave me a chill. I was a little shaky. I knew I didn't dust that case. I just stood there and thought about it. How could the cloth move itself to the other side without any wind? I picked up the rag and said I am going to try this again.

"After opening the museum, I got a hunch that maybe since I've brought Sarah back into view, maybe she is helping me. I thought some more and concluded that I could make this a fearful experience or I can just thank her. So later, when no one was in the museum I said, 'Thanks, Sarah.' I have continued to play the game with her. Five minutes before opening, I'll place the rag on the case and go back downstairs and when I come back up the rag will be moved around and the dust will be gone. It's only on that one case that it works. I do not know why it's just that case in that spot. I know the younger children stayed in that bedroom. Maybe there was a younger child positioned where the case is now."

McDonnell is not disturbed in the slightest that her lighthouse is haunted. Quite the contrary, "I like the notion of the comfort it gives me. It's like a watchman, just making sure everything is OK before it's too late at night."[15]

Some ghosts are less obvious than others, just more reluctant to take center stage. The shade at the old St. Joseph, Michigan, lighthouse depot seems to fall into this category.

The U.S. Lighthouse Service dates from 1789 and the first Great Lakes lights from the 1810s. The first Lake Michigan lights, one of which marked the mouth of the St. Joseph River, were established in 1832. By 1852 there were 76 lights on the lakes, 27 on Lake Michigan. The number on the lakes in 1890 reached 244 with 81 on Lake Michigan. By the turn of the century 114 lights and four light ships guided the booming lake trade. And it was booming! Chicago in 1888 recorded 20,000 vessel arrivals in the eight months of navigation. By contrast, the port of New York had only 23,000 in a full 12 months.

The job of a depot was to serve the lights by providing timely repair, maintenance and resupply services. In addition, they received, stored and overhauled buoys and received, stored and packed supplies and various stores for the far-flung light stations for delivery by the lighthouse tenders.

Originally the Ninth District (Lake Michigan) shared the Eleventh District depot in Detroit, which was established in 1869. Over time this proved to be a very unsatisfactory arrangement. In 1890 the lighthouse board complained "not only is the Ninth District tender obliged to tie up in Detroit and await the full opening of navigation in the most northern waters, viz, at the Straits of Mackinac, where the ice remains for some weeks later than at the head of the lake, but all the lampist and repair work and the distribution of supplies have to be made from the same inconvenient distance and with corresponding loss of time."

After due consideration and an appropriation of $35,000, plans were made to build a new depot at St. Joseph at the south end of the lake, exclusively for the Ninth District. Work started in 1891 and the storehouse, keeper's house and carpenter-lampist shop were finished in January 1893. Located on the north bank of the river and adjacent to the Life-Saving Service station, it provided ready access for supply boats and tenders.

The effectiveness of the depot was short-lived. The Lighthouse Board annual reports for 1899-1903 criticized that it was too distant from Milwaukee where the district engineer had his office and "one of the best markets for materials." There was also too little room on the dock to moor the large tenders for the winter. In April 1904, $75,000 was appropriated to start the construction on a new depot in Milwaukee. Since all these problems were well known before construction, it is obvious St. Joseph was once the political choice, or on the flip side, Milwaukee was the new politically correct choice when politics changed.

Regardless of the new Milwaukee depot, St. Joseph remained active as a depot until 1917 when it finally closed. In 1919, the property was transferred to the Navy Department and was used by the Naval Reserve for many years. In 1952, it was used by the Army

Reserve and, in 1956, was taken over by the Michigan Army National Guard as an armory. In September 1993, the Guard vacated the site.

The ghostly goings-on have been reported not in the large and forbidding three-story brick storehouse as perhaps expected, but instead in the smaller keeper's house. The two-story, cross-gabled-roof dwelling has a brick first story and a shingled second story. Although long abandoned, it is still considered structurally sound.

Inside the house is a wreck, everything a haunted house should be. It obviously has not been occupied for a long period. Windows are boarded over, walls punched through by vandals, rotted floors and stairs, dirt and dust piled high and plentiful. A wind from the right direction can set up an eerie moaning sound that echoes weirdly throughout the empty rooms. Strange cold spots chill the spine. You sense that you are not alone.

Some people have reported curious lights in the old house, mysterious glowing and glimmerings where only darkness should rule. No spirit manifestations have been claimed, nor has any assertion been made for the cause of such unidentified lights or other unnatural events. Is it the spirit of an old keeper still occupying his old home?[16]

The depot building was converted into a restaurant and brewery in 1996. The project apparently failed and in 2005 it became the St. Joseph Yacht Club.

The old light at North Manitou Island isn't there any more. It washed away in the 1970s when erosion destroyed the foundation and the old tower collapsed into the lake. When built in 1896, it was an important aid to navigation for vessels running the Manitou Passage. Many a captain found the trusty beacon a life saver during "dark and stormy nights."

Erecting the light shouldn't have been especially hard. The design was fairly standard and the island, while remote, wasn't a storm-tossed hunk of rock stuck out in the middle of nowhere. It was solid ground and the crew expected little trouble. Little did they know there would be trouble, but not of the engineering kind. They didn't expect the nightly visits of the "Gray Lady."

As the tale goes, back in the 1830s during an especially vicious gale an upbound bark smashed into the shoals off the point where the lighthouse was later built. All aboard were drowned except a young male child miraculously found on a piece of the cabin driven high on the beach when the bark broke up. A party of Indians hunting on the island discovered the child and later brought him to

Mackinac Island. A fisherman's family took pity on the homeless waif and raised the child as one of their own. Certainly it was a happy ending to a sad story. However, the tale didn't end.

In the months and years following the wreck, sailors began to whisper of seeing a mysterious "gray lady" walking the desolate beach where the bark wrecked. The heartbreaking woman desperately searched the lonely shore looking for her beloved child, wailing in anguish over her tragic loss. The ghostly woman wanted her lost child and would not stop looking until she found it, if it took all eternity.

Wandering ghosts were all well and fine as long as they weren't particularly bothering anyone, but when the lighthouse construction crew arrived they were not prepared for a crying ghost wandering up and down the beach all night. It was damned unnerving! Every night the spirit made her way up the sandy beach, sobbing and crying, lamenting her terrible loss.

Soon work on the lighthouse slowed to a crawl. The men were literally "spooked" by the gray lady. Their unusual problem was solved when a Methodist missionary stopped to check on their spiritual needs. Itinerate clergy of various religious convictions were fairly common. Reluctantly the men related their predicament. Just as reluctantly the preacher agreed to see what he could do. Methodists don't perform exorcisms the way the papists do, but he did say a prayer on the beach for the woman's soul, imploring it to find eternal rest.

The prayer worked, at least for a time. The men reported no more unearthly visits of the gray lady and the lighthouse was finished on time.

However, the power of a mother's love for a lost child isn't easily broken and every so often islanders whispered about a strange vaporous image of a woman walking the beach near the old light and the eerie crying riding the night air. The collapse and disappearance of the lighthouse hasn't stopped the strange specter from periodically appearing. It seems every couple of years some island camper will sheepishly report sighting a weeping "gray lady" moving along the sandy shore, knowing nothing about the tale of shipwreck, death, survival and a mother's "undying" love.[17]

Rock Island is certainly one of the smallest inhabited Islands on the Great Lakes. Located directly off the north tip of Washington Island, which itself is just off the tip of Wisconsin's Door Peninsula, it seems to be home to a veritable ghost cavalcade.

Today the island is a state park, which is both good and bad. Good since it works to preserve a historic little island from mindless exploitation and bad because it prevents managed economic development, which could help boost an area largely dependent on tourism. I wonder what the ghosts feel about being permanent residents of a quiet but usually empty park versus members of a vibrant, "living" community?

Getting to Rock Island is an adventure in itself. First take a long winding narrow two-lane road north to the tip of the Door Peninsula, ending at the small community of Gills Rock where an auto ferry will take you across the infamous "Porte des Morts," so named by the old French voyageurs. The term loosely translates as Deaths Door Passage and the "door" part was later applied to the entire peninsula. The small rockbound strait runs between Green Bay and the open waters of Lake Michigan. Since the bones of perhaps more than a hundred ships litter the waterway, the name is entirely appropriate. The ferry will land at Detroit Harbor on Washington Island. A "high diddle-diddle" ride through the middle of the island will eventually bring you to Jackson Harbor and a small "people" only ferry will take you to rugged Rock Island. It isn't the end of the world, but as they say, "you can see it from there!"

As the haunt stories go there seem to be three principal areas of ghost activity on the island.

The old Indian graveyard on the east end of the island is said to be home to a "band" of active spirits. Campers report seeing weird shapes flickering over the graves and hearing voices and unusual noises. It isn't anything threatening, just strange.

The cemetery on the west end has its own crew of spiritual residents. Some observers claim that the ghosts of small children are sometimes playing in and around the graveyard. Historic Pottawatomie Lighthouse is another hotbed of spiritual action. The original light was built on top of a 137-foot bluff giving the beam a focal height of 151 feet, a remarkable elevation for the weak and near useless Winslow reflectors the tower was equipped with. Operational in 1838, it was the first lighthouse on Lake Michigan. The story-and-a-half structure was built of native stone with a low 30-foot attached tower. The government only assigned one keeper to run the light, David Corbin, a veteran of the War of 1812 with the rank of sergeant. Unfortunately, Corbin was a single man and life at the remote lighthouse was very, very lonely. Corbin was usually the only human on the bleak island. The situation was so bad that when the lighthouse inspector arrived on a visit and found Corbin in a deep funk, he ordered him off the island, giving him 20 days to find a wife. Corbin looked high and low, hither and yon, but was unable to find a good woman (or apparently a bad one either) willing to share his monastic existence at the desolate island lighthouse. He reluctantly returned alone to face the utter loneliness of the bleak island. And he died alone on the island on August 7, 1858. His remains are buried in a small graveyard just a couple of hundred feet to the south of the lighthouse. One would have thought that someone would have had the common decency to at least bury him in a village cemetery where he would finally have some company, instead of planting him on the remote island. His grave was unmarked until 2002 when the Friends of Pottawatomie Light erected a gravestone. There are only a dozen remains in the little graveyard. It is believed that seven are shipwreck victims washed ashore on the beach.

The same year that Corbin died, the government tore down the old lighthouse and built a brand new two-story one. The original was in such poor condition that there was little choice. This was typical of nearly all of the early lights built under the inept (perhaps even corrupt) administration of Stephen Pleasanton who served as the de facto General Superintendent of Lights for many years.

Every lighthouse needs a ghost and Pottawatomie is no different. Some campers report strange noises in the lighthouse, doors opening and closing, things going "thump" and even the sounds of heavy walking on the second story. No visual phenomenon has been reported. Is Corbin inspecting the new light or perhaps walking about looking for a wife among the female campers?

There are also claims of hearing children playing on the grounds around the light. The best spectral explanation for the children would seem to be Emily Betts, wife of keeper William Betts who kept the light from 1872-82. Emily bore William nine children, two born in the lighthouse. In addition, she taught school in the basement for her own brood and other island children from the small fishing community. Doubtless recess was spent running around the lighthouse. Are the voices somehow an imprint from the schoolroom past?[18]

There are accounts about peculiar happenings in the old Michigan City, Indiana, lighthouse. The lonely old light isn't quite as quaint as it may seem.

The light has a long and colorful history, virtually all of it intertwined with a sawed-off female keeper named Harriet Colfax. An inch under 5 feet tall and perhaps 90 pounds, she kept the light from 1861 to her retirement in 1903 at age 80. It is fair to say that the light was her life.

The two-story Milwaukee brick lighthouse was built in 1858, replacing a pole light and later small tower in use since 1837. Michigan City was never much of a port, but a reliable beacon was important nonetheless. The new 1858 structure had a small cupola projecting through the roof. The lens was a mere Fifth Order Fresnel, entirely suitable for Michigan City.

Female keepers were rare on the Great Lakes, but not unheard of. Research shows perhaps only 2.5 percent of all keepers, principal and assistant, were female. This was also a time when politics ruled over skill. Prior to 1896 there was no Civil Service system. Your appointment as a lightkeeper, or a galaxy of other federal jobs, was totally dependent on who you knew. In Harriet's case, she knew the right people. Her first cousin was Schuyler Colfax, speaker of the U.S. House of Representatives and later vice president under President U.S. Grant. She was a voice and piano teacher who moved to Michigan City from Ogdensburg, New York, with her brother in the 1850s when he was going to edit a local newspaper. The enterprise failed and he left Michigan City. There was some talk of a failed romance, but there may well have been other reasons to cause Harriet to stay. Although Harriet knew nothing about lightkeeping, she needed a job and Cousin Schuyler came through for her.

Harriet never married but she did form a close relationship with a Miss Anna C. Hartwell, another Ogdensburg native who had come west to teach school. Local folks considered the two women inseparable and they remained together for the rest of their lives.

Starting in 1871, Harriet was also responsible for the small light at the end of the 1,500-foot harbor east breakwater. Reaching the light meant walking on a high wood catwalk intended to allow access during fierce storms. Imagine trying to navigate the catwalk as a frail 90-pound woman with a long billowing dress and carrying a five-gallon can of oil! Several years later the light was transferred to the west pier, which projected 500 feet farther out into the lake, making access even more difficult.

Regardless of the challenges, Harriet managed to get the job done. Fair weather or foul, she kept her light burning. Most of the time she had no assistant. Usually principal keepers were given an assistant, but Harriet rarely had that luxury. It was almost as if the Lighthouse Service wanted her to fail so the job could be given to a "good deserving" man. Now they wouldn't do that, would they?

She was known to run "a tight ship." Everything had a place and was in it. When the lighthouse inspectors came through, her light was always shipshape.

Harriet resigned on October 12, 1904, and died five months later. Generations of lake sailors knew her as the "Grand Old Lady Lightkeeper." Her loyalty, steadfastness and devotion to her light were an inspiration to all.

The old Michigan City Light presently operates as a museum open during the summers. There are those who believe that the light is also home to a ghost or two. Perhaps Harriet and her companion, Anna, are still keeping house.

Objects left out of place have been known to mysteriously move "into place," just as if Harriet were keeping things ready for the inspector. Occasionally steps are also heard on the second floor when no one is there. Even psychics who visit the light claim that, although they sense a spirit, the feeling is pleasant and reassuring. Apparently Harriet and Anna are doing their best to "keep" the old light.

CHAPTER 6

Lakeside Spirits – Mainland

Lake Michigan is not just Lake Michigan. The influence of the lake goes beyond the mere boundaries of the waves and includes those communities, large and small, who owe their existence to the big water. Real estate folks will drum into your head that the only three things that count are location, location and location. In America's Great Lakes heartland, everything connects in some fashion to the lakes.

Just down from the haunted White Lake Lighthouse is the Crosswinds Restaurant, also said to have a resident spirit. White Lake came into being as a lumber town with sawmills dotting the Lake Michigan shore. The old mills are long gone and the buildings reused for other purposes. The Crosswinds, for example, is located in an old sawmill building.

The ghost in question is that of a young boy supposedly killed in some kind of an industrial accident while the building was still a sawmill. This was at an age when young boys were expected to earn their keep early and often worked side by side with adult men. A boy's nimble fingers and quick hands made them ideal for working with fast-moving machinery. Deadly mishaps during this period of unguarded machinery and just plain dangerous working conditions were commonplace. Accidental death at the workplace was regrettable but not unusual or likely to elicit comment.

Restaurant workers claim to have seen the ghost of a small boy out of the corner of their eyes quickly flitting across the dining room. Patrons also have seen the apparition and often asked the wait staff about the running boy. Who is he? Why is he here? The ghost plays a

number of pranks, the most common being pushing a shelf full of glasses to the floor. His antics were enough that the owners, apparently tired of replacing glassware, called in a clairvoyant for a séance during which they asked him to stop breaking the glassware. Their effort was successful since the glassware no longer breaks, although the ghost they named Oscar is still said to be speeding about the dining room.[1]

There is an oft-told tale of the ghost of a beautiful young woman seen flitting over the Indiana Dunes and swimming in the surf along the southern coast of Lake Michigan. Locally the spirit is called "Diana of the Dunes," her name taken from the Greek goddess in recognition of her great beauty. The legend runs through many generations and, as in all such stories, has several variations. Generally though, it goes something like this.

The area surrounding the present-day Indiana Dunes State Park was largely desolate wilderness in the early 1900s. People hadn't yet discovered that the three things that count in real estate are "location, location, location" and living on or near the water wasn't considered desirable. As a result, the dunes area was uninhabited and largely considered wasteland. About this time stories started to spread about a beautiful young woman seen swimming naked in the surf and walking among the lonely dunes. Soon dubbed "Diana," she lived a hermit's life in an old shack far from any human contact.

Why she chose such a solitary existence isn't known for certain, but it is speculated that she was Alice Marble Gray, the daughter of a well-to-do Chicago couple. Educated with a degree from the University of Chicago in 1903 and on and off again graduate work until 1912, she worked in the Windy City as a secretary for a magazine. There are rumors of a failed love affair that drove her "over the edge" and into a reclusive existence in the dunes. Another explanation is that she was losing her eyesight and unable to work, was seeking refuge in the sandy desert. Perhaps neither explanation is correct. No one really knows.

By 1916, the Chicago newspapers picked up the story of a beautiful young woman living alone in the wilds of the Indiana Dunes, swimming naked by the light of a Lake Michigan moon. This was strong stuff for 1916. Given such "facts," reporters took full artistic license with endless stories of the "Nymph of the Dunes." It was said that she magically disappeared whenever anyone approached. Living in an abandoned fisherman's shack, she wore cast-off clothing and didn't care about the material life.[2]

Supposedly she met a drifter named Paul Wilson in 1920. Inexplicably they each found something in the other and paired up, staying together until 1925 or so. As a result, Diana bore two daughters.

All was not well in the dunes, however. When the badly burned and beaten body of a man was discovered on the beach, the police immediately suspected Paul as the killer. Although they questioned him, the police couldn't prove his involvement so he was released.

The relationship between Paul and Diana was, in today's terms, abusive. He beat her frequently and sometimes severely. Even when they moved to nearby Michigan City where Paul made a poor living selling handmade furniture, he continued to beat her. In 1925, Diana died in her humble beach shack shortly after delivering her second child. The cause of death was listed at uremia poisoning, complicated by repeated blows to her back and stomach. Knowing that the police would be looking for him, Paul disappeared, eventually turning up in a

California prison serving a stretch for auto theft. The fate of the two daughters isn't known.

After her death locals began to report seeing the ghost of a beautiful naked young woman cavorting over the lonely dunes and splashing in the cold surf. She appeared from nothing, thin air if you will, flitting over the sand with an effortless motion only to vanish again a moment later. She was there and then gone, a true free spirit released to haunt in death the dunes that she loved in life.[3]

Sand dunes are dynamic, always changing, driven by wind and wave to constantly re-create themselves, morphing into new shapes and sizes. The Bible speaks about building your house on a solid foundation, not on shifting sands. It is certainly "solid" advice.

The Lake Michigan dunes at Sleeping Bear Dunes National Lakeshore are reputedly the largest fresh-water dunes in the world. Astronauts can see them from space. The dunes farther south on the Michigan shore are not as large but are just as dynamic, just as mobile and changing, covering whatever is in their path. Forests have fallen prey to the attacking sand, only to reappear decades later as the dune reformed. In some instances, entire villages were "eaten" by moving dunes.

The community of Singapore just north of Saugatuck, Michigan, is a great example of a buried village. Founded in 1836 by New York land speculators, it was hoped that it would become a major city to rival New York or Chicago. It never realized that hope, but by the 1870s it was a busy lumbering town. During its heyday it had the first schoolhouse in Michigan as well as three lumber mills, two hotels and numerous stores and homes. It also had an infamous bank. After the Civil War, banks were required to maintain a certain level of cash on hand and for many rural banks this was a stiff obligation. Since neither the Singapore bank nor the nearby Allegan Federal Bank was able to maintain it, they worked out a unique cooperative "arrangement." When the Allegan bank heard that the Federal Inspector was coming, the Singapore bank transferred all of its cash to it. After the Allegan bank passed the inspection, bank officials took the inspector out for a night on the town including a full tour of the "red lights." Above all they made certain that they got him very drunk. While the inspector slept it off the following day, bank officials transferred all the available cash to Singapore so it, too, could pass inspection.[4]

With the local timber all cut over, most of the population picked up and moved on, heading for another place to strike it rich. Stripped of trees, the land was easy prey to the hungry dunes. While the living

101

residents fled before dunes overwhelmed the village, it seems that some spirited ones moved in to the abandoned houses. Years after Singapore disappeared beneath the sand, dune hikers reported hearing strange and unattached voices coming from the very sand beneath their feet.

One hiker reported his experience to the authorities that likely viewed his testimony with a bit of skepticism, but, of course, they weren't there, either. "My buddies and I were hiking towards the lake when we started to hear this strange buzzing sound, almost like a swarm of insects, but there weren't any around. A few minutes later we walked down into a depression, a little hollow in the dunes. The air was perfectly still and deadly quiet. It was also hotter than hell. The sun was really reflecting off the sand. Anyway, the three of us started to hear voices. At first they were kinda low and muffled, hard to understand. But pretty soon we could pick out what was being said, something about time to eat again and being hungry. We didn't know what was going on. Suddenly, a bony hand reached up through the sand, then another and another! There must have been a dozen, all reaching for us. We ran like hell and didn't stop till we reached the top of the next dune."[5]

Manistee, Michigan, on the east shore of Lake Michigan got its start as a center of piracy. It wasn't ships, crews and cargos that felt the "sharp end" of a cutlass. It was the vast forest of white pine the thieves were after. Known as timber pirates, their technique was to cut and ship timber from public forestland until they either ran out of trees or were caught, an event of great rarity. Sometimes to add a veneer of honesty, the pirates purchased 40 acres of land in the middle of a virgin forest and cut it, and the 40s bordering it, and the 40s bordering them. In the trade this was known as cutting "round" (from "all around") 40s. When federal lumber agents tried to intervene, the cases were thrown out of court by crooked judges paid off by the lumber pirates, or in some instances key witnesses "disappeared" and were unable to testify. The lifespan of an honest federal timber agent could be short. The pirates killed several lumber agents when they tried to enforce the law.

Over the span of a few years the timber pirates grew very wealthy and throwing on a cloak of respectability were soon referred to as "lumber barons," a more socially acceptable term than "pirate." Suddenly respectable, the old pirates made large contributions to civic organizations to build libraries, schools and, most common of all, "opera houses" to bring a patina of culture to areas notoriously rough around the edges and a thin veneer of honesty to themselves. Of course, the donor's name was always attached to the gift. Manistee, well known as the worst of the worst for stealing public timber, also became the "best of the best" as the home of many lumber barons and benefited from their efforts to buy respectability. The effort has largely been successful, at least locally, since few residents realize the true nature of their timber pirate history.

The historic Ramsdell Theater is just a couple of blocks from the public marina in Manistee. Built in 1902-03 by lumber baron Thomas Jefferson Ramsdell, the century-old ornate theater is a jewel from a bygone era. His friends knew Ramsdell as just T.J. and everyone wanted to be his friend. Reputedly it took three years to build at four times the estimated cost. Some locals soon called it "Ramsdell's Folly."

The theater is home to several performing companies including theatrical productions, dance and music. Out-of-area shows are also booked as time allows between locally produced performances. Recently restored, it is now reflective of the Victorian era of its construction. Red velvet seats, brass rails, a magnificent painted stage drop and decorated balconies testify to past glories and present restoration success. A glorious interior rotunda painted with cherubs, filigree and a naked lady look down on the audience below. The naked lady was painted by T.J.'s son Frederic, an artist of considerable ability. Legend claims that his wife posed for the painting, a topic that certainly gave the proper ladies of Manistee something to "titter" about while waiting for performances to start. What really "cranked up" the local social gossips was in the lobby. Tired of hearing their malicious comments about his wife's painting, he produced two large paintings of classical goddesses cavorting nude in the fields. He cleverly painted the faces of the two worst local gossips on the nudes! Doubtless theatergoers had many good belly laughs every time they passed through the lobby where the paintings were prominently displayed.

Today's performers aren't the only inhabitants in the old theater, however. Theatergoers, actors, stagehands and others have experienced things best explained by a belief in the supernatural. Many think that the ghost of T.J. Ramsdell is still in his theater. Often just referred to as T.J., his spirit is blamed for a variety of inexplicable events.

There are six private boxes in the theater, three on each side of the stage. The lower front one on stage right is T.J.'s old box. As the theater benefactor, a private box was an expected perk. In a spirit of appeasement, a red velvet chair is kept in the box so T.J. always has a seat for every performance.

It seems that if people treat the spirit with the respect T.J. thinks he deserves, he will respond with behavior that is, at best, helpful or, at worst, playful. Examples of such activities are many. One director remembered leaving a prop on the stage near the left stairs when she locked up for the night. Everyone else had already left. Realizing her error when she reached her car in the parking lot, she quickly returned to the stage intending to properly secure it in the prop room. To her surprise the prop was gone from where she left it. However, when she checked the prop room, there it was, right where it was supposed to be. Since she always treated T.J. with respect, speaking aloud to him about the play and making sure that his chair was in his stage right box, she just assumed he took care of her lapse. Other times she would reach for a light switch to turn a set of lights on only to have the lights illuminate before her hand touched the switch. The same thing occurred when reaching to turn lights off. She could only assume that it was T.J. again being helpful.

Sometimes T.J. can be a prankster. While sets are being constructed, tools disappear only to reappear days or weeks later, frustrating working crews.

If not respected, T.J. can be a threatening presence. Staff working high on the rear stage overhead grid systems claim to have occasionally been "pushed" by unseen hands. A fall from such a height could be deadly. The basement-level dressing rooms are very disturbing to some people, who claim that they feel a threatening presence in them. The sensation was so bad at one time a separate set of rooms was built to accommodate actors refusing to use the basement ones.

The theater has two balcony levels. The first is still used today and the plush velvet seats provide a wonderful view of the stage. The second balcony is no longer used since the narrow single stairs violate fire codes. In addition, the seats are narrow wooden benches and very uncomfortable. In the old days, local lumberjacks strictly used the upper level. The story goes that the jacks usually didn't bother to bathe for weeks or months at a time and to keep their stench from regular theatergoers, the men were confined to the upper balcony. Today workers in the theater sometimes report a whiff of indescribably disgusting odor coming from the old upper balcony area. Are the jacks still sitting patiently waiting for the play to begin?

The first balcony, while open to the general public, was also an acceptable area for the town's many "fillies de joile." Manistee businessmen provided a wealth of services to the timber industry, including proper "houses" for those times when the jacks were coming out of the woods with a season's worth of pay jangling in their pockets. The "painted ladies" often used a heavy application of strong perfume and, like the occasional sweaty whiff from the upper balcony, folks on the main floor sometimes got a dose of perfume.

Sometimes T.J. even makes a personal appearance. An apparition thought to be the old timber pirate is also sometimes seen in the old theater. The bearded T.J. is reported occasionally back stage moving silently between the sets as if inspecting their quality. He also has been seen sitting quietly in his chair in his box on stage right. The box sightings are invariably on opening night. He is always clad in a Victorian-style tuxedo. T.J. always was a stickler for decorum and where else should he be for an opening?[6]

A man working in the theater basement saw a longhaired young girl in a white dress standing quietly in a doorway. Wondering why someone would be there, he leaned in for a better look. The girl turned to him, said, "Follow me to your fortune," and vanished before his eyes. Dubbed the White Lady, as people now call her the longhaired ghost is supposedly T.J.'s daughter. She has also been seen in the tower and around the ticket office. Why she haunts the theater isn't known. Perhaps haunting the old Ramsdell is a family affair.

Another man was alone in the theater in the basement straightening things up when the lights flickered and he heard his name being whispered. Needless to say, he left quickly. Whether it was the daughter being playful or another ghost is anyone's guess.[7]

There is a story about a stagehand falling backwards into the orchestra pit and breaking his neck. Whether it was an accidental misstep or perhaps an untimely (and unseen) push is open to speculation, but some people question if the stagehand's spirit is still about the Ramsdell. Yet another tale claims that a stagehand put a noose around his neck, hanged himself in the back stage rigging and his ghost is sometimes seen still "dangling from a rope."[8]

The Ramsdell isn't the only haunted theater on Lake Michigan. The Rhode Opera House in Kenosha, Wisconsin, also has a spiritual cast. Members of the community theater group working in the old theater believe various haunts still walk the stage and enjoy the shows from the audience.

One actor was standing next to the stage when she noticed a man in the back of the auditorium hurrying down a row of seats heading for the exit. He was moving fast and touching the back of each seat as he passed. He had brown hair and wore a blue shirt or jacket. This wasn't unusual except she could see right through him! After he passed half a dozen or so seats, he vanished, just going poof!

Other cast members have seen seats move of their own accord, as if someone were getting up. Perhaps the idea that ghosts may be watching from the audience isn't so far fetched. Another member was sitting in the audience watching a rehearsal when a young man sitting next to her said, "Hey, you're sitting in the ghost's seat, you know." She commented that she wasn't aware of a special seat and she talked with him for a while. Only later when she asked others who he was did she find out no one else saw anyone sitting next to her! Was she speaking with a ghost?

Actors and crew claim to have seen figures moving around backstage when no one was in the area and heard people speaking when there wasn't anyone else around. Once a mother and young daughter were visiting the crew backstage after a show. While the mother was speaking with an actor, the child was eagerly looking around before finally blurting out, "Look at all the pretty ladies." Questioned later, she claimed that she saw several ladies wearing beautiful long dresses. Needless to say, no one else saw any ladies wearing long dresses![9]

One of the most popular ghostly haunts along the Michigan shore of Lake Michigan is the Bower's Harbor Inn on the Old Mission Peninsula near Traverse City. The Inn is a fine restaurant and its resident spook only adds to the legendary ambiance.

Who or what the ghost is has never been determined, but the prevailing thought is that it is Genevieve, the wife of J.W. Stickney, a rich Chicago businessmen. Stickney was said to have made his fortune in lumber and steel. As was common for the times, Stickney and Genevieve decided that they had to have a cottage "up north." The term "up north" loosely defines any place north of Lansing, Michigan. Starting in the 1870s, the Michigan shore of Lake Michigan became a very popular summer spot for people with money fleeing the heat, traffic and general stress of living in Chicago and Detroit. Going "up north" took on a certain social spin too. Vacationing along the same stretch of shore remains very popular today with the old money crowd still at the Old Mission Peninsula while new money tends to flow to new-gated resorts like Bay Harbor, just south of Petoskey.

Anyway, in the late 1890s J.W. and Genevieve built their cottage, really a mansion, and enjoyed the wonderful location. Characterized by high ceilings common to the age, it was a dramatic retreat. It even included an elevator. Genevieve apparently also enjoyed good food and drink, so much so that in time she grew rather large. There are claims that she had a special mirror made to make her appear thinner, much like the old sideshow mirrors common in carnivals. It is thought that her increased bulk caused J.W.'s eyes to wander resulting in the start of a long-time affair with his shapely and willing secretary.

After a time, J.W. took ill and died in a Chicago hospital. Whether Genevieve ever had any knowledge of her husband's wandering is unknown, but the real impact came when his will was read. The secretary, his main squeeze, got all of his money! Genevieve got the boot; not a dime went to her. Legend claims that she went back to the cottage and promptly hung herself in the elevator shaft. While she may have departed the world of the living, there is considerable belief she didn't leave the mansion.

The old mansion was sold several times and in 1959 became a restaurant. It seems that each set of owners reported unusual experiences. Lights turned on and off and the occasional mirrors fell off the wall. Perhaps Genevieve objected to seeing herself since her special "shaping" mirror was long gone. Sometimes the elevator ran by itself, or at least without an earthly passenger, and doors opened and closed on their own volition.

The current owners report much of the same type of activity – lights turning on and off, including pots and pans suddenly flying off their hooks, and even a bowl of salad soaring into the air and overturning.

While "unusual" things happen in many locations in the house, Genevieve's old bedroom, the current women's rest room, is a center of activity. For example, a guest reported that when she was seated snuggly on the "throne" several rolls of toilet paper inexplicably rolled under the stall walls. No one, or at least anyone seen, was in the room. Perhaps the ultimate Genevieve sighting also occurred in her old bedroom. A guest was "fixing" her makeup in front of an antique mirror, reputedly Genevieve's old frame with a normal mirror, when she was surprised to see in it reflecting a woman standing close behind looking over her shoulder. Strangely, the "reflected" woman wore her hair in a tight bun with a large pin and her dress was not in keeping with the Inn's normal clientele. Turning around quickly, the guest was stunned when no one was behind her. After seeing an old photo of Genevieve, the woman was certain she was the woman in the bathroom. Considering the bathroom was once Genevieve's bedroom, was the guest really the interloper? Since then, other people claim to have also seen the strange mirror apparition.

Of course, there are all sorts of other paranormal activities. Strange knocking sounds coming from within the walls, rapping on doors, sounds in closets, are all common manifestations from the world beyond. On another occasion a grandfather clock "leaped" 25 minutes ahead during a five-minute period. It was just as if an unseen hand was pushing the minute hand. Objects left one place overnight will also be found elsewhere in the morning.

Today both restaurant patrons and workers are generally comfortable with Genevieve. While she can be disruptive, the occasions are rare. Usually everyone is at peace with her, but, of course, Genevieve is still mad at J.W.[10]

Today Fayette, Michigan, is a quiet and peaceful place, the silence broken only by the few tourists who take the time to drive the 17 long and twisting miles down the scenic Garden Peninsula to reach the deserted old iron town. For a short period following the Civil War, it was a different place, filled with noisy and smoke chocking industry. From 1867-91, the little port boomed. Shouts of dockhands and sailors loading heavy iron pigs, the roar of iron ore loading into furnaces, yells of children playing in the dusty streets and clatter of horse-drawn wagons all echoed over the busy village. Toxic fumes from smelters and the sick stench of charcoal kilns gave the place an unsettling, disgusting odor defying description. Although long abandoned, Fayette is truly a ghost town in the very traditional sense. Stories abound of sights and sounds long gone, still assaulting the senses, echoing through the long deserted village. But let's start at the beginning.

Iron ore was discovered in Michigan's Upper Peninsula in 1844 and the massive deposits of the Marquette, Gogebic and Menominee ranges were soon providing the muscle for the country's booming steel industry. Much of the ore was shipped to lower lakes mills while some was diverted to local charcoal iron furnaces. This was a period when the steel industry was trying to sort itself out, to determine what was most efficient. Was it better to bring the ore to a central location where it could be combined with coke and limestone to produce steel or should iron be forged nearer the mines, then shipped as "pigs" to lower lakes mills?

Fayette was an example of the latter idea. At its heyday it was a bustling industrial community of 20 buildings, including a furnace complex, town hall, hotel, large dock, company store and workers homes. It was named after Fayette Brown, the local agent for the Jackson Iron Company, who selected the town site. More than 500 people called Fayette home. Over the 24 years the village existed, its furnaces produced nearly 230,000 tons of pig iron. Local limestone deposits were used to help purify the iron.

The problem with the operation was the need for tremendous amounts of charcoal used in the furnaces. The charcoal in turn was produced from the local hardwood forests. During the nearly quarter century of operation, the area surrounding Fayette was denuded of trees, left as desolate as a moonscape. The demand for wood to feed the charcoal kilns was insatiable. Today, the trees have largely grown back so the "look" of the restored village is all wrong, giving the impression of coexisting with the forest in an environmentally friendly state. The reality was much different. When the forests were gone, so was the economic viability of Fayette. In 1891, the Jackson Mining Company closed up shop and Fayette faded into the past, just a memory.

The old village today is operated by the state of Michigan as Fayette State Historic Park. Many of the buildings have been restored and interpreted to tell the story of the days of iron furnaces and sailing ships. Costumed guides walk the grounds to help the visitor better understand Fayette history. But sometimes visitors see other folks in costume who are not on the state payroll.

There are people who maintain there are more than memories at the old ghost town. Some folks claim that the spirits of former residents still roam the streets and buildings. Stories of unexplained sights and sounds are common. Many of the guides have experiences not explained by nature. Tourists come and spend a couple of hours, usually only giving everything a cursory once-over before struggling back up to U.S. 2 to continue their vacation. Park guides are there every day and often detect things missed by the casual visitor.

Shortly after the park opened for the season in 1998, a worker walking along the main street around dusk was startled to hear the "clop, clop, clop" and squeaking wheels of a wagon coming up the street toward him. The sounds continued directly past him, finally fading away after several minutes.

Another worker was sweeping the floor in the company store when he heard the door to the street open behind him. Thinking it was another worker, he turned to greet him. Instead of a park employee he was looking at the figure of a man in the clothing common to the previous century. The figure was only visible for the briefest period, and then vanished.

The sounds of children repeating their lessons have been heard in the old one-room schoolhouse. Blackboards left clean at night will sometimes be filled with lessons the following morning. Did an ambitious guide come in early and chalk them up to add to the visitor's interpretation or was it something else?

A psychic visiting Fayette in 2002 reported several "encounters" with the "other side." She said that the schoolhouse was especially active as might be expected from a group of highly "spirited" children. An unofficial séance (one done without the knowledge of park officials) revealed that the children are apparently the spirits of those buried in the old graveyard. Rather than passing on, they simply returned to the place of their greatest enjoyment.[11]

Perhaps the most spectacular experience involves the sailing yacht *Wind Blown*. The harbor used by the old schooners to deliver ore and load pig iron has been adapted for use by visiting yachts. Called Sea Shell Harbor, it offers fine protection against virtually all winds. On a fine summer night in early June 2000, the *Wind Blown* found herself alone in the harbor. Although being the only boat in the harbor is unusual, it was early in the season and boating traffic was still light. The three-person crew enjoyed an excellent dinner featuring whitefish capped with a bottle of good chardonnay. All was right with the world when they rolled up in their bunks for a good night's sleep.

Everything was quiet until about midnight when an unearthly scream echoed over the harbor. The violent rocking of the boat quickly followed, as if it were a toy in a giant's bathtub. The motion was severe enough for the bowline to snap from the strain. There was no wind or wave action. The nearby trees showed no movement at all. Whatever was happening, only the boat was affected. It was as if it slipped into another dimension. The furious rocking continued for several minutes, then stopped as suddenly as it started. What caused the crazy rocking was never explained.

Folks from another sailing yacht had a different experience in the late 1980s. At the time, the harbor was crowded with boats enjoying the fine summer weather. As sailors are wont to do, a few bottles were cracked and a quiet party was soon in full swing. Cautioned by a park employee to "keep it down," they settled into a quiet session of swapping sailing stories. Around midnight the wine bottles were empty and the sailors crawled to their bunks. However one husband and wife decided to stroll through the old village before turning in, resulting in an experience they will never forget. When they turned on to the old main street, they were greeted not by an empty lane, as expected, but instead by a dozen or so dark forms. All were human size and moving deliberately, as if doing the business of the day. The figures were indistinct, without true definition, much like blurry photos. The couple stood transfixed. Neither spoke, instead just looking on in awe and wonder. The moving forms paid no attention to the interlopers. They just continued their silent ballet. After several minutes, they faded into nothing, leaving no trace. The husband and wife returned to their boat, cutting their evening sojourn short. Secure in the warm glow of their cabin, they discussed what they saw but reached no rational explanation, at least not one that would explain it in acceptable scientific terms.[12]

An overgrown trail runs easterly from the village for a mile or so, eventually ending in a small clearing deep in the woods. When Fayette was booming, a fellow named Jim Sommers operated a small "ranch" there. Locals called it "the hole in the wall." The mining company wanted a perfect town, without any of "those" places around, so it purchased what it thought was all the available property. It missed a piece and that was where Jim established his business. The old stories claim that Sommers was a real bum, cheating customers on the rotgut whiskey he served while they waited for a girl and beating them up if they complained. Since he was off mining company property, it took no action. From the customers' view, the worst part was that he also beat up his girls. And that was downright rotten! There were even rumors that when some of the girls got too difficult to handle, he killed them, burying their bodies out in the thick woods where they would never be found. Eventually, the men of Fayette became so incensed with his murderous ways, a mob attacked the ranch, freeing the girls held there and running Sommers out of town after giving him a severe beating. For good measure, the rough log ranch was burned to the ground.

Fast forward to 2003. A deer hunter working his way down the narrow trail in the predawn hours of November 15, Michigan's traditional start of the firearms deer season, heard several loud screams coming from a point just ahead of him. Unsure what was happening, he moved quickly down the path. Bursting into the small clearing he was stunned to see the shadowy figure of a man dragging the equally indistinct figure of a prostate woman into the woods. Knowing whatever was going on was bad, the hunter quickly worked his bolt, chambering a 30.06 cartridge into his rifle, then yelled, "Stop right where you are!" The man released the woman and turned toward the hunter, pulling a long-bladed knife from his belt. Suddenly he ran at the hunter. Wasting no time the hunter, a Vietnam War veteran, shouldered his rifle and fired, the flash of muzzle blast lighting the entire clearing. When the echoes of the shot cleared, the man was gone. So was the woman. It was as if they never existed. What the hell was it? What happened? The hunter stepped to the edge of the clearing and waited for dawn, chambering another cartridge just in case. Whatever the hell was happening, he needed to be ready. Twenty minutes later, with enough light to see clearly, he cautiously approached the area where the man and woman were struggling. It was empty. Not a shred of evidence suggested anything ever was there. Neither was there a trace of the man he shot, but lying on the ground was an old and much rusted hunting knife. He slipped it into his pocket. The remainder of the day was uneventful other than he did bag a nice eight-point buck. Later that night he related his experience to his friends at deer camp only to be greeted by disbelief. Old John was just a good storyteller. Leave it to him to come up with a good tale. But when he pulled the rusty old knife out of his pocket, their jaws dropped.

I heard the hunter's story from one of the men at the deer camp. While certainly skeptical, he did admit that he tended to think something strange happened in the clearing. I didn't explain the historical connection with the Sommers ranch. No one would believe it anyway.[13]

The sleepy little town of Peshtigo, Wisconsin, was the site of the most horrific disaster ever to strike the Great Lakes. The *Eastland* capsizing pales in comparison and the Great Chicago Fire is nothing more than an out-of-control leaf burning. To know true catastrophe is to understand the appalling Great Peshtigo Fire.

Whether Mrs. O'Leary's cow kicked over the lantern that started the Chicago fire on October 8, 1871, or not is moot. Somehow the fire did start and 300 people perished in the blaze. But the true hell was in Peshtigo, 220 miles north.

All summer long the Great Lakes area suffered through a terrible drought. The forests were tinder dry and the vast quantities of slashings and tops littering the ground were ready to burn with minimum spark. When the lumberjacks cut an area, they left all the unsalable material laying in the woods. Their reckless disregard for fire safety proved deadly to many innocent people. Throughout the summer relatively small fires burned everywhere, but none really caught on.

The same day that Chicago burned, the tinder dry woods west of Peshtigo caught fire. Driven by gale-force winds, the flames flew across the forest and farmland like fiery banshees shot from hell. Hundreds of people desperately ran for safety. Some made it, many by jumping in the river. But an estimated 1,182 didn't. They were burned alive, roasted like a massive cannibal barbecue. When the ashes finally cooled, a million acres were destroyed. The survivors were in appalling shape. All were homeless and had no food. Everything they owned went up in flames. Many lost even the clothes on their backs when the fire burned them off. Unfortunately, most of the relief effort was directed at Chicago, which by virtue of being a big city "made the news." The poor folks in little Peshtigo were largely ignored.

Fires also burned across Michigan. Most of the city of Holland was destroyed in two hours, but with little loss of life. There was even a rumor that a group of Hollanders refused to fight the fire because it would be wrong to do work on the Sabbath. Most of Manistee was also burned up leaving a thousand people homeless. Lansing was saved only because the students from the "Ag" school (today's Michigan State University) turned out to fight the fire. The forests of Midland and Gratiot counties were consumed as well as the towns of Grindstone City, Huron City and Port Hope, all on the Lake Huron shore. Huron, Tuscola and Sanilac counties also burned to ashes. Roughly 2¹/₂ million acres were annihilated. While the economic loss was staggering in Michigan, only 10 lives were lost in comparison to the 1,182 in Peshtigo.

The Peshtigo fire is still very much alive. The town boasts a fine Peshtigo Fire Museum and revels in retelling the terrible story of the blaze. Legend has it that some of the victims still haunt the town. The harbor area is supposedly home to a ghost with an unholy red coloration, instead of the standard issue gray mist. Ghost hunters have captured a strange red orb on their digital cameras in contrast to the normal white ones. Perhaps the red is a spiritual reflection of the horrible fire.

Many of the fire victims are buried in the cemetery behind the fire museum. Some folks living in the neighborhood say that the old burying ground is not always peaceful, with spirits haunting local homes and streets. Sometimes a blue smoke-like mist, much like the legendary London fogs of Jack the Ripper stories, drifts over the area giving it an unearthly appearance. As one old-timer said, "When the fog is up, so are the ghosts."[14]

Haunts and hotels seem to go together and the Lakeside Hotel in Berrien, Michigan, is no exception. Located at the foot of the lake, just a short distance from famous Union Pier, it got its start in 1844 when Vermonter Alfred Ames purchased 78 acres near the area sailors called the Clay Banks, commonly used as a landmark by the old schooner captains. Alfred's son Fisher later established a small hotel on the property called Pleasant Grove. There is a tale that says a local group called the Lakeside Anti-Horse Thief Association used to hold it's meeting there and at least one miscreant did the "Texas two-step" from a tree overhanging the cliffs. They believed that justice should be quick and certain without the interference of meddling "legal beagles."

The Aylesworth family purchased the property, including the old hotel, in 1901. Eventually son Arthur would become intimately involved with the property in this world and the next. Old Arthur was a real character, a man born with the love of adventure. It is claimed that he toured with Buffalo Bill's Wild West Show, hunted big game in

Africa, ran a gambling hall in Las Vegas and trekked steamy jungles of South America. It was a big world out there and he wanted to experience it all.

When improved highways allowed a greater flow of automobiles to reach the area from Chicago, the hotel was expanded several times to accommodate the trade. It eventually grew to three stories in height and included a ballroom, restaurant and health spa. Business boomed in the 1920s, especially with many guests driving over from Chicago. Bootlegging boats unloaded right on the beach and guests eagerly waded into the water to help carry the booze ashore. A chance to participate in a "real" bootlegging job wasn't to be missed.

During the Depression the hotel went into decline and remained "down" for many years. Aylesworth's vivacious second wife, an actress named Virginia Harned, died in 1946. During her days on the stage, a newspaper described her as "a buxom young woman, whose bracing and frank personality carried with it exuberance of spirit, life, freedom and happiness. Her dramatic temperament is sumptuous, warm and full of colour, suggesting voluptuous ease, love of pleasure and a fondness for luxurious refinement. There is nothing spirituelle about her; her stage presence is distinctly material and very much of the world; she seems a woman with a streak of Bohemia in her makeup."

Years before she died, Aylesworth shot her. Supposedly it was an accident. Local people thought different, but since she didn't press charges their theories made no difference. Regardless, the pair had an unusual relationship. Not many marriages survive a bullet wound, accidental or not. It is believed that her spirit still haunts the hotel, especially in and around room 30. Judging from her stage description, she would make a perfect ghost.

In the late 1950s, when the hotel was in deep decline, Aylesworth usually sat in the lobby watching television until he fell asleep. Virginia had long ago taken her last curtain call and there was little else for a broken old man to do. The night watchman, who lived in an out building, would come in and wake him up to go to bed. Supposedly the watchman knew that it was time to put Aylesworth to bed because the ghost of Virginia told him.

After Aylesworth died, the hotel went through several owners and uses, including a baby clothing factory, rooming house and art center. During the winter of 1994-95, a new owner arrived and resurrected it to the glory days. Private bathrooms were added, the entire building rewired, a new heating system installed and old paint stripped to reveal the original fine wood finish. The 31-room inn is now designated as a State of Michigan Historic Landmark.

It is claimed that there are two spirits wandering about in the old Lakeside Inn. Virginia, of course, is felt to be haunting in and around room 30. Her husband is also in the hotel, checking that all is going well. A guest at a recent wedding in the ballroom claimed that he saw his misty form in the corner watching the festivities. Both are harmless and apparently pleased with the return of the inn to grandeur.[15]

Escanaba, Michigan's House of Ludington is another great example of a haunted lakeshore hotel. Like so many of the great ones, it somehow found a way to survive and thrive by providing solid service with an old time ambiance that the new "big box" hotels can't even begin to match.

The original hotel opened in 1864 as the Gaynor House, serving not only the needs of overnight travelers needing lodging but also as an upscale tavern and eatery. In 1871, it was renamed the House of Ludington in honor of lumber barons Harrison and Nelson Ludington. The main street is also named Ludington, showing their local economic power. For many years it was the only real hotel in Escanaba with any level of acceptable accommodation. An advertisement in the 1893 *Michigan Gazetteer and Business Directory* read, "New Ludington Hotel-The Largest and Only hotel in the city having Baths, Steam Heat and Electric Call Bells-$2.00 per day."

Over the years many famous entertainers stayed at the hotel, including John Philip Sousa, Randy Travis, Patricia Neal, Henry Ford, Prince Bertil of Sweden, Cornelius Vanderbuilt Jr., Guy Lombardo, Fred Waring, Jimmy Hoffa, George Gobel, Johnny Cash, Lynn Dickey, Fred Astaire and Jimmy Stewart. The hotel also played host to a galaxy of less savory guests, especially folks from the Chicago underworld. Escanaba was a good place to escape the pressures of the big city and "lay low" for a while and the House of Ludington provided fine quarters while "lay'n." Killers like John Dillinger stayed in the hotel, as did Baby Face Nelson. Locals claim that Nelson's bodyguards used the high cupola as a watchtower, since it had commanding views of the main street as well as harbor. Some maintain that the business end of a Thompson submachine gun always pointed out a window when Baby Face was in residence, but asking too many questions wasn't a healthy thing to do and locals were careful not to inquire too closely about who was currently in residence.

Legend claims that old Scarface himself, Al Capone, also visited the city. Since he is reputed to have owned a house in town, he didn't stay at the hotel but often dined there. Locals knew when he was around since the big black limo parked in front and men with overcoats lounging around the entrance, foyer and back door were all a dead giveaway. The overcoats, of course, concealed their deadly ".45-caliber choppers."

The hotel went through some tough times during the Depression and in 1939 a fellow named Pat Hayes took over. A local wheeler-dealer, he kept the hotel going by hook and crook. Some folks thought that there was more crook than hook, but regardless of how, he did keep it running and pumped its reputation up to legendary proportions. Local politicians and other celebrities were frequent visitors. It is said that he had two mistresses at the same time working for him in the hotel alongside his wife. When Pat died in 1969, he left the hotel to his son and mistresses, cutting his wife out completely. Following his death, the hotel declined significantly, going through rough years and several owners and even a seizure for income tax evasion. In 1996, the present owners took over and returned the House of Ludington to its former glory. Originally the hotel had 100 guest rooms, but over the years the number dropped to 25 as the result of remodeling, combining many into apartments and suites. Renovations preserved the unique history of the hotel while bringing comfort to the guests.

The hotel is the scene of various unexplained phenomena, things that go "bump in the night." Some people believe it is Pat Hayes' spirit causing the bizarre incidents. Others suggest, given its storied guest list, that there are numerous candidates for ghosthood.

Just after the grand reopening, the hotel was hosting a catered affair. One of the owners had just finished wiping off a beautiful crystal punch bowl and handed it to a worker to put away. As she turned her back, the room filled with the sound of shattering glass, the worker evidently having dropped the bowl. But when she turned around to assess the damage, the bowl was safely on the shelf. What caused the noise?

Weird incidents occur in many places in the hotel. Saucers have been known to turn over by themselves and a radio turns itself on and off. Windows in the dining room open of their own accord. Shut 'em at night but by morning they're wide open. Old-timers remembered that Pat always liked fresh air. The lobby elevator has been known to run by itself, suddenly coming to life and delivering an unseen guest to the third floor or back out to the lobby.

A few years ago a guest was startled to see the doorknob to his room turn by itself as if someone who wasn't there was trying to open the door. Intrigued by the incident, a paranormal investigator camped out in the hallway one night to see what would happen. Just after midnight a knob at the far end moved slightly. Hallway lighting was dim and he couldn't clearly see in the deep shadows. A few moments later another knob a little closer to him moved. And then another and another, each time moving closer to him. The moving knobs finally stopped a few rooms away. Whatever it was would not come any closer. He stood his ground, whether showing courage or frozen with terror.

Ghost hunters exploring the narrow tunnel leading between the old section of the hotel and a newer addition videotaped a grainy image of something moving down the dark corridor. Since they shot in darkness, using the camera's low light capability, the image is at best blurry, but something is there moving in the dark.

Is the old hotel still haunted by Pat Hayes, or perhaps several of the Chicago mob who so enjoyed their stay that they returned after death?[16]

The Evergreen Inn in Manitowoc, Wisconsin, is now long closed as a hotel. Many people might suggest while the living guests have left, their places were taken by the dead. There are reports of people in full Victorian dress wandering about in the lounge, dancing and conversing with each other. It is as if a veil to the sights and sounds of a century ago suddenly lifted. The elevator was claimed to run itself on occasion and sometimes when the doors opened the specter of a woman, who hung herself on an upper floor, dangled in the doorway as blood dripped silently to the floor. Good stuff for a Hollywood horror flick. For a while after the hotel closed, a restaurant operated on the first floor. Occasionally customers complained of pounding noises in the empty floors above. When police investigated, including using a special K-9 unit, nothing was ever found. Readers must be cautioned the hotel is closed and trespassers will be prosecuted.[17]

Many people remember the bizarre little car called a Yugo. Starting in 1985, the diminutive autos were imported to America from Yugoslavia. Their cheap price, roughly $3,990, attracted people until the overwhelming poor quality eviscerated further sales. Known as the "lemon on wheels," it was a shattering sales disaster that brought Tito's communist workers "paradise" well-deserved international ridicule. Owners complained of mechanical problems, including premature engine failure, bad brakes, poor shifter and transmission, faulty electrical system and terrible dealer service. The insurance industry also faulted the car's crash worthiness, which didn't help matters. By 1989, Yugo USA was bankrupt. Things got even worse when NATO bombed the home factory during the Bosnia War, since it was also producing weapons (of course if the weapons were as bad as the Yugo, perhaps it would have been better NOT to bomb the factory).

The Yugo entered Michigan legend on September 22, 1989, when 31-year-old Leslie Ann Pluhar of Royal Oak, Michigan, plunged 142 feet to her death off the Mackinac Bridge while driving her 1987 Yugo across during high northwesterly winds. More than a week later, Michigan State Police divers hauled the crushed car, complete with driver, up from the depths adjacent to the bridge. A technical examination revealed that the car was in full working order. There were no mechanical defects causing it to veer out of control and mysteriously climb over the bridge rail.

Considered one of the most beautiful in the world, the five-mile-long Mackinac Bridge was the longest suspension bridge ever constructed when opened in 1957. Bridging the Straits of Mackinac, some of the roughest water in the Great Lakes, was a tremendous engineering achievement. The channel at the middle of the bridge ranges to 295 feet deep. Weather in the Straits can be notoriously bad. Wind speeds in excess of 90 miles per hour have been recorded during autumn storms. Designed to eliminate the fatal flaws of the infamous "Galloping Gertie" as the Tacoma Narrows Bridge in Washington demonstrated when it tore itself to pieces in November 1940, the Mackinac Bridge is solid as the bedrock it is anchored to.

The question of what happened to throw the Yugo off the bridge remains unanswered. A full Michigan State Police accident investigation estimated the car's speed at between "55 and 65 miles an hour," far in excess of the posted 45 mph limit on the bridge. The Pluhar family attorney claimed poor car stability and design flaws in the bridge caused the accident.

Did a blast of high wind pick up the Yugo and casually flip it into the water like a scrap of paper? Did the driver lose control and veer into the low railing, bump upwards and over into the lake? Did the driver commit suicide in this unique way? Or did something else happen, something still unexplained?

A second vehicle went over in March 1997. This time it was a sport utility vehicle, so the light car aspect of the Yugo mystery could not be blamed. The idea of suicide was also considered more likely.

The eerie question with both vehicles, though, is how many more are there? How many unknown cars are rusting on the bottom of the Straits that no one knows anything about? Perhaps they are buried deep in the mud or swept away by powerful currents. What sets the 1989 and 1997 incidents apart is that someone witnessed the cars go flying off. Crossing is not always done in heavy traffic. Late at night, a single car can be on the bridge and unobserved by anyone. If it went over, who would ever know?[18]

The old Grand Haven Theater was claimed by many people to be the home of the ghost of the longtime janitor. Lights went on and off and areas littered with garbage magically cleaned themselves up. Just for good measure, a tale of a body buried in the basement provided a little extra spice to the tales. When redevelopment efforts fell short, as is often the case when communities fail to appreciate intrinsic value of historic structures, the theater was torn down.

The Hackley Public Library on Muskegon's West Webster Avenue has its own resident spirit. As the stories go, the ghost of the benefactor, lumber baron Charles H. Hackley, still wanders around the bookshelves keeping watch on his library.

The North Bluff Cemetery in Gladstone, Michigan, on the south shore of the Upper Peninsula is said to be home to the spirit of a young woman in a flowing wedding dress. Supposedly she is seen wandering through the tombstones searching for the murderer of her husband. Some people claim that she actually comes right up to a person before vanishing![19]

Saugatuck has developed into a fancy little resort community for Chicago. Although in Michigan, it is just around the lower end of the lake so it is common for hoards of Chicagoans to drive over for a summer weekend, week or entire season. It is a role Saugatuck revels in, numerous motels, bed-and-breakfast inns and restaurants all vying for a part of the tourist "trade."

The town also has a share of ghostly visitors. The Felt Mansion is a case in point. Dorr Felt built the Felt Mansion in the 1920s, largely to please his wife, Agnes. She didn't enjoy the magnificent residence long, however, dying of a stroke in her private bedroom soon after moving in. Although Dorr married again, his new wife didn't like the mansion, perhaps because she felt the spirit of Agnes still occupying "her house." The mansion later became a home for boys, nunnery and even a Michigan State Police post. In some fashion all left their imprints on it.

Fortunately, the house is being renovated and ghost tours are even being given as a way of raising additional funds. It is claimed that doors open and close in Agnes's old room, just as if she were still coming and going. Photography also shows strange orbs and mists. Perhaps the most haunted room is the old ballroom, with the spirits of long departed guests still enjoying a night's festivities.

Near the Felt Mansion is a small building locally known as the Junction Asylum. The name is, however, an error since it was never an insane asylum but a "trusty" building for the old Dunes Correctional Facility. Although it is heavily vandalized, psychics claim that spirits of the inmates still roam the desolate and decrepit halls. Sounds of loud breathing, heavy footsteps and screams all echo eerily over the grounds. Strange silhouettes have also been reported, as if only the shadows of ghostly inmates are visible. Unlike most of the Lake Michigan ghosts, these spirits are unfriendly, even downright evil. Men were not sent to the Dunes for having overdue library books. As is common for private property, trespassers can be prosecuted.[20]

Wisconsin's Door Peninsula stretches northeast into Lake Michigan from Green Bay for perhaps 90 miles. Similar to Lake Superior's Keweenaw Peninsula, it is a magnet for shipwrecks, her rocky beaches and offshore reefs catching upward of 100 vessels. While the Keweenaw has never been discovered by the yuppies and remains remote and rugged with little economy and precious few residents, the Door has become Wisconsin's "in" spot for the well-heeled tourist. Once sleepy little villages are now filled with "cute" little bed-and-breakfast inns, restaurants, hotels, condos, marinas, wineries, apple orchards and antique shops. You get the picture.

All this said, the Door does have an exiting "real" history of shipbuilding, commercial fishing, bootlegging and other pursuits. In fact the various ghost stories revolve around the real history as opposed to the current gentrification. All this leads to the question, "Are there any yuppie ghosts?"

Nelsen's Hall Bitters Pub and Restaurant on Washington Island is an example of a business that bridged the gap from the working past to the touristy present. Washington Island is right on the tip of the Door and getting there requires a short ferry ride. Built in 1899 by Danish immigrant Tom Nelsen, the establishment quickly became the social center for residents and visitors. Over time the building was used as a tavern, movie theater, dentist office, pharmacy and even an ice cream parlor. The tavern part never really stopped regardless of what else was going on, including the infamous outrage of Prohibition. The "bitters" part of the name comes from Tom's habit of drinking Angostura Bitters as a stomach tonic. It is said that he drank nearly a pint a day of it for most of his 90 years and credited the libation with his long life. When the dead hand of Prohibition fell across the Nation, Tom obtained a pharmacist's license to allow him to sell the bitters to his customers. Since it was 90 proof, the bitters became an antidote of sorts to the "missing" real stuff. Tom actually became the largest purveyor of Angostura Bitters in the world, a record still held today by Nelsen's Hall. It is also credited with being the oldest "continuously operating tavern" in the United States.

Angostura Bitters were developed in 1824 by Dr. J. Siegert, who intended them for use as a tonic to treat fatigue and stomach ailments. A German national, Dr. Siegert went to Venezuela to join with Simon Bolivar in his fight against the Spanish throne. Bolivar eventually appointed him surgeon-general of the military hospital in the town of Angostura. It is there that he developed his remarkable tonic, which is now the single most widely distributed bar item in the world. Angostura Bitters is named for Angostura, Venezuela, and of course not for the bark of the eponymous tree. It is made from a secret blend of tropical herbs, plant extracts and spices – reportedly more than 40 ingredients. It certainly is a strange libation for a small bar in Wisconsin.[21]

So much of the tavern's history is wrapped up in Tom Nelsen, it would be a shame if his spirit wasn't still around, and many folks claim it still is. Occasionally objects move about and disappear only to reappear a few days later. Strange things have also been reported in the ladies room and someone who wasn't there has tapped people sitting at the bar on the shoulder, as if to say, "Excuse me, but you are sitting in my seat." None of the activity is threatening, rather just the sort of stuff to let people know that someone is still watching over the old place and perhaps looking for another shot of bitters.[22]

The Shipwrecked Restaurant, Brew Pub and Inn in Egg Harbor is another old-time establishment that successfully transitioned to the new age. Built in the late 1800s, it was originally a watering hole for lumberjacks and sailors. With the advent of Prohibition and rise of the Mob, the Door became a good place for the folks from Chicago with music cases to hang out for a while until things cooled off. It is claimed that the big guy himself, none other than the "Pride of Italia," Al "Scarface" Capone, and his henchmen sometimes hoisted a brew or two at the bar.

Former owners of the property as well as the present ones believe a cast of various spooks may haunt it. The divorced wife of a former owner, Verna Moore, is one of the shades. Although she died years ago, folks have seen her walking through the dining room and heard her in the basement. A nice and gentle spirit, she seems to be keeping a close eye on things.

There is a wild tale of a lumberjack being murdered in the bar shortly after it opened. Considered more belligerent, his ghost hasn't made a recent appearance. He is a rare example of an angry spirit.

On one of his trips to the bar, Big Al toted along one of his women with her baby, thought by many to be his illegitimate son. Sometime during his stay, mother and child disappeared. Perhaps he arranged for both to feed the fish in nearby Lake Michigan as a way of getting rid of a couple of problems. Regardless, sometimes the grating screech of a crying baby is heard, giving thought to the likelihood of it being the murdered child. Jason, another of Scarface's illegitimate children, was found dangling at the end of a rope in the attic of the bar. Whether it was murder or suicide can only be guessed. His ghostly image has been seen in the attic as well as on the roof. The roof images were so vivid that locals called the bar to warn that some damn fool on the roof was sure to fall off and kill himself.[23]

Many reasons have been put forward to explain why something or somewhere is haunted. Perhaps it is a powerful sense of vengeance against a person or place, the overriding need to "get even." The ghost may not "know" it is dead and continues with normal actions, just doing what it always did. Guilt could be a factor, too. The ghost did something horrendous in life and is trying to "make up for it" in death. And then there is love and that is the claimed basis of the Castle Park tower ghost.

The castle-like building was built in 1890 on the private estate of Michael Schwarz, a German immigrant who struck it rich in Chicago real estate. Having made his bundle, he moved to Holland, Michigan, in search of a spot to establish a feudal estate like the ones he left behind in Prussia. His overriding concern was to insulate his family, including a wife, six daughters and two sons, from the "uncivilized influences" of America. The result was a three-story "castle" made of brick and stone closely resembling those of his native land.

Supposedly the family lived there for only two years before he gave up on the idea, realizing perhaps that it is impossible to hide from life.

There is a wonderful tale about one of the daughters. Apparently, despite her father's protectionist plans, she met and fell in love with a Dutch boy from nearby Holland. As hard as the father worked to keep them apart, they were attracted to each other. True love will not be denied. Since Schwarz would not allow marriage, the only choice was to elope. One night they decided to sneak away. At this point the story gets muddled. One version claims that the couple made it to the church and finished the ceremony before the irate father showed up. Presented with a fait accompli, he could only accept the marriage. The second version is more popular. The girl escaped from the house and met her beau, who was waiting outside with a carriage. However, the father saw her as she was climbing in and, after grabbing his rifle, ran to stop her. He was too late. The Dutch lover brought the carriage to a fast canter and left the father standing in the dust. Not to be denied, he quickly saddled a horse and took off in hot pursuit, catching them before they reached the church where a preacher was waiting to marry the love-struck pair. The father chased his would-be son-in-law away and forced his daughter back to the castle. To make certain that she never tried it again, he locked the broken-hearted girl in the tower, keeping her confined for years. As time passed and the family moved away, the legend grew that her ghost occupied the tower and on moonlit nights could be seen looking out the window toward Holland, pining away for her young Dutch lover who never returned.

Castle Park subsequently went through a period as a school for boys, then a resort and now is privately owned.[24]

Guests at the Pfister Hotel in Milwaukee, Wisconsin, always appreciate its extra special service. Sometimes it's a complimentary drink at the bar or a rich chocolate candy on the pillow for the evening turndown. But the Pfister has an extra way of checking that everything is just right. The ghost of the founder, Charles Pfister, is said to walk the floors to make sure everything is in order. He may have departed the earth in 1927 but hasn't left "his" hotel.

He has been seen watching the lobby from the grand staircase, walking the minstrel's galley in the ballroom and strolling the halls. Always described as "older, portly, smiling and well dressed," he adds a certain ambiance to this very special hotel. He is never threatening, but always is seen as a quiet guardian spirit.

Since opening in 1893, and just three blocks from Lake Michigan, it has always been the premier hotel in Milwaukee. The Pfister epitomizes a rich tradition of gracious service and impeccable style. And Charles is still there to make certain it always will.[25]

Milwaukee was also home to the famous Giddings poltergeist case in 1874. This baffling case revolved around Mary Spiegel, a servant at the Giddings Boardinghouse. In August, the house became the scene of wild supernatural activity; a cellar trapdoor opening itself, dishes and silverware flying into the air, chairs and food hovering in mid-air and a calliope of sound filling the house. The activity supposedly started suddenly when Mary and the owner's wife, Mrs. William Giddings, were baking pies in the kitchen. When neighbors came over to see what was going on, pails flew at them as if thrown by unseen hands. The wild activity continued off and on for days, but only when Mary was present. Realizing somehow that Mary was the catalyst, Mrs. Giddings fired her, sending her home. What other real choice did she have?

On learning that Mary had been fired, her father severely beat her. Distraught, unable to understand the supernatural devilment, fired from her job and beaten by her father, Mary attempted suicide by jumping in the Milwaukee River. A passerby rescued her.

When he learned of the situation, a prominent Chicago physician took on her case and after an examination diagnosed her as a sleepwalker and neurotic. Considering the stress she was under, this seems an easy evaluation, at least the neurotic part. Whenever he took her back to the Giddings house, all hell broke loose again. Whatever was happening, Mary was certainly the "trigger." Finally, she moved in with his family as a domestic servant and she apparently never returned to the Giddings house or suffered another attack of flying objects.[26]

Chicago is the major Lake Michigan port city. Its connections to the lake are long and deep. In 1871, the year of the Great Chicago Fire, more vessels entered the port than New York, Baltimore, San Francisco, Philadelphia, Charleston and Mobile combined. Today, that rich maritime heritage is largely forgotten despite the glitz of the resurrected Navy Pier.

Today, roughly 2.6 million living souls occupy the city, plus an uncounted number of "unliving" ones. Some psychic authorities believe that ghosts are attracted to water. Since Chicago is on the water and the Chicago River and its various tributaries are such an important part of the city, it is claimed by paranormal investigators that ghosts are especially lured to the area. Some Chicago ghosts are world famous, Resurrection Mary for instance. Others are virtually unknown, quiet spooks that haven't made the "splash" of the others.

Resurrection Mary is perhaps the city's most recognized ghost. Mary is claimed to be the spirit of a beautiful young girl, usually described as having blond hair and deep blue eyes. Outfitted in a white gown and thin shawl, she is often holding a small pocket book. Her skin is always unusually pale. Her name derives from Resurrection Cemetery in Justice, a suburb just south of the city. Legend claims she is buried somewhere within the old wrought iron fence bordering the compound of the dead.

As with any such tale, there are numerous versions, but all agree on the basics. The legend started in the mid-1930s. For some reason Mary got into an argument with her boyfriend after spending the night dancing in the old O. Henry Ballroom. Perhaps he wanted more "action" than Mary was willing to provide or was she flirting with another boy? The result, however, was Mary walking home alone along a dark and deserted Archer Avenue. Suddenly a speeding auto shot down the street, made a quick swerve and ran her down. Smashed and blood soaked, she was dead on the scene. The driver of the mystery auto never stopped, a classic hit-and-run incident. Her grieving parents buried her in Resurrection Cemetery.

A couple of years later, a young man met a beautiful girl at another nearby ballroom. They seemed to hit it off well and spent the evening dancing and talking, although she seemed oddly "distant." He later remembered her skin as being very pale and cool, her deep blue eyes were distant and blonde hair tumbled to her shoulders. When he sneaked a quick kiss, her lips were positively cold. When the dance ended, she asked for a ride home, which he gallantly agreed to. Her directions brought the car to the front gate of Resurrection Cemetery where she asked him to stop. Telling him to stay in the car and not try to follow, she quickly kissed him, ran through the gates and disappeared. The gates of course were locked!

In later years, different variations of the tale developed. Drivers on Archer Avenue reported picking up a girl matching Mary's description and taking her to the O. Henry Ballroom. In other instances, she asked for a ride to the cemetery gates, always vanishing from the car as it pulled up or when running through the gates. Other versions have her picked up in various suburban locations, but invariably taken to the cemetery. Mary was never "vaporous" but always very "solid" until she went "poof." Another variation includes Mary running out in front of a car only to disappear when the vehicle "hits" her.

Mary sightings reportedly increased when the cemetery was renovated in the 1970s. In one instance a motorist claimed to have seen a young girl standing inside the gates grasping the iron bars, evidently locked in. He reported it to the local police who duly investigated but found no one inside, at least no one living. It was claimed, however, that the iron bars the girl held were bent apart, as if tremendous force was used to tear at them. Supposedly, human handprints were imprinted into the cold iron. Skeptics claimed a delivery truck had backed into the bars causing the damage, but locals knew what really happened. It was Mary!

Mary's identity is unknown, although there is speculation involving the deaths of several young women in the late 1920s and early 1930s that generally fit the circumstance. In the end, who she is (or was) makes no difference. The legend of Resurrection Mary continues.

The old Cook County Criminal Courts building and adjoining Cook County Jail reputedly are rife with the wandering spirits of generations of crooks (including local politicians, of course), mobsters and miscreant sailors. Some county employees talk about eerie noises late at night, lights turning on and off of their own accord, elevators running without occupants (at least human ones) and apparitions moving silently down empty halls.

Both buildings have a long and violent history. Blood literally ran in the halls and courtrooms. For example, in October 1970 convicted killer Gene Lewis attempted to shoot his way out of the courthouse with a snub-nosed revolver. His girlfriend smuggled the gun into him hidden in a hollowed-out book of Edgar Allan Poe poetry (fitting, no?). Cornered like a rat in a seventh floor room by police, he died after being riddled with bullets, the cops just standing back and blasting away. One officer later recalled the firing sounded like "popcorn popping." The coroner later counted 70 bullet wounds in the killer's body, moving a courthouse wag to comment, "They had to pick him up with a magnet to get him out of there."

Workers also relate stories of desk drawers opening and closing, jury chairs moving and doors swinging open and shut without benefit of human hands. A custodian claims to have seen the ghost of a man who hanged himself in a room behind a fifth floor courtroom. The gray body swung quietly to and fro before fading away into nothing.

Perhaps the most infamous location is a room in the jail where executions were regularly performed until 1962. The room where "Old Sparky" (the electric chair) once held center stage is now a dreary office. Some folks claim that the room is unusually cold. Certainly its chilling past must influence the present. Others claim to hear chains rattling as if a manacled prisoner was scuffling in to take the seat to electric glory and see the lights flicker as if the "juice" was again driven into the mortal core of another cold-blooded killer. The stench of cooked flesh waft briefly in the stale air.

Although it was torn down in the 1990s, the old Lexington Hotel on South Michigan Avenue south of the Chicago Loop was said to be haunted. During the days when "Big Al" Capone ruled the city, the hotel was his headquarters. Built in 1891 as the Michigan Hotel, it had 370 rooms and was quite a "joint" for the times. Scar Face Al occupied the entire fourth floor and most of the third. After the hotel was abandoned, passersby claimed to see a shadowy figure moving from window to window. Perhaps it was Big Al still watching "his" city or his hoods on the lookout for a possible hit. Considering the number of people Big Al "rubbed out," the ghost (or ghosts) could have been one of his many victims. It was also just a few blocks over on South Dearborn at Madam Emma Duvall's French Elm brothel that the first all-mirrored bedrooms were introduced in the 1890s.

The Prairie Avenue area, once the preferred address of Chicago's rich and famous, including the Palmers, Swifts and Pullmans, has its own collection of spirits. Perhaps the most famous is Marshall Field Jr., heir to the famous department store fortune.

For reasons unknown to this day, on November 22, 1905, he was alone in his mansion, other than for the servants, when a gunshot rang out. Marshall shot himself in the left side of his abdomen while cleaning a revolver in preparation for a Wisconsin hunting trip, or so he claimed as he lay dying in the hospital. This is the official story anyway.

The word on the street was much different, claiming that he had just returned from a night of debauchery at the infamous Everleigh Club, the most famous of Chicago's parlor houses. Marshall was a regular at the very exclusive Everleigh Club enjoying the talents of the very finest young and cultured ladies. Rumors said the shooting was either a botched suicide or perhaps one of the girls took exception at something he said or did. Regardless, the belief was that he was shot in the Everleigh and smuggled home to die, making it all look like an accident. Whether accidental or deliberate, Marshall died and was duly laid out in the parlor for the funeral. Eventually, he was buried in the posh Graceland Cemetery where all of Chicago's elite were planted. After all, the right address in death is just as important as the right one in life. Graceland reputedly has its own host of spirits, including a howling green-eyed dog said to guard the mausoleum of a man named Ludwig Wolff. No explanation for the dog's relationship to Wolff is known or why he deserves such canine protection.

After a time, the Prairie Avenue area changed from ritzy to low class as the cityscape evolved. Today many of the old homes have been renovated since the area is undergoing a resurgence. Marshall's mansion, however, continues to defy efforts to rehabilitate it. Attempts to make it into a nonprofit headquarters, boarding house and restaurant all failed. Some claim it is because Marshall's ghost wants his privacy and chases off those who would interrupt it.

The Iroquois Theater fire on December 30, 1903, was one of the most horrific disasters to befall Chicago, worse than the infamous 1871 fire, which killed an estimated 300 people. The theater was brand new and anxious to impress jaded Chicago theatergoers. The magnificent and ritzy new Iroquois on Randolph Street was designed to rival any theater in New York. Stained glass windows and deeply polished wood were common. A 60-foot-high ceiling graced the lobby and marble walls and huge mirrors accented the palatial theme. Two huge and ornately decorated grand staircases curved upward from lobby to balconies.

It is believed that as many as 2,000 people were jammed into the Iroquois for the afternoon show. Since there were only 1,600 seats, the rest were standing room only. Another 400 performers and stagehands were backstage. Regardless of exactly how many were inside, the theater was certainly jammed. During the middle of the show, a stage curtain caught fire from an overheated spotlight. It spread quickly. An asbestos fire curtain designed to seal the stage (and fire) off from the audience dropped just as it was supposed to, but failed to properly seal against the floor. It was later determined that the curtain was actually not made of asbestos but cotton. It was much cheaper than a real fire curtain and there would never be a fire anyway, so why spend the money? The audience panicked and rushed for the exits, many of which were chained shut. Locking fire exits was a major violation of the fire codes, but the owners were more concerned with people sneaking in via the exits and not paying admission, so the fire inspectors were paid off to look the other way. The illuminated exit signs were also turned off so as not to distract the audience. Other exit doors opened in instead of out. When the panicked crowd pushed to get out, they were just jammed in tighter. The blaze traveled with remarkable speed and soon the theater became a massive oven of fiery death.

When the fire was finally extinguished, firemen discovered that parts of the main floor were 7 feet deep in charred bodies. Roughly 150 people died when they rushed out a balcony fire exit. Unfortunately there were no stairs leading to the ground. It stopped five stories above the street and, pushed by those behind, people fell to their death on the concrete below. When all the grisly accounting was finished, more than 600 people perished in the tragedy.

The building went through several reincarnations. Today it is the Ford Center for the Performing Arts. Regardless of the changes, local legend claims that it is haunted by the spirits of those burned alive in the disaster. Workers and spectators assert disembodied footsteps can be heard echoing up and down deserted halls and lights turn on and off of their own accord. A woman dressed in white is also seen wandering about in an outside alley where so many fell from the stairless fire exit. Other people claim feeling the touch of an invisible hand when no one is around or the "puff" of very hot air. A whiff of acrid smoke no longer sends staff searching for a fire alarm. There are many reminders of its tragic history.[27]

There are ghosts that bridge the gap between land and water. The famous crawling ghost of Calvary Cemetery is one of them. The cemetery, located right on the border between Chicago and Evanston, Illinois, was established in 1859. It is one of the oldest in the area and looks out on Sheridan Road toward Lake Michigan.

While there are variations to the tale, a popular one goes something like this. The ghost of a drowning man is sighted in the lake, just opposite from the cemetery. After the figure sinks for the final time, he seems to crawl up to the shore, cross the road and disappear in the cemetery.[28]

Some sources identify the ghost as a Navy pilot killed in an attempt to land on one of the small training aircraft carriers used on the lake. During World War II, thousands of Naval aviators trained on Lake Michigan. A number were killed in accidents. Is this the ghost of one still trying to make it to safety?

Lincoln Park has its own collection of ghostly tales ranging from groups of people in early 1900s costume to apparitions of World War II soldiers and sailors. Since it was built on the grounds of the old City Cemetery, there certainly is a "foundation" for such ghostly tales. There were also two historic cemeteries located directly on the lakeshores one for Protestants and one for Catholics. High water levels, storms and erosion sometimes resulted in a coffin or two washing out into the lake. Both cemeteries were eventually "redeveloped" and absorbed into downtown Chicago. But do the dead know that?

Harpo Studios on West Washington Boulevard is reputed to be the home of numerous ghosts, likely revolving around the loss of the steamer *Eastland*. When the big steamer capsized in the Chicago River near the Clark Street Bridge on July 24, 1915, she took 841 men, women and children to their death. The *Eastland* was supposed to carry her 2,500 passengers to a Michigan City, Indiana, amusement park for a day of picnics, games and amusement. Instead she plunged the city into deepest mourning.

There are a couple of types of ghosts involved with the *Eastland*. Even today people walking by the site sometimes claim to hear the desperate cry of a person drowning in the river. When they look, no one is there. Was it perhaps an echo from the past? In another instance people looking down from the bridge profess to see bodies floating in the water. When police respond, the bodies are gone. Where they ever there?

Prior to becoming home to the Oprah Winfrey Show in 1989, the building was the old Second Regiment Armory, Illinois National Guard. Following the *Eastland* disaster, the armory was used as a temporary morgue for the victims. Since conversion to a television studio, stories about lights going on and off and doors opening and closing on their own volition began to circulate. Included are stories of strange sobbing, laughing and the eerie sound of ragtime music coming from everywhere and nowhere. Another tale involves hearing dozens of invisible footsteps marching across the empty lobby. An especially creepy account involves a building security guard. Walking his rounds one night, he was surprised by the smell of perfume. Looking around, he saw nothing. When he returned to the security central, the other guards asked why he didn't stop the woman. He replied he saw no one. However, they clearly saw a woman on their camera. She was in a long gray gown and large floppy hat, a costume consistent with 1915. Dubbed the "Gray Lady," her presence has since been reported several times.

The Red Lion Pub on North Lincoln Avenue is also said to be home to a couple of spirits. One is reportedly a bearded man dressed like a cowboy seen wandering around the bar. Perhaps he is a holdover from the days when Buffalo Bill's Wild West Show toured the city or a spiritual "urban cowboy." There is also the tale of a woman murdered in an upstairs room whose playful ghost reportedly takes perverse pleasure in locking women in the rest room.

There are even claims that the Hooters on North Wells is haunted. Before being converted to the current use, the building was home to numerous businesses, all of which failed for various reasons. Employees claim to hearing footsteps in the basement storerooms or their name called when they are alone. Electrical equipment comes on and off, including a corner jukebox.[29]

About halfway between the lake and the north branch of the Chicago River is the old Biograph Theater, well known as the location where the villainous killer John Dillinger met his just deserts on the evening of July 22, 1934. If the ghost stories are true, he is reliving his bullet-ridden death again and again.

The John Dillinger story is at best confusing. Whether he was responsible for all the crimes he was charged with, or even more, isn't known for certain. There is a tendency to blame any unsolved bank robbery on the most famous crook of the time. If Dillinger did it, then surely the local cops couldn't be blamed for failing to catch him. Nobody ever caught Dillinger. Dressed in a stylish straw boater hat and known for his athletic jumps over teller cages, his flamboyant style constantly drew attention to his crimes. He was a crook bigger than life, a living legend. There are even tales that it wasn't Dillinger killed at the Biograph.

Dillinger's life of crime began in 1925 when he robbed a grocery store in his hometown of Mooresville, Indiana. Quickly nabbed, he spent eight years in prison, released in May 1933. Despite his initial failure, he must have decided that being a criminal was good career choice. Once he was back on the street, he charged off into a spree of bank robberies and murder. In little more than 14 months, he knocked off 11 banks (with his own gang or in cooperation with other gangs), killed four law enforcement officers and four innocent citizens. He also shot his way out of half a dozen ambushes and police traps as well as escaped twice from behind bars. His gang broke him out of prison in Lima, Ohio, and he "faked" his way out of the Crown Point, Indiana, jail with a gun carved from a bar of soap (although some said it was actually wood).

He was an embarrassment to law enforcement everywhere and FBI Director J. Edgar Hoover declared him "Public Enemy Number One" and loosed the agency dogs to catch him. Heading up the federal effort was Special Agent Melvin Purvis.

In an effort at disguise, Dillinger paid a doctor of dubious distinction to alter his face with plastic surgery. He wanted several moles eliminated, the deep cleft in his chin and bridge of his nose changed. An unsuccessful attempt to eliminate his fingerprints was also made. There are doubts how successful the surgery was.

The story goes that Purvis convinced Anna Sage, a girlfriend of Dillinger, to set him up for the Biograph ambush. She convinced him to take her to see the new Clark Gable movie "Manhattan Melodrama." Perhaps anticipating the need for a spare later, Dillinger also brought along Polly Hamilton, another girlfriend. Sage, a Romanian immigrant, was being threatened with deportation for running a string of bordellos in Gary and East Chicago. If she fingered Dillinger, Purvis would see that the deportation process would be dropped. The cops weren't sure what Dillinger looked like after his surgery, so Sage was important to the plot.

When Dillinger and the women left the theater, Purvis and another agent walked up behind and a little to the left of him. Purvis claimed that he said in a nervous voice, "Stick'em up Johnnie. We have you surrounded." Dillinger ran for the alley a couple of storefronts down from the Biograph and supposedly reached in his jacket for his gun. The alley was a shortcut to North Halstead, next street over. With 20 federal agents around the theater, it was a hopeless try. Although sources differ, there were reportedly no Chicago Police present, reflecting a deep schism between the federal and local law enforcement. It is believed that J. Edgar Hoover wanted full credit for bringing Public Enemy Number One in and there would be no sharing with local police.

Shots rang out and Dillinger dropped, perhaps dead when he hit the alley concrete. A wide pool of his blood soon covered the pavement. Reports vary on the number of shots striking him, but at least three are for certain. There are also conflicting stories that the agents never identified themselves, but simply started firing. With a character as dangerous as Dillinger, shooting first and asking questions later was a wise course. Regardless, two innocent women bystanders were wounded by the agents who couldn't shoot straight.

Some Dillingerologists claim that he tripped and fell in the alley and agents shot him while he was laying helpless on the concrete. Supposedly the autopsy report supports the claim.

Chaos followed the shooting. Women ran forward and dipped handkerchiefs in the blood as if to capture a macabre memento. Sopping up blood from a public execution was an old European tradition. During the French Revolution when thousands of innocent people where sent by the mob to meet Madame Guillotine, crowds surged forward to soak handkerchiefs or other cloths in the gushers of bubbling blood. The French thought the blood had healing powers.

Immediately following the shooting, Sage ran home and grabbed Dillinger's arsenal of guns. With the help of a friend, she carried them off to Lake Michigan and threw them into the water. She desperately wanted to be as far from any incriminating evidence of her relationship with Dillinger as possible. In the end, it did her no good. Purvis reneged on his immigration promise and she was shipped back to Romania. She did, however, receive $5,000 in reward money.

Dillinger was carried off by the FBI to a local hospital where the body was dumped on the front lawn until a doctor came out and officially pronounced him dead. The corpse was then taken to the Cook County Morgue. After the autopsy, the body was propped up on the slab and the room opened for public viewing.

The morgue was complete pandemonium. Thousands of people trooped to get a good look at the infamous Dillinger. The morbidly curious knew no class or age. Rich stockbrokers and bankers and society matrons rubbed shoulders with shopkeepers and street bums. Mothers happily brought along young children to see the dead gangster so they could proudly tell their children that they saw the great man. Showgirls, hookers, pimps, pickpockets, cops and cheap politicians all shuffled past, craning their necks to gaze at the lifeless, bullet-ridden lump inert on the coroner's slab. Some women cried, whether in shock or grief is anyone's guess. The public showing was great theater and everyone loved it.[30]

It is believed that Dillinger's body was robbed, too. A large ring he was wearing somehow disappeared during the movement from alley to hospital to morgue. He was also known to carry thousands of dollars in money on his person at all times. Yet when the official search was conducted, only $7.70 was supposedly found in a pocket. More ominously, no gun was ever entered into evidence at any inquest or official proceeding, which leads to the question, did he ever have one?

Some sources claim that the man killed wasn't Dillinger at all, but instead a lookalike who recently moved to Chicago. When Purvis leaned on Sage to lure Dillinger into the ambush, she double-crossed the agent with a smalltime hood bearing a close resemblance to Dillinger. To back up their claims, they point to discrepancies in the autopsy report. However, the FBI claimed positive fingerprint identification regardless of the botched effort to eliminate them. Some Dillingerologists claim that the real Dillinger moved to Oregon, married a nice local girl and faded away into obscurity. Believe that and I have any number of bridges to sell you cheap.

Regardless of the identification problem, the body was eventually taken home to Indiana where a crowd of thousands attended the funeral and subsequent internment at Crown Hill Cemetery. To make certain that his son's remains were not disturbed, three feet of reinforced concrete was poured on top of the grave. That should keep Dillinger in his coffin. The real fear wasn't for John coming out, but thrill seekers digging up the body for "kicks."

Businesses around the Biograph theater soon capitalized on the notoriety. The bar next door advertised itself as the place Dillinger had his last drink. Theater customers could sit in his seat and see the same last flick he did.

There didn't seem to be any ghost stories about the death until the 1970s when some people started talking about seeing a misty figure running down the old alley, falling to the ground and disappearing. Others talked about cold spots and a feeling of dread and apprehension in the alley. Is Dillinger back and "reliving" his death again and again?[31]

The most notorious killing ground in Chicago is just a couple of blocks south of the Chicago River, near the corner of Randolph and Clark streets. If there is any place in the city cursed with ghosts of the past, it is the site of the infamous St. Valentine's Day massacre.

The victims were clearly the scum of the earth, men who needed to be sent directly to hell without passing go, or collecting $200. But even with the despicable character of the victims considered, the method of killing was brutal.

It all started on the snowy morning of February 14, 1929. The seven men hanging around the small SMC Cartage Company garage at 2144 North Clark Street represented the typical thugs working Chicago's gangland, with a single exception. One was a safe cracker, two brothers were bootleggers and three were "muscle" enforcers for gang policy and decisions. All were thugs of the lowest order, ready to roll a drunk, and drop a "swell" with a sharp rap of a blackjack on the skull. All, too, made their living by stealing from honest men. No tears should be shed for such human garbage. The exception of sorts was the seventh man, an optometrist who liked to hang out on the fringe of gangs. Today he could be called a "groupie." Whatever the reason he had for his dangerous hobby, he paid full measure that day.

The thread that bound all seven together was their association with George "Bugs" Moran, one of Chicago's most infamous mobsters. Bugs used the old garage as his head office. The men were sitting around waiting for a shipment of booze supposedly coming from Detroit. Being a mobster wasn't an easy career. Not only were the authorities out to get you (especially when you didn't make a protection payment), but so were other mobsters. If gangster one can eliminate gangster two, then gangster one can take over gangster two's "territory." The booze shipment was a setup. Big Al Capone wanted to "rub out" Bugs and so laid an ambush. At stake was the vice trade on the north side of Chicago. It was simple. Bugs had it. Al wanted it. Since Bugs tried to "put a hit" on Big Al in Cicero on September 20, 1926, revenge certainly played a part. It went down something like this.

A police car parked outside the garage and three "uniforms" plus two "plain clothes" exited and walked into the garage. Likely the men inside anticipated a simple arrest for bootlegging, a "rap" that Bugs would easily have a "mouthpiece" (lawyer) beat for them. Alternatively, they could have thought it was a simple shakedown. The various gangs always paid the local cops for "protection." Perhaps the local precinct just wanted a bigger cut. The cops expected to find Bugs in the garage, but he was late. It saved his life, for a while.

When the cops entered, they ordered the men to line up against a brick wall. Probably the men expected the cops to throw some "bracelets" on them and drag them "downtown." Instead, the plain clothes cops pulled "choppers" and "sawed off" shotguns out from beneath their topcoats and started blasting away. The uniforms drew .38-caliber revolvers and added to the hail of lead. The concentrated firepower was awesome. Slugs tore through the gangsters and struck the brick wall. Some ricocheted off, others dug deep into the brick. Thick pools of blood pooled on the floor. The acrid smell of cordite filled the garage. Satisfied the men were "rubbed out," the cops left. The killers were never identified until years later. Eventually it was determined that Big Al's personal killer, "Machine Gun" Jack McGurn, planned and participated in the "hit." McGurn later died in a hail of machine gun fire on St. Valentine's Day 1936. Fred Goetz, aka "Shotgun George Ziegler," was another of the killers. An unlikely mobster, Goetz was a graduate engineer who served as a flyer in World War I. After jumping bail for raping a 7-year-old girl, he pursued a life of crime. Eventually, he hooked up with the infamous Barker gang and ran with the notorious killer Alvin Karpis. Karpis became famous after he sold the public a sob story about really being a nice guy, just misunderstood. The truth, of course, was the opposite. Karpis was one of the most vicious killers ever to walk into "The Rock" (Alcatraz prison.) Goetz was eventually gunned down, on orders of Big Al, to prevent the slim chance that his "amnesia" about the massacre might undergo a miraculous cure. In other words, Capone was afraid he would "rat" to the cops.

Incredibly one victim survived just long enough to gasp to police, "Nobody shot me. I ain't no copper." Although it was widely known Big Al was responsible for the slaughter, he was safely in Florida at the time of the shooting and it couldn't be "pinned" to him. No one was ever convicted of the crime.

Bugs took the hint from Big Al and backed off from getting in his way. He eventually died in prison in 1957, a penniless small-time crook.

The old Moran garage was torn down long ago and is now the front yard of a nursing home. But the ghosts of the victims still haunt the area. People strolling by claim to have heard screams and groans coming from the yard, the area where the infamous wall actually stood, as well as unearthly gunshots echoing down the street. Cold spots are also said to be present.

A curse is also associated with the garage. It seems that when it was torn down in 1967, a Canadian businessman decided there was a clear opportunity to cash in on a grisly piece of American history. He purchased the bricks and sold them as vulgar souvenirs. So far so good, except the story soon made the rounds that buying one, or even having one around, brought bad luck. Stories of financial ruin, poor luck and even death added to sales woes. The curse extended to the Canadian entrepreneur who suffered financial ruin.

There is another version of the brick tale. When the garage was torn down, the 417 bricks of the massacre wall were carefully numbered and placed into storage. In 1972, the wall was reassembled in the men's room of a Roaring Twenties-themed restaurant. To make sure everyone had a fair opportunity to see the death wall, three days a week the men's room was open to women patrons. When the restaurant failed, the wall was disassembled and bricks sold for $1,000 each. As in the previous version, bad luck followed the purchasers. Like the massacre itself, the truth seems elusive. What is rock solid, though, is the real belief that the old garage site is beset with the spirits of the machine-gunned "hoods."[32]

Navy Pier is a popular Chicago tourist destination filled with many exciting attractions. The most eye-catching is the 148-foot Ferris wheel, modeled after the first Ferris wheel built for the 1893 World Columbian Exposition. There are also two museums, shops, restaurants and taverns. The Pier is also a starting point for many boat trips, including two four-masted schooners and a variety of sightseeing and dinner cruises.

Originally known as the Municipal Pier Number Two, it is one of two piers called for in Daniel Burnham's 1909 Chicago plan. The other pier was never built.

Construction started May 1914 and in 1916 it was opened to the public. At the time it was the world's largest pier, 292 feet wide and 3,000 feet long.

The pier was designed as a shipping and entertainment area. In its first decade, the Municipal Pier was successfully attracting both visitors and ships. It was also temporarily used as a military facility during World War I.

By the end of the 1920s, the Navy Pier's success started to decline. The introduction of automobiles and the opening of movie theaters created more competition for the Pier. Shipping dropped off in the 1930s due to the Depression and competition by trucks.

In 1927, the pier was renamed Navy Pier in honor of World War I veterans. It would turn out to be a prophetic name change, as the Navy Pier again was used as a Navy training facility during World War II. After the war, it served as the Chicago branch of the University of Illinois. In 1965, the university moved to its new location and the Navy Pier started to decay.

The major step to redevelop the pier was taken in 1989, when the city of Chicago and the state of Illinois teamed up to commit $150 million for reconstruction of the pier as a recreational center. The renovation finished in 1994. The result is a tremendously successful recreational center next to Chicago's downtown area. With many attractions and 50 acres of parks and gardens, it is a magnet for more than 8 million visitors each year.

There are two major buildings on Navy Pier, Headhouse and the Auditorium, both constructed in 1916. Headhouse on the land end of the pier has no interest to us, but the auditorium is a different story. This beautiful building with a magnificent Grand Ballroom measures 138 feet by 150 feet with a half-domed ceiling 100 feet high. Located on the extreme end of the pier, it provided dramatic views of both lake and cityscape.

The auditorium is a perfect location for dances. With large windows overlooking the lake it is a great place to spend a wonderful evening with your favorite girl. During the big band era, it was a popular place to swing with the best of the big sound. It seems some of the dancers enjoyed it so much that they never left! More than one security guard has been startled to hear the faint whisper of music and see a ghostly pair of dancers on the floor still "tripping the light fantastic." There is even a tale of a guard who was so rattled by the experience that he fired several rounds from his revolver at the ghosts, of course to no effect other than jeopardizing his job. It is one thing to see ghosts, but quite another to shoot at them.

The industrial city of Gary, Indiana, at the foot of the lake is home to a female ghost. Much like Chicago's Resurrection Mary, she will stop cars in the Cudahey neighborhood, usually near the intersection of Cline and Fifth avenues and ask for a ride to Calumet Harbor. Before arriving at the harbor, she vanishes. Often called the "woman in white," one local legend claims that she is searching for her children she drowned in the Calumet River. A variation maintains that the children were killed in an automobile crash in the 1930s, thus explaining her appearance on Cline and Fifth instead of just near the water.

Folklorists draw the close analogy to the famed ghost La Llorona, subject of an old Mexican legend. As with most ghostly tales, there are several variations. One claims that a beautiful girl named Maria lived in a small country village. She was so vain, she refused the romantic advances of local men, vowing to only marry someone worthy of her great beauty. One day the son of a rich ranchero rode into the village on a spirited white stallion and she knew he was the one she had to have. Instead of throwing herself at him, she acted very strangely, refusing to speak with him and turning away his gifts. Such behavior made him want her all the more for being so "hard to get." She played her game well and soon she roped the wild young buck into marriage. Life went along fine for the couple and soon Maria bore him two children. But the young man grew bored with the tame life of a husband and father, and perhaps a bit bored with Maria, too. She was far below his station in breeding and sophistication and likely he yearned for someone more his equal. He often left home for months at time and, when he returned, only paid attention to his children, not Maria. There was even talk of annulling the marriage to Maria and marrying someone of his own class. Certainly the beautiful Maria raged at her husband and likely transferred her anger to the children. After all, he valued them more than her.

As the legend goes, Maria and the children were walking along the river when her husband drove by in a carriage with a fashionable high-bred lady seated beside him. He reigned up and spoke with the children, but said nothing to Maria. After a few minutes he snapped the reigns and trotted on, leaving Maria in the dust.

Livid with rage, Maria grabbed the children and tossed them into the river where both drowned. Although she quickly realized the horror of her terrible deed, it was too late to save them. The next morning, villagers found Maria dead on the riverbank.

Funerals were quick and simple in old Mexico and within a day Maria was buried deep in the parched earth. The following night people heard the eerie sound of wailing down by the river. When a brave villager investigated, he claimed that a woman wearing a long white robe was walking up and down the riverbank crying and sobbing. When they buried Maria, she was dressed in the same robe. Thereafter, the ghost of the sobbing woman was often seen walking along the river looking for her lost children. She soon gained the name La Llorona, "the weeping woman." The tale became a Mexican legend and children everywhere were warned to stay at home at night or the ghost of La Llorona would steal them away forever.

How a Mexican ghost came to Indiana is easy to explain. Years ago, when the Indiana steel plants were booming, the Cudahey area was made up mostly of Mexican immigrants. It is logical to assume that the La Llorona legend came with them. It is also possible that the immigrants transposed the La Llorona story on to an existing local ghost tale. Because the stories were so similar, they simply called it La Llorona.

Another version claims that a beautiful Indian princess fell in love with a debonair Mexican nobleman and had two children with him. The nobleman refused to marry the princess regardless of her beauty. When he finally deserted her and married a woman of his own class, she went berserk and stabbed the children to death. She was later found wandering the streets, crying and covered with her children's blood. After due consideration a noose was slipped around her neck and she did the "Texas two-step." Thereafter, her wandering specter was seen moving silently though the streets searching for her murdered children. She is always reported as covered in blood.

The La Llorona legend is common not only to Mexico but also the American southwest and as far west as the Philippines. Some folklorists claim that it dates from the deepest recesses of Aztec mythology. La Llorona's dress varies also. Usually she is seen in either white or black with long black hair. Her fingernails are long and sharp, sometime even described as claws. She either has no face or has a bat or horselike face. Sometimes she is also described as a female vampire.[33]

Be she Mexican, Indian, or American, the ghost of the wailing woman still haunts the streets of Gary.

Lakeside Spirits – Islands

Native Americans rarely visited the Manitou Islands. Hunting wasn't especially good with a limited deer population and it was a hazardous crossing from the mainland. If the Manitou Passage was dangerous for commercial freighters, as evidenced by scores of shipwrecks, just think about the dangers an individual faced in a frail birch-bark canoe.

There is one story of tribal activity on the islands. It seems a Native American band raided another band living on the mainland opposite the islands, killing all but seven who were out of the camp when the attack occurred. Flushed with success, the attackers canoed to South Manitou Island to spend the night and rest before returning home. Doubtless they thought that they were safe. After all, their enemies were dead, right?

When the seven Indians returned to camp and discovered the bloody carnage, they swore vengeance. By the gods the murderers would pay for their dastardly attack. Carefully they followed the retreating band to South Manitou Island, arriving after the raiders landed then warily finding their camp. The seven waited very patiently until the marauders finished their wild celebration and fell into a deep sleep. One by one the group of seven avengers crept silently into the enemy camp and with their razor sharp knives slit the throats of the sleeping killers. The only sound was the soft gurgle of warm blood as it boiled out of the severed arteries. All night long the seven men wreaked their terrible vengeance, dispatching one at a time. With the first streaks of dawn painting the sky, they left. Behind was a scene of utter massacre, much of the ground stained red with the fresh blood of the slain attackers.

142

There were a few survivors. In the dark of the night some who were sleeping were missed and therefore spared retribution. When they awoke to the horror of the sleeping dead, gaping red smiles open across their necks, they could only attribute the deed to evil spirits. Somehow they had offended them and this was the appalling result. Hurriedly they fled the evil island. When word of the terrifying slaughter spread, other Native Americans also avoided the islands of evil spirits.

During the 1830s and 1840s, vast numbers of immigrants flowed west over the Great Lakes. Although some settled in the area, the majority continued on to the new western lands. In many ways the highway to California ran west on the Erie Canal then via boat over the Great Lakes to Chicago. Period newspapers wrote of steamers running from Buffalo to western lakes ports often crowded with 1,000 or more passengers. In 1834 alone, approximately 80,000 men, women and children passed through Buffalo for points west. By 1836, the number doubled. During the same period, 1,000 immigrants a day were arriving in Detroit. Many continued on by ship, others by slow and laborious wagon train. At one point wagons were rolling out of the city on an average of one every five minutes. Small frontier towns boomed with phenomenal growth. Milwaukee, Chicago and Detroit quickly became cities in every sense of the word. On Lake Michigan, places like the Manitou Islands, especially South Manitou Island, became important stopping points for steamers, not only as a handy place to shelter from a storm, but also to replenish the cords of hardwood that fed their voracious boiler fires. The old steamers wheezing along with their inefficient low-pressure engines needed to refuel approximately every day and a half,

South Manitou Island, about 3.5 by 3 miles in size, is 6.8 miles north of Sleeping Bear Point. Hilly with high bluffs on the west side, it is lower and wooded on the east. North Manitou Island, also wooded and hilly, is 3.9 miles to the northeast. A deepwater channel runs between the two. South Manitou has an excellent harbor on the southeast side, providing first-rate protection and good holding ground for anchored ships.

An island legend persists that immigrant ships infected with cholera occasionally stopped at South Manitou, a conveniently remote location before reaching Chicago, and used the opportunity to bury their dead in hasty mass graves in the timber line along the sandy shore. The story is also told that some especially callous captains also included those about to die with the dead, literally burying them alive. "Why wait for the inevitable? Surely it was better to just get rid of them now." Supposedly on the anniversary of their burial, the restless spirits of the tormented victims rise up from their sandy graves and walk again. Whether it is in protest over their poor treatment or in a hopeless attempt to complete their voyage can only be speculated.

There is also the tale of a young and handsome captain who would never go ashore. It was said he could see misty specters moving about the beach and was afraid of their vengeance. A beautiful dark-haired woman in a black dress especially haunted him. He supposedly had a shipboard romance with her and as she died in his arms, she swore never to leave him. He callously had her buried in the dunes with the other dead. On later trips when he looked ashore he saw her standing at the edge of the harbor staring forlornly at him, then glide slowly into the watery depths as if trying to walk to his ship. He was a haunted man.

There is also the story of a sailing ship sinking in a storm near the entrance to the bay. About 15 Native Americans, traveling to logging camps in Michigan's Upper Peninsula, were sheltering in her hold when she suddenly plunged for the bottom. None of the men ever got out of their death trap. They could have been cowering in fear from the cold blasts of the hell-spawned wind, or perhaps they were locked below by a captain who didn't want landlubbers running amok on his deck when he needed working space for his sailors. Reportedly, after due consideration by the islanders, it was decided to leave them in their impromptu tomb. What was the value in an expensive salvage operation just to recover the bodies of some dead lumberjacks? They too are now part of the island's spirit world.[1] Although modern scuba divers have looked for the wreck, she remains elusive.

There are other ghosts on South Manitou besides massacred Indians, cholera fatalities and shipwreck victims. One of the old farms on the island is known as the Hutzler place, established in 1860. All the windows of the house are boarded up, which locals claim is to stop the ghost sightings. "If the ghosts are looking out the windows, if we board them up the ghosts will not be seen, therefore there are no ghosts." It seems that too many island tourists have reported seeing the image of someone peering out a window. Tired of dealing with the stories, it was easiest just to "board'er up."

Another story involves the ghost of 16-year-old Ronald Riker. The son of an island farmer, he drowned in August 1967 while swimming near the dead hulk of the *Francisco Morazon*. This steel steamer wrecked on the southwest end of the island during a roaring gale on November 14, 1960. Her rusting remains still protrude from the water and are a popular sightseeing attraction for island visitors. The tale goes that on dark and dreary nights, the boy's ghost has been occasionally seen lurking in the shadows on the beach near the wreck. At other times his vaporous image is seen walking from beach to home. Some folks even claimed to have heard a swimmer crying for help near the wreck. Of course, the mysterious swimmer could never be found. For a while the ghost was reported to the park rangers so often, they stopped even logging the incidents. Why bother? Ghosts aren't part of any federal management plan.

Some people believe ghosts are the result of change. A way of life is interrupted which somehow changes the balance between dimensions, the barrier weakens and fractures with the resulting spirits becoming visible. Taking the islands from a place of working human habitation to a largely deserted National Lakeshore is an argument for this vein of reasoning.

While the year-round population of South Manitou Island was never larger than 98, it was a complete community, including a small schoolhouse once serving 30 youngsters. Built in 1899, the old school presently is closed but there are hopes of restoring it. Hikers claim to see the shadowy faces of children peering out from behind shuttered windows. Another group camping nearby heard the distinctive voices of children playing, but on investigation discovered only an empty yard and a single old rubber ball lying in the grass. How the ghosts will respond to the change is anyone's guess.[2]

Other visitors talk of hearing the horrible shouts of people drowning on long-ago island shipwrecks. But when they investigate, no one is there, just an empty lake befit of sight or sound, other than the constant lapping of the waves.[3]

The first lighthouse at South Manitou was a 35-foot tower erected in 1839. The present brick keeper's house was added in 1858. The redoubtable Dr. Alonzo Slyfield, the island's only physician, served as keeper for a dozen years, 1848-1859. Together with the North Manitou Shoal Light, the South Manitou Light helped guide ships through the infamous Manitou Passage, one of the most hazardous stretches of water on the Great Lakes. The route is a shortcut between Gray's Reef Passage to the north and the south end of Lake Michigan. In places the deepwater channel is less than 2 miles wide. The original tower was replaced in 1871 with the present 104-foot brick tower with a Third Order Fresnel lens. On a clear day the view from the lamp room at the top is remarkable. Eight miles across the passage is Sleeping Bear and Pyramid points. To the north is Cat Head Point at the top of the Leelanau Peninsula and to the south, Point Betsie. The terrible passage runs the gauntlet between the islands and mainland. In the 1870s, 100 ships a day often ran through the passage. In 1958, the Coast Guard abandoned the light station and it presently is part of the Sleeping Bear Dunes National Lakeshore.

In 1988, the passage was designated as the Manitou Passage State Bottomland Preserve. More than 50 known shipwrecks, dating from 1835 to 1960, litter its bottom, reefs and shoals. And there are those still not discovered, ones that seemingly sailed off, as the old time sailors said, "into a crack in the lake." That so many ships met disaster as did is not surprising. There is little room for navigational error. Even today it is a popular shortcut for the big freighters and every once in a while one will "find bottom."

Strange sounds have been reported in the old South Manitou light tower. In one incident, two National Park Service maintenance workers were in the keeper's residence when they heard strange noises and voices in the tower. Although they couldn't make out what was being said, they were certain that it was coming from the lamp room at the top of the tower. Thinking that someone unauthorized had gained entry, they climbed the winding iron stairs and checked but found no one, just an empty tower. The only sound was the empty echo of their footsteps. The exterior tower door at the base of the tower was also still securely padlocked. It was impossible for anyone to enter through that door. Nor could anyone have come past the two men in the house without being noticed. No rational explanation for their unearthly experience was ever made.

Other world spirits also reportedly occupy the old U.S. Life-Saving Service building. The life-saving station on South Manitou became operational in 1902, in contrast to the one on North Manitou dating from 1877. Together they provided vital assistance to vessels wrecked in trying to run the Manitou Passage. The facility consisted of a boathouse to keep the various boats and other equipment and a station house as a combination office, mess and quarters for keeper and crew. As time passed, additional out buildings were added. In 1915, the U.S. Life-Saving Service and

U.S. Revenue-Marine were combined to form the new U.S. Coast Guard. The mission of the South Manitou station continued largely unchanged until the station was finally abandoned in 1958. North Manitou station was abandoned 20 years before. Both are presently used as seasonal quarters for National Park Service personnel.

When ghostly activity first started in the old Life-Saving Station isn't clear, but National Park Service employees have heard loud footsteps pacing on the second floor. The footfalls were so distinct to one man that he was absolutely certain another park employee was upstairs. When he looked, there was no one there, at least no one he could see. Doors also opened and closed, room lights turned on and off and knocking was plainly heard at the front door. When he told his supervisor what happened the boss laughed and replied that others had heard the strange sounds too, but there was no real explanation for it, other than ...[4]

A female ranger showering in the upstairs bathroom of the North Manitou Life-Saving Station was startled to hear male voices coming from the old crew room just on the other side of the door. Knowing that she was alone in the house, the ranger listened closely and could clearly hear the men discussing the upcoming day's drill activities. Whether the voices seemed to resonate from the old Life-Saving Service days or newer Coast Guard era wasn't known. When she pulled the door open, the crew room was empty. On other occasions the sounds of someone knocking at an exterior door were heard. When the door was opened, no one was there.[5]

Neither of the Manitou Islands have any year-round residents. Park personnel only live on the islands from May through October. The rest of the year, they are desolate, without human habitation. At one time, however, before the park took over the islands, there were a number of small farms, some lumbering and fishing. They were places where people lived, worked and died. Today they are mere open-air museums. Peak population now might reach as high as 320 souls on a warm summer day when day-trippers make their way over from the mainland. Most undoubtedly have little idea of the other side of the peaceful islands, the spiritual one. On the Manitou Islands, the ghosts still walk.

In the early 1920s, the son of the South Fox Island lightkeeper remembered seeing the specter of a strange "woman in black" eerily floating across the island's shallow flats. The phenomenon was observed numerous times, not only by the one boy but also by his brother. The woman always dressed in black clothes from a bygone

era with a short, shoulder-length black cape hanging from her shoulders. The ghost seemed to come right at them, only to disappear just before reaching the pair. She wasn't threatening, just spooky. The boys never knew a reason for the haunting, but that never stopped the woman in black from her nightly sojourns.[6]

From additional research it appears that she could be the spirit of one of a number of shipwreck victims washed ashore on the desolate island. Most received proper Christian burial, either on the island or returned to grieving families for internment, but not all. Some washed ashore and were never discovered, left to quietly decay into the lonely island helped along by winged scavengers. Perhaps she is the spirit of a forgotten victim begging for discovery and burial.

Considering all the supernatural activity on Lake Michigan, fair questions would be, "What is the most haunted area? Where are the most ghosts?"

There is no clear answer. Certainly the Door Peninsula is in the running as are the Manitou Islands and Manitou Passage. But I feel the locale with the greatest potential for haunting activity is likely to be Beaver Island. No other area has the history of conflict, trauma and the interplay of people as the Beaver Island area. I believe the island is filled with spirits and wandering specters, but many of the stories go unreported. They certainly exist but have not been publicized.

Beaver Island is roughly 20 miles off Charlevoix, Michigan. A number of smaller islands surround it. Three of them, High, Garden and Hog, at one time had minor settlements. Beaver Island is roughly 53 square miles and by far the largest of the group.

While much of island history is established, a great deal is still a mystery. For instance, it is known, based on Ottawa oral tradition, that Native Americans visited Beaver Island roughly 2,200 years ago. Archaeologists have discovered arrowheads, spearheads and small pieces of Woodland period pottery, all clear proof of an earlier aboriginal occupation.

The island also has a Stonehenge-like ruins. Consisting of 39 stones ranging from 2 to 10 feet in length, the circle has a diameter of 397 feet. Archaeologists think that the circle of boulders might be a primitive calendar allowing Indians to track the movement of the sun and determine growing seasons. The center boulder has a hole that may have held a wooden post, possibly serving as a sundial. The largest boulder in the circle is the eastern rock, which may line up with the rising sun at the seasonal equinoxes. If this theory is correct, it is the only one of its kind found in the Great Lakes region. Many native people also believe that the circle has spiritual significance.

Small bands of Ottawa were on the island when Europeans arrived in the middle 1700s. Bishop Frederic Baraga, the famous Jesuit snowshoe priest, converted a small number of them to Christianity, but the ones living out on Whisky Point refused to follow the new God, preferring to remain with the old ones. Follow-on missionaries finished the job, however, including the roughly 200 inhabitants living on Garden Island, just to the north. Garden is also the site of more than 3,000 Indian graves, mute testimony to long habitation as well as the sacred nature of the island.

European traders and trappers arrived in the early 1800s eager to barter with the natives for fur. The island also became a popular stop for the old wood-burning, smoke-belching steamers making runs from Buffalo to Chicago and other points. The steamers needed to refuel with cordwood every day-and-a-half or so and Paradise Bay was good place to load up.

Beaver Island's rich forests provided a boundless supply of wood, far exceeding the depleted forests of Mackinac Island just east of the Straits of Mackinac in Lake Huron. Soon Beaver Island became the economic center of the upper Great Lakes, to the loss of the old interests on Mackinac Island. It was a change that the business interests from Mackinaw would not forget.

It is at this point that the island's history becomes forever intertwined with one Joseph Smith, ex-felon, ex-fortune teller and full-time local joker, from the sticks of western New York. Smith was a fascinating character, truly an American in the mould of P.T. Barnum. And like Barnum, he knew that a "sucker is born every minute."

In 1820, at the age of 14, he claimed that both God and Jesus visited him, telling him that all the accepted churches were wrong and he should steer clear of them. Three years later Smith claimed that the angel Moroni came calling and told him of a secret cache of mysterious gold plates that related the story of the ancient inhabitants of North America.[7] Because the plates' inscriptions were in an unknown language, claimed later to be "Reformed Egyptian," two mystical stones, Urim and Thummin, were conveniently buried with the plates to aid in the translation.[8] Four years later the location of the extraordinary plates and magic rocks were mystically revealed to Smith. Shovel in hand, Smith went out to the woods and dug up his treasure. Of course, Smith was alone when he unearthed the plates, other than his wife, Emma, who he instructed to turn her back so she couldn't see him work. Cult leaders are always very trustworthy, so don't question them on such actions. Using the magic stones, Smith labored for three long years before he was finally able to finish translating the script. The result was the Book of Mormon.

Once his new religion took off, Smith took the title, "Prophet, Seer and Revelator" and claimed that he alone spoke with God. If you want to know what God wants, just ask old Joe!

Smith found a soul mate in 1844 when James Jesse Strang, an ex-lawyer, ex-postmaster, ex-Baptist preacher and generally lost soul, decided to join the Mormons. Within a month, Joe made James an Elder of the church and turned him loose on an unsuspecting world. When Smith was killed in a shootout with local authorities in 1844, Jesse produced a letter he claimed was from Smith, appointing Strang the new leader of the church should anything happen to him. Whether the letter was real or a forgery is unknown, but Brigham Young's reaction was immediate. He had slaved in Smith's shadow for years and, with Smith out of the way, no "Jesse"-come-lately was going to steal the Mormon gold mine from him! After a vicious and raucous leadership fight, Young emerged victorious and Strang led a small group of followers to several settlements before reaching Beaver Island. Smith's own brother, William, took off with Strang, apparently unable to stomach Young's "leadership." Young, of course, ended up virtually taking over the state of Utah. Like old Joe Smith, Strang, too, found mysterious plates in the ground that only he could decipher. The only difference was that Jesse was much poorer than Joe and could only afford to have six brass plates as opposed to Joe's gold ones. Both men, of course, were the only people who could "decipher" the mysterious hieroglyphics!

Strang and his small flock arrived at the island in 1848 after he had a vision telling him to take his followers there. Incidentally, the same vision told him that he didn't need to bother about land deeds or other legal mumbo jumbo. The island was his by divine right. Within several years the Mormon count increased to approximately 2,000, enough voters to have him elected to the Michigan Legislature.

The Mormons exerted tremendous pressure, psychological, financial and physical, to force the non-Mormons off the island. The non-Mormons, or Gentiles in Strang's parlance, soon fled. Strang not only forced tithes from them, but also made use of flogging to encourage proper action and thinking. There were even rumors of an iron cage that he locked malcontents into, both Mormon and Gentile. Just to make certain of his place in history, Strang named the small settlement St. James and the adjacent water Paradise Bay.

James Strang and Brigham Young were cut of the same cloth. Both had massive egos and incredible confidence. Doubtless, as each was in direct contact with God, this was quite reasonable. While Young's "stage" was larger and Strang's limited mostly to Beaver Island, both men knew what they wanted – absolute power over their followers.

Strang and his industrious Mormons carved a community out of the Beaver Island wilderness, building homes, docks, farms and roads. They actively fished the nearby waters harvesting rich hauls of lake trout and whitefish.

The island was always a popular place for the old steamers to stop for cordwood. During the Strang era, selling cordwood to them was an important source of sparse hard currency. Strang was in large measure an active supporter of lighthouses at St. James and Beaver Head. He wanted to make it as easy as possible to increase commercial activity at the island.

The light at Beaver Head at the south end of the island became operational in 1851, but due to poor construction was rebuilt in 1858. The old Lewis reflectors were replaced by a Fourth Order

Fresnel lens providing a nominal range of 16 miles. The lighthouse was discontinued in 1962 and taken over by the Charlevoix Public Schools for use as an educational opportunity for disadvantaged youth. While there are no spectacular tales of ghostly figures looking down from the lantern room, there are murmurings about footsteps on the iron spiral staircase winding up to the tower. Footsteps have also been heard in the second floor. A few years ago a visitor noticed a downstairs doorknob turning like someone was trying to enter the room. When she pulled the door open, no one was there. Like many ghost stories the world over, no one is ever seen. It's all unexplained noise and movement. Is it just the normal creaks and groans of an old house or something else? Lighthouses are perhaps, next to castles, the most haunted structures on earth. Is an old keeper still on watch?

By contrast, the light at Whisky Point, the long arm extending north of Paradise Bay, seems to be "dead" of all spirits. The original light was built in 1856 and replaced with a new structure in 1870. From 1872-1884 it was the domain of Elizabeth Whitney Williams, one of the legendary female lightkeepers of the Great Lakes. Elizabeth's first husband, Clement Van Riper, was killed while trying to rescue the crew of a storm-wrecked schooner, and she was appointed in his place. The lighthouse was automated in 1927 and keepers house and other structures, other than the tower, torn down by the Coast Guard in the 1940s. With the buildings gone, there isn't any place for a respectable ghost to haunt.

There were also dark accusations of "mooncussing," luring ships into offshore reefs by showing false lights. Once the ship was wrecked, Mormon pirates killed the passengers and crew, stole the cargo and destroyed the vessel so evidence was forever gone. Mormon pirates were also said to have raided mainland communities, stealing supplies and causing general havoc. Perhaps such tales are nothing more than lies spread by non-Mormons. On the other hand, perhaps they are true. There are arguments on both sides.

Fed by an increasing ego, on June 8, 1850, Strang had himself crowned "King of the Kingdom of God on Earth." Even Young was never a crowned king, so Strang was one up on his old nemesis. In terms of wives, though, Strang couldn't keep up with old Brigham, who collected an estimated 55 spouses bearing him 57 children. Strang only managed five wives, but since two were sisters, extra points should be awarded. Then again, wife one left as soon as wife two appeared on the scene. (Doubtless she said something like, "I married you when you were a good God-fearing Baptist, not some shyster Mormon wife-collector. I'm taking the kids and going home to mother!")

As Strang's grip on his followers tightened several decided it was time for rebellion from his tyranny. On June 16, 1856, while the King was walking down the street, two men leaped from behind a pile of wood and emptied their revolvers at him. Several bullets found their mark and the king died a week later. There are many tales as to why the king was "done in." One involves an edict he issued that island women all had to wear bloomers. Two of his follower's wives took exception to his royal interference in the fashion world and talked their husbands into shooting him. The men were never punished.

When the news reached Mackinac Island that the evil king was dead, the folks Strang threw off the island returned with a vengeance. One source described them as a mob. Within a couple of days, all of the Mormons were forced onto steamers and shipped off to Chicago or Detroit, taking with them only what they could carry on their backs.

After a short period Irish fishermen moved to the island and found rich hauls of lake trout in the offshore waters. More important, they found that the place reminded them of the "Old Sod" and wrote home, giving appealing descriptions of the new "Emerald Isle." Soon the island was overrun with Gallaghers, O'Donnells, Boyles and other sons and daughters of the shamrock.

The influence of the Irish is everywhere, from the names of businesses to the ferryboats that carry passengers and freight. Make no mistake, Beaver Island is a hunk of Ireland far removed. If archaeologists dig deep enough, they will surely find evidence of St. Brendan having visited, not to mention a pot or two of leprechaun gold.

The fishing economy thrived until the late 1880s when over-fishing and the introduction of the steam tug allowed mainland fishermen to reach the rich Beaver grounds. There were too many fishermen for too few fish. The arrival of the sea lamprey in the 1940s was the coupe de grace.

Farming was important, but only at relatively low levels. Fields cultivated by the Mormons were used until the 1950s. However the island's poor soil made serious cultivation tenuous at best.

In 1901, the Beaver Island Lumber Company started a "big time" operation on the island, even building a small railroad through 10 miles of the interior to haul the logs to their mill, but the island was too small to support sustained logging and the lumbering business ended in 1916. The tracks were pulled up and worthwhile machinery loaded onto boats and taken away. Some small operators tried to hang on, but their hold was tenuous.

Electricity finally came to the island in 1939 with construction of a local plant. Prior to then only the Coast Guard station on Whisky Point had a generator. Oil lamps ruled the rest of the Island. By the 1940s, population dropped off to 200 or so people. Opportunity wasn't on Beaver. It lay in the outside world, especially for the young, and many left to find it. Taking jobs on the lake freighters or joining the Coast Guard were common.

Beaver Island was "saved" by this strange new thing called "leisure time." Starting in the 1970s, people "discovered" Beaver Island. Folks wanting to enjoy solitude and quiet and get away from the hordes of mainland vacationers headed for northern Michigan resorts. Today, the major activity on the island is construction of summer homes. The danger, of course, is for every new arrival. The island takes a step closer to being what folks wanted to get away from. As the old cartoon "Pogo" said, "We have met the enemy and he is us!"

Considering the long and colorful history of the Beaver Island group, it is only fair that it is a "spirited" place. While doubtless many tales are still hidden away in the memory of old-timers, there are those in the public venue. There are stories of ghostly activity at a number of island locations.

The Old Mormon Print Shop is the only building left from the King Strang era. Built in 1850, the white clapboard structure housed the island newspaper as well as published religious rants and raves from the pen of the illustrious king. When Strang was finally assassinated in 1856, the deadly deed occurred at the small beach just in front of the print shop. Today, a sign marks the location. The Print Shop is now the Beaver Island Historical Society Museum and houses many unique artifacts sharing the island's rich heritage.

Given the spot's close relationship with King Strang, one might suspect a specter or two wandering about. Apparently there are. Late night strollers claim to have seen the misty image of a bearded man sitting on one of the rocking chairs in the shadows of the Print Shop front porch. When approached, he just fades away. The King had a full beard. Considering that his Beaver Island colony was the only success in life he ever had, is it reasonable to think that his spirit returns for a peaceful visit?

154

Another visitor alleged that she saw two figures moving about in the bushes by the water, just in the area that the King's assassins would have hid waiting for him to approach. Over several years of visiting the island, she claimed to have seen them at least twice. It was always in mid-afternoon, and when she walked over to investigate, no one was there. Was she seeing something that wasn't there?

While there are no allegations of haunting within the Old Print Shop, the place gives some visitors the feeling of always being watched. Whether there alone or with others, someone is always keeping an eye on you. The feeling on the second floor is especially strong. Another visitor claimed, "the whole place gave me the creeps."

The island was also home to a strange and mysterious man called Feodar Protar. It is thought that he immigrated to America from Estonia in 1874, arriving on the island in 1893 after working on stage and editing various newspapers. Protar is a difficult man to explain. He doesn't fit into a neat hole. Perhaps it is best to say that he pursued a spiritual quest in a self-sufficient environment, growing his own food as much as possible. He went to a considerable length to disguise his identity. Some folks thought he was being pursued by the Russian government, thus was trying to hide on Beaver Island. And considering all, Beaver Island is a damn good place to hide! Unlike the typical weird recluse, Protar was anxious to help islanders seeking his aid. While not a physician, his remedies and unusual healing power usually worked the trick for the ill. He also refused all pay for such service.

Protar was beloved by the people and on his death in 1925 they built a field stone enclosure and tomb to the west of his home. Inscribed on a nearby bronze plaque is "To our Heaven-Sent Friend from the people of Beaver Island."

The tomb was not something Protar wanted. He wanted his body buried "at sea" between Beaver and High islands. If he died in the summer, just row him out and dump the remains overboard in a "strong bag" with a heavy stone weight to keep him down. If he died during the winter, throw his body on a sleigh and run out to a good place to cut a hole and slip it into the depths. No coffin, special dress or flowers were wanted. However, since Michigan State Law prohibited such burial, the islanders built the fancy tomb. This strikes me as strange. First, because having held Protar in such deep respect, it seems inconsistent that the people would ignore his burial wishes. Second, although a burial "at sea" was against the law, since when did old time Beaver Islanders give 2 cents about a "mainland" law?

An air of mystery still enshrouds his house and tomb. Is Protar's spirit still watching over the island? Or is he making his presence known as a way of objecting to the extravagant burial.

Based on the overwhelming Irish heritage, the island must be awash in the supernatural. Perhaps no land on earth has as many tales of fairies, goblins, leprechauns, mermaids, dragons, superstition and ghosts as Ireland. And we can't forget the banshees!

Irish Banshees (literally "women of the other world") are generally thought to call out in lamentation in their ghostly voices at the imminent death of an Irish person. When a member of the Emerald Isle is dying, banshees prowl the darkness around their house, their white figures sharply contrasting against the night's blackness. Their silver-gray hair streams to the ground and gray-white cloak of a cobweb texture seductively clings to their tall, thin bodies. Their faces are deathly pale and eyes run red with centuries of crying. Banshees also attend the funerals of the beloved dead, but always unseen, although sometimes they can be heard wailing, their voices blending in with the mournful cries of others.

It has long been my belief that the true center of the island's cultural and social activities is the Shamrock Bar, more properly the "Shamrock Restaurant and Pub", although that name has too much of a high flaunting air to it. The Shamrock, established in 1935 and just across from the ferry dock, is one of those unique corners of America not yet captured by the corporate world. On any given night you can find any combination of staff and students from the Central Michigan University biological research station, townsfolk, visiting sailors and boaters, summer people and lost tourists all imbibing friendly spirits. The amount of "spirits" consumed doubtless can account for a number of "spirited" tales, but certainly not all. No bar like the immortal Shamrock can survive so long without having a ghost or two somewhere. Who says that the quiet guy in flannels drinking a pint of beer at the end of the bar isn't the shade of old Clyde O'Boyle, or Paddy Sullivan, Mick O'Rourke or even old Protar himself enjoying a cold brew? By all accounts, Strang was far too uptight to savor a good ale, so his ghost wouldn't be caught dead in the Shamrock.

One of the island spook tales involves the old Beaver Island Lumber Company and its railroad. Since the priority was getting the timber to the mill, the rail tracks were quickly laid but not well ballasted. When the timber trains rumbled along the tracks, they shook with the stress and sometimes the cars jumped the rails. Often the trains ran too fast and on April 17, 1908, the result was deadly. The engine derailed near the end of Kuebler Road, killing engineer David Chase. A small white wood cross marks the spot, which is just across the field from Protar's tomb. Although many folks think the cross marks his grave, in fact the body was shipped back to Grand Rapids for internment. Nevertheless, on dark and stormy nights some claim to have again heard the sound of the train chugging along the tracks, the screech of steel as the wheels jump the tracks, and the crash of trees as she comes to rest in the woods.[9]

With all the conflict of cultures – Indian, French, Jesuit, Mormon and Irish – Beaver Island has to be a boiling pot of spirits. So when you visit the island, be aware of them!

Not all ghost stories are widely known. Many like the ghost of Marion Island are recognized only in their local area.

Marion Island is in the West Arm of Grand Traverse Bay near Bowers Harbor on the Old Mission Peninsula, north of Traverse City, Michigan. It's just a little place, but with an intriguing history. The island was locally called Hog Island for many years, certainly well before the Traverse City area became the trendy upscale place it is today. In 1872, it was purchased by Frederick and Ann Eager Hall of Ionia, Michigan, and given to their daughter, Marion, as a gift. Since the Halls owned it and didn't want to give their child anything named after a pig, they had it legally renamed "Marion" Isle.

Marion was the wife of an Army officer. When her husband died in 1898 returning from Cuba and combat in the Spanish-American War, she moved to California. Although she had fond feeling for the island, especially since it was a gift from her parents, she wasn't in a position to manage it. Just to the northeast of the isle is tiny Bassett Island. When lake water is low, a small sand beach connected it with the big island. By 1901, the Chicago Yacht Club owned Bassett and it made overtures to Marion about buying her island. The story of why the deal didn't go through is murky, but it didn't happen. If it had, the club planned to build a resort complex including docks, hotel cabins, and more between the two islands. Regardless of the failure, both places were popular for local camping and day trips.

In 1906, a large 50-by-100-foot, two-story pavilion was built on Bassett Island. The first level included a restaurant and kitchen and the second a dance floor. While many people came, in the end it wasn't profitable and failed.

The island was purchased by Henry Ford in 1917 and became a playground for Henry and his cronies, including Thomas Edison and Harvey Firestone. Common folk need not apply. For a time there were rumors of great plans for the island. With Henry and his buds summering there, surely hordes of other rich folk would follow and all the locals would get rich, too. It didn't happen. Ford certainly stopped by a few times traveling north on his 200-foot yacht *Sialia*. When he "roughed it" on the island, his wife and her friends roughed it in the Park Place Hotel. Ford's ownership resulted in locals calling it "Ford Island."

The island was sold again in 1944 to logging interests and some cutting was done. In the 1970s, the local chamber of commerce formed a non-profit corporation to buy the island and maintain it as a nature preserve. As a major part of the funding came from a gift from Glenn and Annette Power, the name was officially changed to "Power Island" in their honor. To this writer's mind, Marion Isle is a far better name, marking parental love for a daughter in a most unique way. But then, again, old Bill Shakespeare muttered something about "What's in a name? That which we call a rose by any other word would smell as sweet." (From "Romeo and Juliet" (II, ii, 1-2)).

Both islands have their legends. Locals often called Bassett Island the "Isle of the Dead" because of a legend claiming that an Indian woman was decapitated there for "misbehaving." Some folks claim that her headless ghost still walks the shore on dark and storm-lashed nights, looking, of course, for her missing noggin. The story certainly evokes more questions than provides answers, but often the background to such tales is long lost in the mist of memory.

At one time, Indians claimed that Marion Island was home to the ghost of an evil blacksmith. It seems that the tribe used to live on the west side of the island but then fled to the east when the ghost started haunting their camp. They told tales of a spirit wearing bib overalls and rolled-up shirt sleeves walking along the lakeshore and stopping ever so often to fill a pail with water. He left no footprints, sure evidence of his spectral nature. The loud thundering of this powerful hammer could often be heard echoing over the island at night.

There is also a lodge on Marion Island with its own spectral presence. Supposedly the ghost of the owner's wife is still occupying it. The tale goes that the owner became infatuated with one of his beautiful young chambermaids. The affair spun out of control and his wife closed herself off in the attic in shame. It is entirely possible that her husband just locked her up there, too. "How can I cavort with a chambermaid if my wife is always underfoot?" What happened next is unknown. Whether he murdered his wife to free him to marry the maid or whether she just conveniently "up and died" is also a mystery. Perhaps he and his vivacious new fluff doll just took off for parts unknown, he to enjoy her special charms and she to take pleasure in his wealth.

Eventually the lodge came up for sale. As the story goes a potential buyer and his son went out for a look but were scared away by a galaxy of ghostly occurrences. Strange sounds, unexplained slamming of doors and other disturbing events drove them from the building. Ever since, the lodge has had the reputation of being haunted by the old owner's distraught wife.

Just to add a dash of greed, there are also rumors of a treasure buried on the northwest corner of Marion Island. Legend claims that it was placed there by nefarious James Jesse Strang, the Mormon king of Beaver Island.[10]

The waters of Green Bay were often filled with small fishing boats and the loss of one on November 12, 1874, was not especially noteworthy. It was just another small Great Lakes tragedy that would soon be forgotten except for what happened next. The Sturgeon Bay *Expositor* of February 4, 1876, recorded the unusual event.

A Washington Island mystery: "Lights floating over the waters of the harbor near where it is supposed two men were drowned and the circumstances connected therewith, as related to us by Mr. E.W. Steward of Washington Island. It will be remembered that in the fall of 1874 two men, Halley and Root, went out in their fisherman's boat and never returned. The oars, net boxes, etc. coming ashore made it evident they were drowned during a terrible snow storm that arose soon after they went out. This occurred on Thursday, November 12. Some weeks previous to this, on Sunday evening, Halley had an altercation with a neighbor, who struck him with a stone on the head, injuring him severely that he was partially insane at the time he went out in the boat. It is supposed by the people on the island, that had it not been for Halley's partial insanity, the unfortunate men would have weathered the storm and returned safely to shore. Soon after this disaster, a mysterious light was seen moving along the ice on Thursday evening, followed again on Sunday evening. These lights appeared during the whole winter regularly on Thursday and Sunday and occasionally during the summer and have been seen every Thursday and Sunday during the present winter. The light usually has the appearance of being at the mouth of the harbor, about a mile to a mile and a half away. It usually has the appearance of a lantern moving along, about as a man would carry it, sometimes moving along four or five miles, but usually passing back and forth over a space of about a mile near the bluff at the mouth of the harbor. Sometimes it will flare up and look as large as a basket and again it will rush along at railroad speed for a mile or two. The light is usually pure white with never a halo. William Betts pursued the light one night last winter. He left his house for that purpose, but was unable to get any nearer than apparently one-half to one-fourth mile from it. When he went faster the light moved faster and when he slackened his pace the light would follow suit. Finally it turned and moved off toward St. Martins Island and led him onto such poor ice that he could not follow it further. Now the mystery about this is, its appearance on Thursday and Sunday nights, the one day of the week on which Halley was hurt and the other on which he and his companion were drowned, and its being seen in winter mainly when the atmospheric lights were not produced by natural causes. Nearly every person on the island has seen it several times and many have seen it dozens of times and there is no doubt of its regular appearance as stated above."[11]

No other explanation for the mysterious lights was ever offered. Neither is there a report about sightings today, but given the vast amount of light pollution prevalent today, perhaps they are simply overwhelmed by the bright loom. The question remains however. Do the lights represent the souls of the two lost fishermen trying to find their way home?

CHAPTER 8

Monsters — Sea, Air & Land

All the Great Lakes have stories of monsters of various descriptions. Some are long snakelike creatures undulating through the water. Others present themselves as horse-headed monsters with burning eyes. Strange birds dive from the sky and weird lizardlike beasts scuttle off into the dark. Lake Michigan and its shores is no exception, perhaps even having more than any other lake.

When the early Jesuit missionaries arrived in the Great Lakes area they reported Indian tales of a host of different fantastic sea monsters. One was known as Mishegenabeg, or "great snake." In the adult form it was claimed to have antlers like a deer and large, hypnotic eyes. Supposedly it could change form, including taking that of a human. While many reports place it in the Apostle Islands and Pictured Rocks areas of Lake Superior, others trace it to northern Lake Michigan.

It was said that only the most capable Indian wizards would summon the great serpent and thus obtain its supernatural power for their own use. It was a very dangerous fiend and difficult to control. A single error meant a death too horrible to contemplate for the manipulating medicine man. Mishegenabeg was not all-powerful, however. It was claimed that the great thunderbird was its natural enemy and sought every chance to attack it. Should there be such a battle, mortals needed to stay clear of the bloody combat.

One of the stranger Indian monster tales involves the notorious Piasa bird. It is one of those marvelous tales mixing both fact and fable into a devil's brew of confusion bubbling with equal parts of reality and fiction.

In 1673, Jesuit priest Jacques Marquette and his companion Louis Joliet were shocked to find the colorful but bizarre rendering of the Piasa bird monster on a bluff overlooking the Mississippi River near today's Alton, Illinois. Marquette was exploring the river when he stumbled across the ancient pictograph high on a rock bluff. It was claimed that the image was terrible, "upon which the boldest Indians dare not long rest their eyes." The drawing was so high on the bluff that the local Indians said the gods must have made it, since no man could climb to such heights. In many ways the bird is similar to the phoenix of the southwest and creatures attributed to other areas of the world. Said to have a wingspan of more than 50 feet, it was large enough to carry off a human. Before leaving on his trip, Marquette was warned by the Menominee he would see the horrible Piasa, so its fame certainly extended to the Lake Michigan area.

Other travelers beside Marquette claim to have seen the rendering. French missionary St. Cosmo recorded it in 1686 and a college student named Spenser Russell in 1836. The horrible illustration seemed to appear and disappear. Most travelers never saw it, passing by the site without note, while others were startled by the powerful image.

It was claimed that the name Piasa was given by the Illini Indians and translated to, "the bird that devours men." The local Indians claimed that the Piasa lived in the valley of the Illinois River and from ancient times it fed on living creatures. A huge beast, its talons were big enough to spear a full-sized deer. But after it tasted human flesh, it would feed on nothing else but the flesh of man.

Spenser Russell's father, a professor at Shurtleff College, wrote a report containing additional details of the horrible creature. Shurtleff College is now part of Southern Illinois University. He related how an Indian chief named Ouatoga dreamed a scheme to kill the beast by offering himself as a decoy. When the Piasa attacked, his companions sprang from ambush, killing it with poisoned arrows. The professor claimed that he later explored a cave near the pictograph and made a horrifying discovery. The mouth of the cavern was 150 feet above the ground and rather small, but inside he measured the height at 25 feet. Human bones littered the bottom of the cave. He dug test holes in several locations to a depth of 4 feet, finding nothing but bones, the estimated remains of thousands of humans devoured by the Piasa.

According to legend, the monster ate at least five or six people daily, so bone residue accumulated quickly.

No one was safe from the creature's steel-like talons. No matter where they were or what they were doing, the Piasa could swoop silently down from the sky, grasp them in its claws and fly away to its cave. Professor Russell's account, of course, is not universally accepted. Since he was known to have an imaginative streak, some people thought he was just playing an elaborate prank. Others view his work more seriously. Regardless, the American Legends Society completed a 48-foot-by-22-foot painting of the Piasa on the Mississippi bluffs just north of Alton in recognition of this unique tale of our first Americans.

There is also some doubt as to where the original pictograph was located. Marquette's descriptions were vague enough to suggest that he may have seen it on the Missouri River instead of the Mississippi.

The Piasa was not believed to have any progeny. Once it was killed, the threat was forever removed. But then again, who is to say that a winged monster does not still exist, living on deer and other forest animals, perhaps with a careless camper or two as an occasional delicacy?[1]

Not far to the west of Green Bay, Wisconsin, is the city of Rhinelander. The city has two primary claims to fame: good beer and a mythical creature known as the hodag. The creature is described as roughly 7 feet long and 30 inches high with bristly spikes like a dinosaur projecting along its back and tail. The jaws are said to be viselike and capable of crushing anything unfortunate enough to be "munched." Just to add to its ferocity, the claws are razor sharp and long tusks hang down from the upper jaw. Honest folk don't have to worry about it, though, since it reputedly only eats white bulldogs on Sundays.[2]

There are several varieties of hodag: black, sidehill and cave. The black hodag was discovered in the woods of northern Wisconsin in 1893 and is usually considered the largest. Its name is derived from its black fur.

The sidehill hodag is common to the hills and bluffs of southeastern Wisconsin and is characterized by shorter legs on one side than the other. The imbalance helps it run around hills but limits it to running left or right only. It can grow to the size of a white-tailed deer. Unlike the Rhinelander variety, it lives on a steady diet of rocks.

The cave hodag seems to be a sidehill hodag with mutated glowing eyes intended to help it see in the dark caves that it commonly inhabits. Early explorers told of seeing them along the lake bluffs north of the Milwaukee River. Some authorities have also placed it as far away as Virginia, West Virginia, Tennessee, Kentucky, Indiana and Missouri.[3]

After a series of sea monster reports in Lake Michigan in 1867, a Milwaukee saloon owner offered a reward of $1,000 for its capture. None of his patrons took up the challenge to go after the horrible serpents. He reportedly claimed he wanted to serve it as a barroom lunch, putting a whole different twist on the old institutional joke of "mystery meat."[4]

A 1908 sea monster scare in Grand Traverse Bay was finally cleared up in 1938 when a newspaperman admitted he paid a photographer to fake the photo of the beast. After sketching the monster on a picture of the bay, the man rephotographed it, producing a somewhat blurry but very believable "monster" that was widely circulated. In our age of digital wizardry, such manipulations seem childlike in simplicity, but for the period, it was high technology.[5]

In the early 1930s, another mystery was solved when the remains of a 30-foot long wooden serpent were discovered scattered on the sand beach at Ludington, Michigan. Made in numerous sections and wired together, it was carefully designed to give the appearance of swimming when pulled through the water. Although crude in design and construction by today's standards, it was effective enough to scare many local swimmers and spawned monster stories for years afterward.[6]

In 1910 an unidentified creature was reported in Lake Leelanau in Leelanau County, Michigan, just to the northwest of Traverse City. It seems that a dam was built to increase the level of the lake 10 to 12 feet to provide a better head of water for a water-powered sawmill. A young man fishing for perch in the lake near the present village of Lake Leelanau was the first to find the creature. The flooding of the lake produced a large number of stumps and trees sticking out of the water. When the young man attempted to tie his boat to one, he was startled when two big eyes opened on the log looking right at him. With a sudden splash, it submerged and swam off. Judging the size was impossible, but the youngster remembered that the head was past the boat while the tail still hadn't moved. While other people admitted to having seen the creature, none would do so publicly for fear of ridicule.[7]

Between 1869-1917, southeast Wisconsin was inundated with tales of slithering giant serpents wrecking havoc across the countryside. The story goes that a huge snake (perhaps several) was

166

sighted lying in thick weed beds in inland lakes and occasionally striking at trolling lures and bait. One fisherman claimed that a monster snake took his bait and dragged him merrily along in his boat for a mile before spitting out the hook and swimming away. Another declared that he harpooned it, but the serpent was too tough and escaped.

The snake's appetite apparently grew as the tales did. In the Red Cedar Lake area, its powerful jaws grabbed wandering pigs and sheep from nearby farms and it hauled them off to the water for breakfast, lunch or dinner as appropriate. Once in a while when a dog disappeared, it was thought to be a snack food for the snake. Mangled animal bodies were often discovered in shallow water. Eyewitnesses claimed that the snake was 40 feet long.

Later reports placed it at lakes Koshkonong, Elkhart, Pewaukee, Oconomowoc, Delavan and Geneva. The steady diet of pigs and sheep must have agreed with it since witnesses now claimed it had reached 70 feet long! Said to be greenish in color, it swam with its head out of the water, as if to survey its domain. Whatever happened to the great serpent isn't known. Reports dwindled off and soon stopped altogether. Perhaps it died of old age, or just found a big enough cave to take a nice long hibernation.[8]

It seems that several years ago two young men were fishing in Lake Michigan just a few miles north of Milwaukee. Their boat was about 350 yards offshore. Both later claimed that they were not drinking or using illegal drugs, but just spending a pleasant afternoon floating along on a calm lake. Since the fish were not biting, there wasn't much to do but enjoy the weather. After a time the sky began to darken and a rainstorm moved in from the west. Deciding to head to shore, they prepared to get under way. One of the men started to haul in the fish stringer dangling in the water. Since they hadn't caught anything, it was empty. As the man leaned over the side, a huge black shape glided by just under the surface. The second man laughed, claiming it was just a fish and nothing to be excited about. Before they could start the outboard motor, both were shocked to see a serpent like head break the surface moving fast across the water away from the boat. They watched in awe until it slowly submerged.[9]

Not all monsters were myths. On November 17, 1903, the men on the dredge tug *Mentor* had an unusual scare. Running about two miles off South Chicago they were startled when a sea lion, recently escaped from the Lincoln Park Zoo, attempted to climb aboard. Fireman Charles Kimball was standing at the door of the fireroom when the sea lion shot up to the rail of the tug. Kimball instinctively jumped back, only to tumble backwards and fall 7 feet into the stoke hold, bruising himself badly about the head and shoulders. Meanwhile, the sea lion had managed to flop its flippers over the rail and was attempting to climb aboard. Seeing the struggle, Capt. McGregor grabbed a rope and tried to lasso it in an effort at capture, but only succeeded in frightening the animal, causing it to slip back into the lake. The eventual fate of the sea lion is unknown.[10]

The *Chicago Tribune* reports that "Lake Michigan is inhabited by a vast monster part fish and part serpent, no longer admits of doubt. We have already published the fact that the crews of the tug *George W. Wood* and the propeller *Sky Lark* had seen him off Evanston, lashing the waves into a tempest. It is regretted that those vessels were not able to approach nearer to him, as from the culled testimony of so many persons we might have been able to obtain an accurate idea of the nondescript. As it is the evidence of the crews sufficiently establishes the fact that the animal is within 40 and 50 feet in length, his shape serpentine, the size of his neck about that of a human being and the size of his body about that of an ordinary barrel.

"The monster was not seen again until Wednesday morning when he suddenly made his appearance just below Hyde Park, about a mile and a half from shore, where the bed of the lake suddenly dips to a great depth. The facts that we are about to state we have derived from a fisherman living in that vicinity named Joseph Mulke. Mr. Mulke is an intelligent German who gains his living by fishing and is well known to the residents of the southern part of the city, where his cart and fish-box have been constant callers for the past three or four years. We have no reason to doubt his statement. While their general statement is confirmed by him, he adds many details, which are new.

"Mr. Mulke, as is his custom, took boat and lines at daybreak yesterday morning, nearly to the edge of the flats, where fish are abundant, threw out his anchor and set his lines. It was a bright, clear morning, a gentle south breeze just rippling the surface of the lake, but not sufficiently strong to impart any motion to the boat. For some reason, his usual good fortune did not attend him. He fished on for about half an hour, and still no bites. It was now growing light very fast and he determined to go in nearer to shore and fish a while for perch and return to his grounds after the sun was up. He therefore drew in his lines and was about to weight anchor when he became aware of a singular motion of his boat.

"The ripple of the lake was not sufficient to cause it. There could not be a swell on the lake as the weather had been very still during the past two or three days. Again, the wind was from the south and his boat was headed to the north so that if the disturbance had been the result of natural causes, his boat would naturally have had a corresponding motion, while in reality the motion was lateral, or from east to west and different from that caused by a swell, not being long and gradual, but abrupt and broken. He turned his eyes to the eastward, but could see nothing and still the motion of the boat increased. Alarmed by this phenomenon, he again commenced pulling in his anchor but he was this time interrupted by a sound to the eastward – a peculiar noise, half puffing like a heavy breath and half an actual vocal sound, harsh and grating as the fisherman described it, like the noise a catfish makes when first caught, only a great deal louder and more frightful.

"He immediately let go the rope and turned his eyes in the direction of the sound, and for the first time became aware of a dark object in the water, oval in shape, resembling very much a boat keel upward and only about 80 rods distant.[11]

"At first the object seemed stationary, but as he watched it, it gradually increased in bulk, still preserving an oval, or rather the segment of a circle in form. Suddenly the motion ceased, the object rising out of the water at its highest point, three or four feet. In a very short time another object commenced rising about 20 feet nearer to him, as he judged, which he could clearly see was the head of some animal, as the eyes were plainly visible. Almost at the same time the tail became apparent, equidistant from the first part of the animal he had seen. As he judged about two-thirds of the monster was out of the water. Thus far the animal had made no forward motion and manifested no disposition to do so, the only signs of activity displayed being a gentle motion of the head, north and south, as an occasional uplifting or stretching of a long neck out of the lake and a few splashes of the tail upon the water, but not by any means with that fully described by the crews of the *Wood* and *Sky Lark*. The fisherman, rightly judging that an animal so huge would not approach the flats, determined to watch him until he could get a good idea of his general appearance.

169

"As we have said, his estimate of the length, which he informs us was five times the length of his boat, very nearly tallies with the previous accounts, while his estimate of the circumference is equally confirmatory. The general color of the animal was bluish black, darkest in the center, graduating to nearly blue at the head and tail. The underside of the animal was only visible as he lifted his head and tail occasionally and this appeared to be of a grayish white, resembling the color of the dog-fish somewhat. The head was a little larger than the human average head, growing smaller toward the mouth and sloping gradually toward the neck, somewhat like a seal's. Toward the snout, which was triangular in shape, the head was very much depressed and on the extreme end of the snout, Mr. Mulke thinks there were barbels, but of this he is not sure. No teeth were visible.

The eyes were large, larger than the human eye, but of their color or shape Mr. Mulke could form no idea whatever. Only a portion of the neck was visible. This appeared to be rough and along its upper surface and extending nearly to its tail was a series of what looked like the bony plates of a sturgeon. This ridge extended over the first section of the animal, which Mr. Mulke saw, but apart from this there was no appendage visible on the forward end of the animal. Mr. Mulke, however, was confident that there were either fins or legs, toward the head and under the water, as there was a constant wash of the water on either side of him, near that point, as if he was sustaining this huge bulk by the motion of such appendages. A few feet forward of the tail there was a well developed fin of a grayish hue, corresponding with the dorsal fin of the sturgeon, but many times larger and evidently more powerful. The entire fin had a lateral motion and the various spines of which it was composed had an individual longitudinal motion, so that sometimes the fin was almost closed up like a fan. Immediately beneath this was an anal fin, possessing the same characteristics but different in shape, being very long and the spines of equal length. Immediately in front of this were two well-developed legs. Mr. Mulke thinks they ended in a webfoot. In any event they were jointless, but were so flexible that the animal could draw them up to the belly when they were not in use. By analogy, therefore, we should infer that the animal had similar legs at his other extremity, which favors the supposition that he walks at time on the bed of the lake, in search of his prey and at once banishes the supposition that he might be of the sturgeon family. The tail itself was of great size and strength, very unsymmetrical in shape, with something resembling long hair covering its entire upper surface, the under surface being diversified with sharp ridges, radiating to the outer edge."[12]

There is no record of Mulke's monster appearing again, at least in the form he reported it. Was it all nothing but an illusion or perhaps spun from the pen of a bored newspaper reporter? We will never know.

In the late 1890s, however, another sea serpent was reported by some Milwaukee commercial fishermen. They were setting their nets off Jones Island when the large head of a sea serpent broke the surface not far away. They all got a good look at the beast before it submerged, but made no guess of its color or size. As expected, when they repeated the story ashore, they were laughed at.

A few days later several young men were sailing a catboat in the bay when they saw what they thought to be a wood cask floating not far from the boat. As they drew near, the cask was revealed to be the head of a large serpent floating on the surface. Afraid to go closer, they carefully sailed away.

A few mornings later a "serpent" was sighted in the river. A man loafing on the Michigan Street Bridge claimed that he saw a large grayish-green body move down the river in the shadowy depths before it dove out of sight. Later that morning another man claimed to have seen it down near the river mouth. Other reports made the rounds, but no "hard" evidence was ever found. The mystery of what they saw remains unsolved.[13]

In 1992, the *Weekly World News* reported that a 140-foot-long snakelike creature was captured by the U.S. Navy in northern Lake Michigan near the Manitou Islands. By all accounts it fits the legendary description of Mishegenabeg but, of course, since the U.S. Air Force will reveal nothing about the space aliens they captured in Roswell, New Mexico, in 1953, so the Navy is keeping quiet about its sea monster.

There is a mythical fable about whales in Lake Michigan. Obviously most mariners give such claims a snort of derision, but yet a few tipsy sailors believe it to be true. Certainly having a couple of shots of "Old Fog Cutter" rum helps the concept go down. Regardless of the veracity of the issue, you be the judge.

There are many variations to the tail of Lake Michigan whales. This is only one and doubtless others will be promulgated as experienced sailors ruminate a bit.

While the whales can range most anywhere in the lake, they mostly stick to the warmer southern waters except when migrating in the spring and fall. They rarely appear in full daylight and usually surface only during fog and mist. The mournful exhalations from somewhere out in the gray cotton can be very disconcerting to the inexperienced sailor.

Although very little research has been done, some scientists think they are a subspecies of sperm whale. The white lab coat crowd crayoned in the genus "whalusreallyreallybigushoaxus" when completing the tentative identification of the species on the periodic table of elements. It is thought they migrate from the southern part of the lake to Hudson's Bay in the fall and return in early spring. Since few are seen in the Sault Locks, it is assumed they travel by underground rivers from Lake Michigan to Lake Superior, coming up near the Pictured Rocks, then into another underground river near Outer Island and on to Hudson's Bay. A few with confused internal navigation systems sneak out via the Seaway, but they are very rare indeed. The whales are very rarely sighted in Lake Superior. The belief is that the generally rough water makes them hard to spot and the lower level of shipping traffic means that there are less eyes to see them. Paleontologists conclude that there must be huge underground caverns in the underground rivers allowing the whales to surface and catch a breath, otherwise such a long underwater migration would be impossible. This theory meshes well with the core concepts of the Hollow Earth Society whose original research has been groundbreaking in its interpretation of demented logic.

Observers report they look like a sperm whale although about 20 percent smaller. The size difference is accounted for by the general lack of biomass in the lake. Their diet consists of salmon, lake trout, alewives, herring and increasingly zebra mussels and goby. Since the whales are practically the only creatures munching on the miserable little invaders, if the mussels and goby continue to increase in number, the whales could become a critical control challenge.

The whales are protected by an unwritten, verbal subsection of the Volstead Act, as amended by Part A, 45, (d), ii, Title 7, USC 98. Harvesting the whales would be devastating for such a small population, thus protecting them is critical for future population maintenance.

There is some evidence of a very early Native American whale fishery in the area around Indiana Dunes. Imagine the bravery of trying to slip a shell-tipped harpoon into a whale from a birch-bark canoe. While blubber was considered a real delicacy, whalebone was vital since it was used for dice manufacture, critical, of course, for the development of the Indian gaming industry.

There is a fair degree of archeological evidence for whales in the Great Lakes. Fossilized whalebones have been found in several sites in Michigan. In 1928, the bone of either a right or bowhead whale was found while excavating for a school building in Oscoda. A tooth from a sperm whale was also found in the Pine River in the northeast corner of Lake Michigan.

Some folks consider it quite possible that at least several shipwrecks were caused by the whales. Imagine a small sailing ship fighting through rolling seas suddenly smashing into a surfaced whale. Since the whale never hung around, the case was never proved.

There are also those who think La Salle's *Griffon* wasn't lost in a storm while returning from the Door Peninsula, as popularly thought, but rather as the result of a whaling effort gone bad. Native American tradition holds that Luke the Dane, the headstrong captain of the *Griffon,* decided to add to the cargo of beaver furs by catching a whale or two on the way back. The valuable oil would add to the trip's profit. Apparently the whale was only angered by Luke's harpoon and instead of dutifully dying, turned and rammed the *Griffon,* staving in her hull, sinking her.

So are there Lake Michigan whales or not? Archeological evidence proves that whales were in Lake Michigan, so the real issue is whether there still are. The truth is perhaps in the mind of the believer.[14]

CHAPTER 9

We Are Not Alone

"Unknown objects are operating under intelligent control,"
Admiral Roscoe H. Hellenkoetter, Director, Central Intelligence
Agency, 1947-50.

If you believe the reports, and that is strictly up to the reader,
Lake Michigan is frequently visited by tourists from Outer Space,
aka, "Flying Saucers" or UFOs. The number of incidents of strange
lights and shimmering saucer-shaped objects published in
newspapers and various "UFO journals" is mind-boggling. These
are only some of the perhaps thousands of stories. Perhaps Lake
Michigan is a vacation destination for space aliens on holiday. You
be the judge.

When the UFO phenomenon started after World War II, Lake
Michigan was in on the ground floor of the action. The recently
publicly accessible Project Blue Book files, the special U.S. Air Force
investigation of UFOs, provides a wealth of data on early reports.

On April 21, 1949, two sophomores from Ludington
(Michigan) High School stated they saw two "flying discs" pass over
the town and disappear over Lake Michigan. Note the term "flying
saucer" wasn't in general use yet. On the same day, employees at the
Pet Milk Company in Homer, Michigan, claimed that six "flying
discs" passed over the village.[1]

On July 24, 1952, a man 40 miles north of Chicago reported
seeing five to seven luminous spots in the sky flying in an irregular
horizontal line, roughly north to south. They were very high and
moving at an estimated 1,500 to 2,000 mph.[2]

A woman living in a high-rise apartment on North Sheridan

Road in Chicago made a unique UFO report on April 8, 1954. It seems that she saw a parachutelike object skipping over the waterfront. Since it was over water, she telephoned the Coast Guard on Navy Pier. She stated to the startled Coast Guardsman that a humanlike form dangled beneath the parachute and it was presently hovering over the Belmont Harbor Yacht Club at an altitude of 300 feet. The Coast Guard immediately dispatched a boat, reaching the area about 20 minutes later. They found nothing, no parachute or pilot. Whatever the woman saw was gone.

Four days later the woman was interviewed by an Air Force investigator and revealed more details. A brilliant white light illuminated the parachutelike object and she pointed it out to two of her neighbors. Since it was about 6:30 p.m., it was dark enough for the white light to really stand out against the dark lake. As the Coast Guard boat approached the area, the object moved to shore and landed in a group of trees. The humanlike form beneath wore a green one-piece jump suit and a helmet of some kind. She stated that until this event, she never believed in "flying saucers." After the Coast Guard boat left, the parachutelike device rose slowly into the air and hovered off the water until the airman elevated into it. It then zoomed off in a tremendous burst of speed. There was no noise.

The following day the investigator returned, but was unable to have the neighbors corroborate the sighting. Perhaps they suffered from a temporary lapse of memory as a way of "not getting involved." Although the woman was apparently financially well off and had solid credentials, the investigator clearly tried to cast doubt on her mental stability. Whether she actually saw what she claimed or not is unknown, but it is an atypical sighting.[3]

Scores of Chicago area residents were startled to see a brilliant unidentified object over Lake Michigan on September 24, 1966. Police and radio stations were jammed with calls from excited Chicagoans. One observer described it as "a large black object with a white ring around about 4,000 feet in the air. It didn't make any noise and was traveling east." Four airline pilots reported to O'Hare control tower that they spotted a brilliant light at that same altitude 100 miles east northeast of the city.[4]

Many folks around Holland, Michigan, in the southeast corner of the lake were amazed to see a "string of Christmas lights way up in the sky" during the evening of March 8, 1984. Reported as being blue, red, white and green, some sources claim that more than 300 people reported the strange lights to various law enforcement agencies up and down the lake, but they were especially brilliant over Holland. It was claimed that an Ottawa County Sheriff 911 operator questioned the National Weather Service radar technician at Muskegon Airport concerning the lights and was told that there were multiple objects on the screen and they were making very abrupt movements, one traveling 20 miles in 10 seconds. The technician also said at one point that he had three objects on the screen. They were triangular in shape, hovering over Holland then moving quickly off to the southwest. When one moved into the pattern, another moved out of it. Altitude varied from five to 12,000 feet. Even though the conversation between the dispatcher and radar technician was recorded, the technician's manager quickly backed away from endorsing the radar readings, claiming that there was no relationship between the radar images and what people on the ground were seeing.[5]

In the following days, hundreds more reports of eerie lights in the sky poured in to the authorities. At least one UFO group sent a team to the area to gather information and try to solve the mystery.

Radar continued tracking unknown objects out over Lake Michigan. Witnesses claimed that the lights were "oscillating." But the speed was incredible, zipping from South Haven, Michigan, on the eastern Lake Michigan shore to 10 miles west of the city in an astounding 10 seconds. Unlike known aircraft, the mystery objects could also suddenly hover, something even high-performance military craft were incapable of doing. No sonic booms were reported, either.[6]

Some sightings were decidedly weird. One witness reported a huge object 500 feet long moving just above the trees. Most sightings were only of mysterious lights in the form of triangles. Some were low to the ground and others 1,000 feet high. All were inexplicable, at least as far as the witnesses were concerned. Lights were seen also over Whitehall and Muskegon, both Michigan cities about midway up the lake.[7]

Six years before, on July 23, 1978, men from four Coast Guard stations witnessed a spectacular UFO sighting on Lake Michigan. The crews from St. Joseph and Ludington, Michigan, and Two-Rivers and Sturgeon Bay, Wisconsin, all reported sighting a cigar-shaped object with colored lights traveling at a speed in excess of 1,200 miles per hour.

At 3:53 a.m., Station Two-Rivers received a radio call from Station Ludington asking them to look out over Lake Michigan between Rawley Point and Big Sable for an apparent UFO. When

the radio call was made, Ludington had the UFO in sight. They
described it as flashing red, white, orange and green lights and
moving west at a high rate of speed. Six minutes later Two-Rivers
called Sturgeon Bay asking it to keep a watch for the UFO.

At the same time Station St. Joseph received a call from two
residents of nearby Benton Harbor, Michigan, stating that they
sighted a long silver cylinder-shaped object hovering at a height of
approximately 2,000 feet. It remained stationary for about half an
hour then moved off to the southwest heading out over Lake
Michigan. At 4:00 a.m., the men at Sturgeon Bay sighted the object
or perhaps a second or even third. They couldn't determine distance
from the station but it was about 25 degrees above the horizon. A
minute later, Station Ludington saw the object moving westerly
toward Sturgeon Bay at a very high speed. It had red lights and a
very bright strobelike light flashing erratically. The station soon lost
track of it.

At 4:25 a.m., the Green Bay Lighthouse reported to Two-
Rivers seeing the object still moving very fast to the west. Twenty
minutes later, Two-Rivers sighted a white light moving toward the
station and flashing in a nonrhythmic manner. The light then
turned northeast and went straight up and out of sight. Station
Ludington received a telephone call from a local resident that a
UFO had hovered over U.S. Highway 31 then shot off to the west

at high speed. It, too, had flashing white lights with an occasional red flash. Men at Station Two-Rivers observed it and reportedly took 10 35mm pictures.

There were additional sightings on July 28. The crew at St. Joseph reported a long cylinder hovering at 6,000 feet over Lake Michigan at 4:23 a.m. It shot off to the north at high speed. St. Joseph notified Two-Rivers and reportedly it reached there in three minutes, a distance of 200 miles. Two and a half hours later, a similar object was sighted by a Coast Guard craft off the Apostle Islands in Lake Superior. It was observed five times for a total of five or six minutes and was always directly overhead.[8]

The Coast Guard wasn't finished with their UFO however. During a 10-day period in early October 1978 the object(s) returned. One of the Coast Guardsmen from Station Ludington reportedly shot motion picture film of the object, which he dutifully sent to Headquarters in Cleveland. And just as in any made-for-TV government coverup movie, it was "lost" in the mail and reputedly never arrived. No film means no evidence and therefore no UFO.

Nevertheless, deputy sheriffs from Oceana County as well as Coast Guardsmen watched the strange fast-moving object flashing green, white and red lights hovering just offshore for half an hour. One deputy later stated, "Whether it was something from another planet or from another country, I don't know. But it sure made a believer out of me." A Coast Guardsmen related that he and his men saw the lights "moving at a high rate of speed, horizontally, then stopping, then moving vertically and stopping." Other witnesses reported weird lights over Silver Lake on the Michigan shore. The sheriff himself saw the objects, but wouldn't report them until others saw them, too. Seeing UFOs is not a career-enhancing achievement. A deputy put it best when he said, "You don't want to get too excited about this because people think you're goofy, but I saw it and it made a definite believer out of me."[9]

In early November, a woman claimed seeing UFOs near the Cook Nuclear Plant in Berrien County, Michigan, on Lake Michigan's southern shore. She and her two sons watched spellbound from her porch as five UFOs hovered above the plant at 10 p.m. and shot blue, green and red beams into the facility. The UFOs were observed for an hour before they finally shot off into the night. Some UFO experts claimed that such a craft often visited nuclear power plants. Why atomic facilities are hot spots for UFOs was never specified.[10]

UFOs have also been sighted around the Green Bay, Wisconsin, area. (Perhaps they are Packer fans? Could the local tradition of wearing a cheese head for games come from visitors from the moon? After all, the moon is made of cheese.) On June 10, 1997, a local clergyman driving northeast of the city at 5 p.m. saw a "metallic object that was illuminated by the sun but also threw off its own light." It was the classic saucer shape and vanished after a couple of minutes.[11]

Two months later a man and his two sons sighted a UFO while driving near Manitowoc, Wisconsin. It was 11:35 p.m. and the strange object, which looked to be triangular in shape and illuminated with three reddish-orange lights, hovered silently for a few minutes then dove for the ground as if it were going to crash, before pulling up.[12]

If UFOs fly in the sky where airlines fly, it is logical to assume that commercial pilots must see them from time to time. And indeed they do. On July 4, 1981, a Lockheed 1011 Tristar was flying along at 37,000 feet from San Francisco to New York – Kennedy. As it approached the east shore of Lake Michigan the pilot was startled by a silvery disk that "splashed into view full size … like the atmosphere opened up." He recalled that it looked like a sombrero viewed from the top. It rolled as it came up to the plane, then darted quickly away. Viewed from the side, it had six evenly spaced jet black portholes on the outside edges. A flash of sunlight bounced off the top and it disappeared in a shallow climb. A slight contrail seemed to be behind it. The copilot remembered only seeing the bright flash. The flight engineer, sitting well to the rear of the cockpit, saw nothing. For obvious reasons neither the pilot nor airline is identified. We can't have the passengers frightened by reports of hot-rodding Venusians can we?[13]

The eastern shore of Wisconsin is the locale of story after story of UFO sightings. Many follow the pattern of triangular objects, often silver colored and glowing or reflecting internal illuminations while ringed with colored lights. Maneuvers are invariably erratic and rapid, impossible for aircraft to perform. So what are they and what is the attraction to Lake Michigan?

Epilogue

Many of the tales in this book are historic, passed down generation to generation. Others are contemporary, from either the recent past or still "occurring" today. The thread binding them together is Lake Michigan. They either happened on the lake, over the lake or immediately surrounding the lake.

While not the biggest of the Great Lakes, a distinction that belongs to Lake Superior, it is still a massive body of water. Fall storm winds can build over a sweep of more than 300 miles north to south. The resulting seas can be terrific, pounding hard against the shore and destroying ships and crews. Wind and wave are well understood by sailors and scientists. It's the "weird" aspect of the lake presenting the real challenge.

I have sailed Lake Michigan for a number of years suffering through a few bouts of stormy seas as well as stumbling through a few "unusual circumstances" defying logical or conventional explanation.

I am not a "ghost hunter" or especially "sensitive" to things from the "other side," but that said, I have experienced things I can't explain. I do not believe in ghosts, sea monsters, UFOs or the like, but I do believe there are things we do not yet understand.

For example: a few years back I was sailing on a small cruise ship approaching Beaver Island in the northern end of the lake. Just before midnight the captain and I were in the pilothouse discussing the upcoming arrival when we noticed a target on the radar approaching us at high speed. The full story of the remarkable incident and it's more remarkable aftermath is in Chapter 2, in short however, our mystery target tracked right up to the ship, passing close aboard our port side only to disappear just astern, but we never saw a thing. It was a modern day electronic ghost ship! If I hadn't seen it, I would not have believed it.

I had the good fortune to be aboard the World War II submarine USS *Cobia* at the Wisconsin Maritime Museum at Manitowoc, Wisconsin, when her volunteer crew fired up her engines. The volunteers work hard to keep *Cobia* in "fighting trim," including maintaining the big diesels in flawless running order. The loud hammering of her engines is a powerful link to the past, keeping not only the sub's history alive but some folks think it energizes the spirits of the old combat crew, too. *Cobia*'s only casualty occurred during a night surface attack on a small Japanese naval convoy. In the resulting tracer-streaked firefight a gunner was killed by enemy fire. Considering the ghostly activity reported on board the sub today, a few docents believe the lost crewman still stands his watch, keeping *Cobia* safe from harm but not resisting the temptation to pull a good joke or two. Standing between the trembling diesels with the old steel hull shaking hard beneath my feet, the tales of ghostly goings on are very believable! The spirit of the *Cobia* is still alive and so is at least one of her crew. When you consider the reports of ghostly activity aboard the USS *Silversides* in Muskegon, Michigan, and the German *U-505* in Chicago, the *Cobia* haunting becomes part of a pattern.

Other people experienced phenomena that can best be explained as ghostly. The halting steps of a long gone keeper at White Lake, Michigan, echo in the second story and locals claim old Captain Bill Robinson still stands duty at "his" light. Some folks think longtime keeper Harriet Colfax still tends the old light at Michigan City, Indiana.

It seems the harder you look, the deeper you dig, the more questions asked, strange and weird stuff bubbles up around Lake Michigan. There are indeed things that go splash in the night in the lake.

If stories from the "other side" bother you, then this book should make you afraid, very afraid because Lake Michigan spirits still roam wild and free.

SO ——————————— CR

Endnotes

CHAPTER 1
[1]Ivan Walton Collection, Box 4, Bentley Historical Library, University of Michigan, Ann Arbor, Michigan.
[2]Manistique Courier (Michigan), December 15, 1899.
[3]Also listed as Mueller and Bernaitorio.
[4]Iron Port (Escanaba, Michigan), December 2, 1897, March 12, 1898.
[5]Stonehouse Collection, Escanaba; Escanaba, www.boatnerd.com/news/archives/10-03-.htm.
[6]Interview, unidentified.; Weekly Maritime News, n.d.
[7]Authors notes – Ghosts and Sea Monsters.
[8]The contribution made by the Great Lakes built submarines is often overlooked by naval historians. The very idea of building deep sea going warships on the Great Lakes somehow seems ridicules. The hulks of dead Jap ships rusting on the bottom of the Pacific Ocean testify loudly to the contrary, www.wisconsinmaritime.org/sub.htm; U.S.S. Cobia, SS 245, www.copperas.com/ss245/; Warships Associated With World War II in the Pacific, www.cr.nps.gov/history/online_books/butowsky1/cobia.htm.
[9]Ships and Tonnage Sunk or Damaged in WW II by U.S. Submarines, www.rddesigns.com/ww2/ww2sinkings.html; Silent Hunters,Submarines of the US Navy in the Pacific War, www.mikekemble.com/ww2/silent.html; The Silversides is one of the most remarkable tales to come out of the Pacific War and her subsequent survival and restoration into museum ship only accentuates it., www.silversides.org/silversides.html;en.wikipedia.org/ wiki/USS_Silversides_(SS-236a0.
[10]Hans Goebler: U-505 Submariner, www.feldgrau.com/interview7.html; Stonehouse Collection – U505.

CHAPTER 2
[1]Wallace J. Baker, Sr., "On Manitoulin Island," Inland Seas, (October 1947) pp. 211-217; Dwight Boyer. Great Stories of the Great Lakes (Cleveland: Dodd, Mead, 1966), pp. 215-230; Dave Stone. Long Point, Last Port of Call (Erin, Ontario: Boston Mills Press, 1988),pp. 22-25; Frank A. Meyers, compiler, "The Manitoulin GRIFFON vs the Tobermory GRIFFON," Inland Seas, (Winter 1956), pp. 275-284. Rowley W. Murphy, "The GRIFFON Wreckage at Tobermory," Inland Seas, (Summer 1956), pp. 142-149; Walton, box 4.
[2]Geri Rider, Ghosts of Door County, Wisconsin (Sioux City, Iowa: Quixote Press, nd), pp.31-34.
[3]Frederick Stonehouse, Went Missing II (Au Train, Michigan: Avery Studios, 1984), pp. 137-147.

[4]Ivan Walton Collection, Box 7, Bentley Historical Library, University of Michigan, Ann Arbor, Michigan.
[5]Stonehouse, Went Missing II, pp. 155-157.
[6]*The State Journal* (Lansing, Michigan), December 4, 1938.
[7]Stonehouse, *Went Missing II*, pp. 155-161; Great Lakes Journal, February 1919.
[8]*Milwaukee Journal*, January 24, 1895.
[9]Stonehouse Collection, clipping, unidentified, not dated.
[10]Steve Harold, Shipwrecks off Sleeping Bear (Traverse City, Michigan: Pioneer Study Center, 1984), pp. 6-7.
[11]Interview, Anna Hoge, March 12, 1996, Anna is a lighthouse keepers daughter with extensive experience, especially growing up on lonely and forsaken Passage Island, north of Isle Royale, Lake Superior.
[12]Mackinac Island is strictly non-motorized other than for several carefully hidden emergency vehicles. All transport is by foot, bike or horse powered. The latter mode usually leaves large deposits which visitors should avoid accidentally finding.
[13]Interview anonymous, July 15, 2001.

CHAPTER 3
[1]Richard M. Dorson, *Bloodstoppers and Bearwalkers* (Cambridge, Massachusetts: Harvard University Press, 1952), pp. 244-245.
[2]Ivan Walton Collection, Box 7, Bentley Historical Library, University of Michigan, Ann Arbor, Michigan.
[3]John Mansfield, History of the Great Lakes, Volume I.(Chicago: J.H. Beers and Company, 1899), p. 723.
[4]*Milwaukee Journal*, September 10, 1860; Edward N. Hoare, *Perils of the Deep, Being an Account of Some of the Some of the Remarkable Shipwrecks and Disasters at Sea Over the Last Hundred Years*, no publisher given, n.d., pp. 258-259.
[5]C.H.J. Snider, "Schooner Days," *Toronto Telegram*, March 16, 1946, DCCXXXV.
[6]Walter Havighurst, *The Long Ships Passing* (New York: MacMillian, 1975), pp. 68-71.
[7]Walton, box 4.
[8]C.H.J. Snider, "Schooner Days," *Toronto Telegram*, January 28, 1933, LXXII; Chicago Inter-Ocean, March 22, 1875.
[9]Dwight Boyer, *True Tales of the Great Lakes* (New York: Dodd, Mead and Company, 1971), p. 208; Mansfield, History, p. 862.
[10]James Donahue, "Cursed Ship Goes Down, 287 Killed," *Marquette Mining Journal*, October 15, 1994.
[11]*Milwaukee Journal*, September 2, 1854.
[12]*Milwaukee Journal*, October 30, 1857.
[13]Marion Morse Davis, *Island Stories* (Lansing, Michigan: Marion Morse Davis,), pp. 71-73; Mansfield, History, p. 881; David Swazye. *Shipwreck* (Traverse City, Michigan: Harbor House, 1982), p. 204.
[14]C.H.J. Snider, "Schooner Days," *Toronto Telegram*, December 8, 1934, CLXV; Swayze, *Shipwreck*, p. 87.
[15]Karl Baarslag, *Coast Guard to the Rescue* (New York: Farrar and Farrar, 1936), pp. 222-232; John O. Greenwood, *Namesakes 1930-55* (Cleveland: Freshwater Press, 1978), p. 259; John H. Wilterding, *Jr. McDougall's Dream, the American Whaleback* (Duluth: Lakeside Publications, 1969), pp. 41-42.
[16]George W. Hilton, *The Great Lakes Car Ferries* (Howell-North: Berkley, California, 1962), pp. 195-196, 118-120, 124-128; Rev. Peter Van Der Linden, *Great Lakes Ships We Remember II* (Cleveland: Freshwater Press, 1984), p.p. 311-312.
[17]Arthur C. and Lucy F. Frederickson, *Frederickson's History of the Ann Arbor Auto and Train Ferries* (Frankfort, Michigan: Gull's Nest Publishing, 1994); Hilton, *Car Ferries*, pp. 82, 89-90, 95-97; Van der Linden, *Great Lakes Ships We Remember II*, p. 28.
[18]Walton, box 4.
[19]*Great Lakes News*, August 1926.
[20]Walton, box 7.
[21]Toronto *Evening Telegram*, May 15, 1937.

[22]Rev. Peter J. Van der Linden, *Great Lakes Ships We Remember* (Cleveland: Freshwater Press, 1979), p. 292; Stonehouse Collection.
[23]Donald L. Cannery, *U.S. Coast Guard and Revnue Cutters, 1790-1935* (Annapolis, Maryland: U.S. Naval Institute Press, 1995), p. 60; *Grand Traverse Herald* (Traverse City, Michigan), June 12, 1899, June 25, 1917; Record of Moments, U.S. Coast Guard, 1790-1933 (Washington, DC: Treasury Department, 1989), pp. 277-282.
[24]*Detroit Free Press*, May 5, 1902.
[25]VERNON File, Stonehouse Collection.
[26]*Chicago Tribune*, August 26, 1886.
[27]*Milwaukee Sentinel*, October 31, 1887.
[28]*Chicago Tribune*, September 3, 1886.
[29]*Chicago Tribune*, June 21, 1887.
[30]*Chicago Tribune*, June 18, 1887.
[31]*Milwaukee Sentinel*, November 2, 1887.
[32]VERNON File, Stonehouse Collection; Milwaukee Sentinel, November 8, 1887.
[33]Annual Report, U.S. Life-Saving Service, 1898, Treasury Department.
[34]Blazing Star File, Stonehouse Collection.
[35]William Home File, Stonehouse Collection.
[36]Superior File, Stonehouse Collection.
[37]James L. Donahue, *Steaming Through Smoke and Fire, 1871* (Sanilac, Michigan: James L. Donahue, 1990), p. 85.
[38]Great Lakes and Seaway Shipping, www.boatnerd.com/.
[39]Author Files; Pete Caesar, Lake Michigan XV, (Green Bay: Pete Caesar, n.d.),pp. 41-44.
[40]Author Files; Pete Caesar, Lake Michigan, XV, pp. 25-29.
[41]Author Files; Detroit Free Press, June 2, 1874.
[42]Detroit Free Press, May 12, 1895.
[43]Stonehouse File – Material Service.
[44] Andaste Disappears, September 9, 1929, 25 Lives Lost, www.macatawa-org/-crich/andaste.htm; Stonehouse File – ANDASTE.

CHAPTER 4
[1]Dwight Boyer. "Strange Adventures of the Great Lakes" (Cleveland:Freshwater Press,1974), pp. 223-225; Author files.
[2]A flag of convenience is a flag of one country, flown by a ship owned by a citizen of another country. The ship owner is able to often avoid taxes and make registration easier; the country providing the flag charges money for that service. The use of a flag of convenience in order to take advantage of laxer registration and safety standards is frowned upon for two reasons: The practice causes nations with stricter requirements to lose income and safety/work conditions of shipboard employees suffer.
[3]Stonehouse Collection - SERIUS.
[4]*Milwaukee Journal*, October 8, 9, 10, 12, 1999.
[5]1950 Last Call For Northwest 2501, UFO Roundup, v. 2, no. 24, June 15, 1997; *Detroit Free Press*, May 1, 2005; The Disappearance of Flight 2501, www.hope.edu/resources/arc/quarter/spring05/flight.html; www.numa.net.
[6]Inland Seas, Great Lakes Historical Society, Winter 1998, p. 267.
[7]Escanaba Daily Press, n.d.
[8]NTSB Identification: CHI92FAMS1, Aircraft: BEECH 95-BE55, registration: N1123B, www.ntsb.gov/ntsb/brief.asp?ev_id=20001211x14079&key=1.

CHAPTER 5
[1]Charles K. Hyde, *The Northern Lights* (Lansing, Michigan: Two Peninsula Press, 1986), p. 153.
[2]Interview, Joel Blahnik, June 1, 1994.
[3]Interview, Doug McCormick, May 21, 1994.
[4] Seeing the Light, Lighthouses of the Western Great Lakes, Grand Traverse Light, www.terrypepper.com/lights/michigan/gdtravers/gdtravers.htm; Stonehouse File – Grand Traverse Light.

[5]Hyde, *The Northern Lights*, pp. 66; Laurie Penrose and Bill Penrose, *A Traveler's Guide to Michigan Lighthouses* (Davidson, Michigan: Friede Publications, 1992), p. 33.

[6]ET1 Joseph P. Gilmartin, Sr. USCG (Ret.), The Keeper's Light, Shipmates, October 1994, p. 7.

[7]Correspondence, Mr. Luther Barnett to Author, November 3, 14, 1994; Jack Edwards, "The Mystery of Sand Point Lighthouse," Great Lakes Cruiser (June 1995), pp. 20-32; Iron Port, Escanaba, March 5,13, April 10,17, 1886; Marquette Monthly, November 14, 1994.

[8]Seul Choix Point Lighthouse File, Stonehouse Collection; Interview, Marilyn Fischer, October, 1997.

[9]Interview, Marilyn Fischer, October 2005.

[10]Interview, Marilyn Fischer, October 2005.

[11]Interview, Marilyn Fischer, October 2005.

[12]Interview, W.C. Adams, May 17, 1994.

[13]Hyde, *The Northern Lights*, pp. 109-110; Seul Choix Point Lighthouse File, Stonehouse Collection; Interview, Marilyn Fischer, October, 1997.

[14]Jack Edwards, Waughoshance, A Nautical Gravestone, Great Lakes Cruiser, October 1994, pp. 14-23; Hyde, *The Northern Lights*, pp. 66, 103; Stonehouse file; Walton, box 4.

[15]Hyde, *The Northern Lights*, p.122; Interview, Karen McDonald, September 9, 1994.

[16]Annual Report, U.S. Light-house Establishment, 1890-1903; author's collection.

[17]Manitou Island File, Stonehouse Collection.

[18]Chad Lewis and Terry Fisk, *The Wisconsin Road Guide to Haunted Locations* (Research Publishing Company, 2004), pp. 195-199; www.terrypepper.com/lights/michigan/pottawatomie/pottawatomie.htm; Lighthouse Digest, December 2002, p. 29; Stonehouse Collection – Pottawatomie.

CHAPTER 6

[1]"Oscar of the Crosswinds," Great Lakes Cruiser, October, 1995, pp. 34-35.

[2]Dave Dempsey, "On the Brink, The Great Lakes in the 21st Century" (East Lansing, Michigan: Michigan State University Press, 2002). Pp. 88-92.

[3]Author notes – Diana of the Dunes; Haunted Places in Indiana, www.juiceenewsdaily.com/0305/news/haunted_indiana.html.

[4]Singapore, www.ghosttowns.com/states/mi/singapore.html

[5]Anonymous, Stonehouse File, Singapore.

[6]Some folks are happy to be quoted concerning their "unusual" experiences. Others are more reluctant and only really open up when no attribution is assured. Interview, Anonymous Source, August 12, 2005: Stonehouse File, Ramsdell Theater.

[7]Interview, Anonymous Source, August 12, 2005: Stonehouse File, Ramsdell Theater.

[8]www.ghostzoon.com/forum/Partagium/viewthread.php?tid=139.

[9]Rhodes Opera House, www.weird-wi.com/ghosts/fhodesoperah.htm.

[10]Gary Barfknecht, Unexplained Michigan Mysteries: Strange but True Tales from the Michigan, pp. 52-54; Bowers Inn, www.prairieghosts.com/bowers.html; Bowers Harbor Inn, www.members.tripod.com/jayboy74/story32.html.

[11]Authors Field Notes - Fayette.

[12]Authors Field Notes – Fayette.

[13]Authors Field Notes - Fayette.

[14]Burned Across the State, ncha.ncats.net/data/Burned_Across_The_State; Author file, Peshtigo.

[15]Author Notes – Lakeside Inn; History of the Lakeside Inn, www.lakesideinns.com/history.htm.

[16]Stonehouse Collection - House of Ludington File; House of Ludington, www.houseofludington.com/.

[17]Haunted Places in Wisconsin, www.theshadowlands.net/places/wisconsin.htm.

[18]Stonehouse File – Yugo; Detroit Free Press, October 1, 6, November 7-9, 1989.

[19]Haunted Places in Michigan, www.theshadowlands.net/places/michigan.htm.

[20]Haunted Michigan, www.juiceeenewsdaily.com/0205/news/ haunted_michigan.html.

[21]The History of Angostura Aromatic Bitters, The history of this remarkable concoction is nearly as good as a good ghost story. www.angostura.com/flash/history.shtml.

[22]Hotels and Inns, Washington Island, www.ghosttraveller.com/wisconsin.htm#hotels; Nelsen's Hall, the Original and Only Bitters Pub and Restaurant, www.washingtonisland.com/nelsens.
[23]Shipwrecked Brew Pub, Restaurant and Inn, www.shipwreckedmicrobrew.com/brewery.html.
[24] Castle Park, www.dupontcastle.com/castles/castlepa.htm; Haunted Places in Michigan, www.theshadowlands.net/places/michigan.htm.
[25] The Pfister Hotel, www.allstays.com/Haunted/wi_milwaukee_pfister.htm; Pfister Hotel,www.pfister-hotel.com/hotel_overview.asp.; Milwaukee's Founding Familes, www.widenonline.com/pdfs/foundingfamilies.pdf.
[26]www.praireghosts.com/hauntwi.html.
[27]*The Great Chicago Theater Disaster.* The Complete Story Told by the Survivors by Marshall Evert (1904). Publishers Union of America. *Almanac, Chicago Daily News* (1905, 1906); www.inficad.com/~ksup/iroquois.html; Chicago (III.). *Fire Marshall Annual Report.* 1903; Cook County (III.). *Coroner. Iroquois Theater Fire,* Chicago; *Chicago Tribune,* December 30, 1903 – January 15, 1904.
[28]Calvary Cemetery, www.graveyards.com/IL/Cook/calvary/
[29]The Haunted Walmart and Other true Tales of Terror, www.gapersblock.com/airbags/archieves/the_haunted_walmart_and_othertrue_tales_of_terror/.
[30]Sage & Zarkovich, www.images.google.com/imgres?imgurl=www.crimelibrary.com/graphics/photos/gangsters_outlaws/outlaws/dillinger/10a.jpg&imgrefurl=www.crimelibrary.com/gangsters_out laws/outlaws/dillinger/10.html%3Fsect%3D17&h=216&w=150&sz=7&tbnid=YUuC hYs24tgJ:&tbnh=101&tbnw=70&hl=en&start=4&prev=/images%3Fq%3Danna%2Bs age%2Bdillinger%26svnum%3D10%26hl%3Den%26lr%3D%26sa%3DG; Girardin, George Russell, with William J. Helmer, *Dillinger: The Untold Story,* Indianapolis:Indiana University Press, 1994.
[31]The Biograph Theater, www.praireghosts.com/dillinger.html; Chicago: Public Enemy, www.travel.discovery.com/convergence/hauntedtravels/interactives/chicago/biograph.html; Girardin, George Russell, with William J. Helmer, *Dillinger: The Untold Story.*
[32]Chi Town Spooks, www.wormwoodchronicles.com/lab spooks/spooks.html; Haunted Traveler, www.travel.discovery.com/convergence/hauntedtravels/interactive/chicago/html; The St. Valentine's Day Massacre, www.praireghosts.com/valentine.html; Find a Grave, St. Valentine's Day Massacre, www.findagrave.com/php/famous.php?page=pr&FSctf=109.
[33]www.literacynet.org/lp/hperspectives/llorona.html; Llorona Legend, www.travel.discovery.com/convergence/hauntedtravels/interactives/llorona.htiml; La Llorna, Gary Indiana, www.praireghosts.com/lalloron.html; La Llorona, www.khpindustries.com/forums/showthread.php?t=5; The Spirit of La Llorna, www.lallorona.com/La_index.html.

CHAPTER 7
[1]Glenn Furst, "I Remember, Mass Burials on South Manitou," Vol. 5, No. 2. n.p.
[2]Interview, anonymous, September 10, 2004.
[3]Interview, unidentified, September 15, 1995.
[4]Interview, unidentified, August 21, 1995.
[5]Interview, unidentified, September 15, 1995; being female has no bearing on the story other than being factually correct.
[6]Interview, Doug McCormick, May 21, 1994.
[7]Old Joe had a real sense of humor. Drop the "i" and Moroni become MORON!
[8]What is "Reformed Egyptian?" Is there an "Unreformed Egyptian?" Doesn't the whole thing seem just absurd?
[9]Stonehouse Collection – Beaver Island; The Beaver Island Historical Society, www.beaverisland.net/history; Brigham Young's Wives and His Divorce From Ann Eliza Webb, www.utlm.org/onlineresources/brighamyoungswives.htm; Seeing the Light, Lighthouses of the Western Great Lakes,

www.terrypepper.com/lights/michigan/beaverhead/beaverhead.htm; Anjte Price, "F. Protar: The Heaven Sent Friend," The Journal of Beaver Island History, Volume One, 1976, pp. 51-67; The Church of Jesus Christ of Latter Day Saints – Mormon, www.americanreligion.org/cultwtch/mormon.html. [10]Stonehouse Collection – Marion Island; Have You Explored Michigan's Grand Traverse Bay Yet?, www.uswayfarer.org/cruising_logs/grand/grand.html; Kathleen Craker Firestone, An Island in Grand Traverse Bay, Lake Michigan Islands, Volume I. (Northport, Michigan: Michigan Islands Research, 1992), pp. 24-29, 31-36, 73, 50-54. [11]*Sturgeon Bay Expositor*, February 4, 1876.

CHAPTER 8
[1]The Piasa Monster Bird, www.angelfire.com/electronic/bodhidharma/piasa.html.
[2]The Famous Hodag, www.members.aol.com/joviko/hodag.html.
[3]Hodag, www.en.wikipedia.org/wiki/Hodag
[4]*Milwaukee News*, August 9, 1867.
[5]*Great Lakes Journal*, October 1938.
[6]*Great Lakes Journal*, October 1938.
[7]www.canadiancontent.net/en/jd/go?
[8]Wisconsin's Monsters of the Deep, www.atthecreation.com.
[9]www.canadiancontent.net/en/jd/go?
[10]*Detroit Free Press*, November 18, 1903.
[11]80 rods equals about a quarter mile.
[12]Detroit Free Press, August 9, 1867.
[13]Lake Monsters, www.weird-wi.com/lakes/brown13.htm
[14]Lake Michigan Whale Watching, www.geocities.com/lakemichiganwhales; Stonehouse Collection – Lake Michigan Whales; The Hollow Earth, Subterranean Populations, www.crystalinks.com/hollowearth.html; Theories of the Hollow Earth, www.fiu.edu/~mizrachs/hollow-earth.html; Michigan Whale Fossils, www.sentex.net/~tcc/michwls.html; Interview, April 1, 2003 – professor I. M. Nutz.

CHAPTER 9
[1]Project Blue Book Archive, NARA-PBB88-694, www.bluebookarchive.org/page.aspx?PageCode=NARA-PBB88-694.
[2]Although attacked by critics of UFOs as a waste of money and lambasted by UFO supporters as a government whitewash, Bluebook was an honest effort by the Air Force to investigate UFO sightings, Project Blue Book Archive, www.bluebookarchive.org.
[3]Project Blue Book Archive, www.bluebookarchive.org.
[4]Sunday American (Chicago), September 25, 1966.
[5]Spirits in the Sky, www.ufos.about.com/library/weekly/aa01210a.htm; Transcript of the 08 MARCH 1994 Ottawa County 911/National Weather Service tapes, www.ufocasebook.com/hollandmichigantranscript.html.
[6]*Grand Rapids Press*, March 13, 1994.
[7](Domain no longer active), www.ufobbs.com/ufo, The coming and going of Internet sites presents a challenge to the researcher. Regardless of the veracity of the information, should it be ignored because the "owner" allowed the site to lapse? For the purpose of this book I choose to include the information with the understanding readers can make their own judgements.
[8](Domain no longer active), www.michiganufos.com/1978.htm#lakemichigan.
[9]*Detroit Free Press*, October 11, 1978; *The Star* (Terre Haute, Indiana), October 13, 1978.
[10]*Grand Rapids Press*, November 2, 1978; *Grand Haven Tribune*, November 3, 1978.
[11]Cigar-Shaped UFO Sighted Over Southern Ontario, UFO Roundup, v. 2, no. 25, June 22, 1997.
[12]UFOs Sweep Canada, UFO Roundup, v.2, no. 17, August 17, 1997.
[13]When Pilots See www.UFO's,theshadowlands.net/airspace.txt.

Bibliography

BOOKS

Almanac, Chicago Daily News (1905, 1906).

Annual Report, U.S. Light-house Establishment, 1890-1903.

Baarslag, Karl. *Coast Guard to the Rescue.* New York: Farrar and Farrar, 1936.

Boyer, Dwight. *Strange Adventures of the Great Lakes.* New York: Dodd, Mead and Co. 1974.

Boyer, Dwight. *True Tales of the Great Lakes.* New York: Dodd, Mead and Company, 1971.

Cannery, Donald L. *U.S. Coast Guard and Revnue Cutters, 1790-1935.* Annapolis, Maryland: U.S. Naval Institute Press, 1995.

Caesar, Pete. *Lake Michigan XV.*

Clary, James. *Superstitions of the Sea.* St.Clair, Michigan: Maritime History in Art, 1994.

Coroner, *Iroquois Theater Fire,* Chicago, 1903.

Davis, Marion Morse. *Island Stories.* Lansing, Michigan: Marion Morse Davis, n.d.

Dempsey, Dave. *On the Brink. The Great Lakes in the 21st Century.* East Lansing, Michigan: Michigan State University Press, 2002.

Donahue, James. *Steamboats in Ice 1872.* Cass City, Michigan: Anchor Publications, 1995.

Dorson, Richard M. *Bloodstoppers and Bearwakers.* Cambridge, Massachusetts: Harvard University Press, 1952.

Everett, Marshall. *The Great Chicago Theater Disaster: The Complete Story Told by the Survivors.* Chicago; Publishers Union of America, 1904.

Fire Marshall Annual Report 1903, Cook County, Illinois.

Firestone, Kathleen Craker. *An Island in Grand Traverse Bay, Lake Michigan Islands,* Volume I. Northport, Michigan: Michigan Islands Research, 1992.

Frederickson, Arthur C. and Lucy F. *Frederickson's History of the Ann Arbor Auto and Train Ferries.* Frankfort, Michigan: Gull's Nest Publishing, 1994.

Girardin, George Russell, with William J. Helmer. *Dillinger: The Untold Story.* Indiana University Press, 1994.

Harold, Steve. *Shipwrecks off Sleeping Bear.* Traverse City, Michigan: Pioneer Study Center, 1984.

Heyl, Erik. *Early American Steamers, Volume IV.* New York: Erik Heyl, 1965.

Hilton, George W. *The Great Lakes Car Ferries.* Berkley, California: Howell-North, 1962.

Hoare, Edward N. *Perils of the Deep, Being an Account of Some of the Remarkable Shipwrecks and Disasters at Sea Over the Last Hundred Years.* No publisher given, n.d.

Hoge, Anna. *Childhood Memories of a Lighthouse Keeper's Daughter.* No publisher, n.d.

Hyde, Charles K. *The Northern Lights.* Lansing, Michigan: Two Peninsula Press, 1986.

Lewis, Chad and Fisk, Terry. *The Wisconsin Road Guide to Haunted Locations.* Research Publishing Company, 2004.

Lytle. William M and Holdcamper, Forrest R. compilers. *Merchant Steam Vessels of the United States*. Staten Island, New York: Steamship Historical Society of America, 1975.

Mansfield, James. *History of the Great Lakes*. Chicago: J.H. Beers Company, 1899.

Record of Moments, U.S. Coast Guard, 1790-1933. Washington, D.C.: Treasury Department, 1989.

Rider, Geri. *Ghosts of Door County*. Wisconsin. Sioux City, Iowa: Quixote Press, n.d.

Edward Rowe Snow. *Mysterious Tales of the New England Coast*. New York: Dodd, Mead, 1961.

Stone, Dave. *Long Point, Last Port of Call*. Erin, Ontario: Boston Mills Press, 1988.

Stonehouse, Frederick. *Haunted Lakes, Great Lakes Ghost Stories, Superstitions and Sea Serpents*. Duluth: Lake Superior Port Cities, 1997.

Stonehouse, Frederick. *Haunted Lakes II, More Great Lakes Ghost Stories*. Duluth: Lake Superior Port Cities, 2000.

Van der Linden, Rev. Peter J. *Great Lakes Ships We Remember*. Cleveland: Freshwater Press, 1979.

Van Der Linden, Rev. Peter. *Great Lakes Ships We Remember II*. Cleveland: Freshwater Press, 1984.

COLLECTIONS

Andaste, Stonehouse Collection.

Beaver Island File, Stonehouse Collection.

Blasing Star File, Stonehouse Collection.

Grand Traverse Light File, Stonehouse Collection.

House of Ludington File, Stonehouse Collection.

Material Service File, Stonehouse Collection.

Marion Island File, Stonehouse Collection.

Seul Choix Point Lighthouse File. Stonehouse Collection

U505 File, Stonehouse Collection.

Vernon File, Stonehouse Collection.

Walton Collection, Bentley Historical Library, University of Michigan.

William Home File, Stonehouse Collection.

INTERNET

Beaver Island Historical Society, www.beaverisland.net/history

Black Death Books, www.khpindustries.com/forums/showthread.php?t=5

Bowers Harbor Inn, www.members.tripod.com/jayboy74/story32.html

Bowers Inn, www.prairieghosts.com/bowers.html

Brigham Young's Wives and His Divorce From Ann Eliza Webb, www.utlm.org/onlineresources/brighamyoungswives.htm

Burned Across the State, www.ncha.net/data/Burned_Across_The_State

Calvary Cemetery, www.graveyards.com/IL/Cook/calvary/

Chicago Ghosts, www.travel.discovery.com/convergence/ hauntedtravels/interactive/chicago/html

Chicago: Public Enemy, www.travel.discovery.com/convergence/hauntedtravels /interactives/chicago/biograph.html

Chi-Town Spooks. www.wormwoodchronicles.com/lab/spooks/spooks.html

CHI92FAMS1, www.ntsb.gov/ntsb/brief.asp?ev_id=20001211x14079&key=1

Church of Jesus Christ of Latter Day Saints – Mormon, www.americanreligion.org/cultwtch/mormon.html

Dillinger, www.praireghosts.com/dillinger.html

Disappearance of Flight 2501, www.hope.edu/resources/arc/quarter/spring05/flight.html

Find a Grave, St. Valentine's Day Massacre, www.findagrave.com/php/famous.php?page=pr&FSctf=109

Great Lakes Seaway and Shipping News, www.boatnerd.com/

Hans Goebler: U-505 Submariner, www.feldgrau.com/interview7.html

Haunted Hotels and Inns, www.ghosttraveller.com/wisconsin.htm#hotels

Haunted Places in Indiana, www.juiceenewsdaily.com/0305/news/haunted_indiana.html

Haunted Places in Michigan, www.theshadowlands.net/places/michigan.htm

Haunted Places in Wisconsin, www.theshadowlands.net/places/wisconsin.htm

Haunted Michigan, www.juiceenewsdaily.com/0205/news/haunted_michigan.html

Haunted Walmart and Other Tales of Terror, www.gapersblock.com/airbags/archieves/the_haunted _walmart_and_othertrue_tales_of_terror/

Have You Explored Lake Michigan's Grand Traverse Bay Yet? www.uswayfarer.org/cruising_logs/grand/grand.html

Haunted Wisconsin, www.praireghosts.com/hauntwi.html

History of Angostura Bitters, www.angostura.com/flash/history.shtml

History of Lakeside Inn, www.lakesideinns.com/history.htm

Hodag, www.en.wikipedia.org/wiki/Hodag

Hollow Earth, Subterranean Civilizations, www.crystalinks.com/hollowearth.html

House of Ludington, www.houseofludington.com/

Lake Michigan Whale Watching, www.geocities.com/lakemichiganwhales

La Llorona, A Hispanic Legend, www.literacynet.org/lp/hperspectives/llorona.html

La Llorona, www.praireghosts.com/lalloron.html

Legend of La Llorona, www.travel.discovery.com/convergence/ hauntedtravels/interactives/llorona.html

Michigan Haunted Places, www.theshadowlands.net/places/mich.htm

Michigan's Fossil Whales, www.sentex.net/~tcc/michwls.html

Milwaukee's Founding Familes, www.widenonline.com/pdfs/foundingfamilies.pdf.

Nelsen's Hall, the Only Original Bitters Pub and Restaurant, www.washingtonisland.com/nelsens

No Title, www.llorona.com

Pfister Hotel, www.allstays.com/Haunted/wi_milwaukee_pfister.htm

Pfister Hotel, www.pfister-hotel.com/hotel_overview.asp

Pfister, www.wideonline.com/oldmilw/hotels.htm

National Underwater and Marine Agency, www.numa.net

Piasa Monster Bird, www.angelfire.com/electronic/bodhidharma/piasa.html

Project Bluebook, www.bluebookarchive.org

Rhodes Opera, www.weird-wi.com/ghosts/fhodesoperah.html

St. Valentine's Day Massacre, www.prairieghosts.com/valentine.html

Seeing The Light, Lighthouses of the Western Great Lakes, Beaver Head Lighthouse, www.terrypepper.com/lights/ michigan/beaverhead/beaverhead.htm

Seeing The Light, Lighthouses of the Western Great Lakes, Grand Traverse Lighthouse, www.terrypepper.com/lights/michigan/gdtravers/gdtravers.htm

Seeing The Light, Lighthouses of the Western Great Lakes, Pottawatomie Lighthouse, www.terrypepper.com/lights/michigan/pottawatomie/pottawatomie.htm

Ships and Tonnage Sunk By WWII Submarines, www.rddesigns.com/ww2/ww2sinkings.html

Shipwrecked Brew Pub, Restaurant and Inn, www.shipwreckedmicrobrew.com/brewery.html

Silent Hunters, www.mikekemble.com/ww2/silent.html

Singapore, www.ghosttowns.com/states/mi/singapore.html

Spirits in the Sky, www.ufos.about.com/library/weekly/aa01210a.htm

Theories of the Hollow Earth, www.fiu.edu/~mizrachs/hollow-earth.html

Transcript of the 08 MARCH 1994 Ottawa County 911/National Weather Service tapes, www.ufocasebook.com/hollandmichigantranscript.html

Unofficial Hodag Home Page, www.members.aol.com/joviko/hodag.html

U.S.S. Silversides, www.silversides.org/silversides.html

U.S.S. Silversides, SS236, www.en.wikipedia.org/wiki/USS_Silversides_(SS-236a0

Warships Associated With World War II in the Pacific,
www.cr.nps.gov/history/online_books/butowsky1/cobia.htm
When Pilots See UFOS, www.theshadowlands.net/airspace.txt
Weird Wisconsin, www.weird-wi.com/lakes/brown13.htm
Wisconsin's Monsters of the Deep, www.atthecreation.com

INTERVIEWS
Adams, W.C., Interview, May 17, 1994.
Barnett, Luther to Author, Correspondence, November 3, 14, 1994.
Blahnik, Joel, Interview, June 1, 1994
Fischer, Marilyn, Interview, October, 1997.
Hoge, Anna, Interview, March 12, 1996.
McCormick, Doug, Interview, May 21, 1994
McDonald, Karen, Interview, September 9, 1994.

NEWSPAPERS
Chicago Inter-Ocean, 1874, 1875.
Chicago Daily News, 1903, 1904.
Chicago Tribune, 1886, 1903, 1904.
Detroit Free Press, 1867, 1874, 1895,1902, 1903, 1978, 1989, 2005.
Grand Haven Tribune, 1978.
Grand Rapids Press, 1978, 1994.
Grand Traverse Herald, (Traverse City, Michigan), June 12, 1899, June 25, 1917.
Great Lakes Journal, 1938.
Great Lakes News, 1919, 1926.
Iron Port, (Escanaba, March), 1886, 1898.
Manistique Courier, (Michigan), 1899.
Marquette Mining Journal, 1994.
Marquette Monthly, 1994.
Milwaukee Journal, 1854, 1855, 1857, 1860, 1887, 1999.
Sunday American, (Chicago), 1966.
Sturgeon Bay Expositor, 1876.
The State Journal, (Lansing, Michigan), 1938.
Toronto Telegram, 1933, 1935, 1937, 1946.
The Star, (Terre Haute, Indiana), 1978.

PERIODICALS
"Oscar of the Crosswinds." Great Lakes Cruiser. October 1995.
Baker, Sr., Wallace J. "On Manitoulin Island," Inland Seas. October 1947.
Edwards, Jack "The Mystery of Sand Point Lighthouse," Great Lakes Cruiser. June 1995.
Edwards, Jack "Waughoshance, A nautical Gravestone," Great Lakes Cruiser. October 1994.
Furst, Glenn "I Remember, Mass Burials on South Manitou," Vol. 5, No. 2.
Gilmartin, ET1 Joseph P. Sr. USCG (Ret.), "The Keeper's Light," Shipmates, October 1994.
Lighthouse Digest, December 2002.
Meyers, Frank A. compiler, "The Manitoulin GRIFFON vs the Tobermory GRIFFON," Inland Seas.
"The MAROLD II," Journal of Beaver Island History, 1976.
Murphy, Rowley W. "The GRIFFON Wreckage at Tobermory," Inland Seas, Summer 1956.
Price, Anjte "F. Protar: The Heaven Sent Friend," The Journal of Beaver Island History, Volume One.
1976.
UFO Roundup, v. 2, no. 24, June 22, August 17.

Index

A

A. Booth 50
Alcatraz prison 137
Allegan Federal Bank 101
Alpena 23
Alpena Storm 24
Altamha 55
Alton, Illinois 163
Amelia 48
American Legends Society 164
American Shipbuilding Company 42, 46
Ames, Alfred 114
Ames, Fisher 114
Andaste 58
Anderson, Albert L. 58
Angostura Bitters 121
Angostura, Venezuela 122
Ann Arbor No. 4 44
Anna C. Minch 46-47
Apostle Islands 162, 178
Arnold, Thomas 23
Astaire, Fred 116
Atlantis 62
Augusta 1, 38
Aylesworth, Arthur 114
Aztec mythology 141

B

Bannockburn 20
Baraga, Frederic 149
Barnum, P. T. 150
Barrnett, Luther 74
Bassett Island 158
Bataan Death March 13
Battle Creek, Michigan 63
Battle of the Atlantic 16
Bay Harbor, Michigan 107
Beaver Head Lighthouse 151
Beaver Island v, 21, 34, 51, 70, 86, 148-160, 180
Beaver Island Lumber Company 153, 157
Beaver Island ruins 149
Beechcraft 66
Belleville, Ontario 2
Belmont Harbor Yacht Club 175

Bennett & Schnorbach 48
Benton Harbor, Michigan 25, 41, 64, 177
Benton Harbor airport 66
Bermuda 17
Bernstein, Peter 2
Berrien County 178
Berrien, Michigan 114
Bertil, Prince of Sweden 116
Betts, Emily 96
Betts, William 96, 160
Big Sable 176
Biograph Theater 132, 135
Bismark archipelago 15
Bissell and Davidson 40
Blahnik, Joel 68
Blazing Star 51-53
Bolivar, Simon 122
Booth Fishing Company 49
Booth, Vernon 49
Bower's Harbor Inn 106
Bowers Harbor, Michigan 158
bowhead whale 173
Brown, Fayette 109
Bruce Peninsula 21
Buffalo Bill's Wild West Show 114, 132
Buffalo, New York 37, 39, 41, 143, 149
Burnham, Daniel 138
Bush, William 88

C

California 101, 143, 158
Cal-Sag Canal 57
Calumet Harbor 140
Calumet River 57, 140
Calvary Cemetery 130
Camp Manistique Prison 76
Cape Horn 20
Capone, Al 116, 122, 128, 136
Carolines island 15
Carpenter, Wellington 37
Cash, Johnny 116
Castle Park, Michigan 59, 124
Castle Park tower 123
Castro, Fidel 67

Cat Head Point 146
Cavalier, Rene, Sieur De La Salle 20
Cayman Islands 61
Cayuga Creek 20
Cedar Point, Ohio 28
Central Intelligence Agency 67, 174
Central Michigan University 157
Chambers Island, Wisconsin v, 66, 68
Chambers Island Lighthouse 68
Champlain 51
Charlevoix Public Schools 152
Charlevoix, Michigan 51, 149
Chase, David 157
Cheboygan, Michigan 51
Chicago & Northwestern Railroad 72
Chicago v, 6, 15, 19, 23, 27, 30, 37, 44, 51, 55,
    57, 61, 91, 106, 113, 120, 125, 130, 135,
    138, 149, 153, 175, 181
Chicago Drydock Company 49
Chicago Northwestern Railroad 3
Chicago River 27-28, 31, 56-57, 125, 131, 135
Chicago Sanitary and Ship Canal 57
Chicago Tribune 168
Chicago Yacht Club 158
Chicago, Northwestern Ore Dock No. 4 2
Chicora 20, 24-26, 58
City Cemetery 131
City of Cheboygan 45
City of Ludington 26
City of South Haven 28
Civil Aeronautics Administration 64
Clark, James R. 26
Clay Banks 114
Cleopatra 41
Cleveland, Ohio 28, 44, 51
Cleveland Cliffs Iron Company 58
Cleveland Shipbuilding Company 58
Cobia 10-11, 15, 181
Colchester Lighthouse 42
Coleridge, Samuel Taylor 20
Colfax, Harriet 96, 181
Colfax, Schuyler 96
Colonel Cook 1, 39
Combat Insignia Battle Stars 14
Conneaut, Ohio 42
Cook County Criminal Courts 127
Cook County Jail 127
Cook County Morgue 134
Cook County Sheriff 57
Cook Nuclear Plant 178
Corbin, David 95
Cornwall, England 9
Courier (Manistique, Michigan) 1
Craig Shipbuilding Company 43
Crosby 26
Crosswinds Restaurant 98
Crown Hill Cemetery 135
Crown Point, Indiana 132
Cuba 158
Cudahey, Indiana 141
Cussler, Clive 65
Cuyahoga River 58

D
Dartmouth, Massachusetts 72
Death's Door Passage 9, 22, 36, 41, 94
Delta 3
Delta County Historical Society 73
The Depression 115, 117
Destination Tokyo 14
Detroit 4, 39, 62, 67, 91, 136, 143, 153
Detroit Free Press 48, 55
Detroit Harbor 94
Deutsche Werft 16
Diana of the Dunes 99
Dickey, Lynn 116
Dillinger, John 116, 132, 136
Donner, George R. 60
Door Peninsula v, 9, 21-22, 41, 45, 70, 94,
    121, 148, 173
"dreaded Manitou" 32
Duluth, Minnesota 61
Dunes Correctional Facility 121
E
East Saginaw 27
Eastland 27-28, 30, 113, 131
Edison, Thomas 158
Edwards, Jack 81
Electric Boat Company 11
Eleventh District depot 91
Ella Ellenwood 27
Ellen Spry 27
Emerald Isle 156
Empire, Michigan 27
Erie Canal 143
Erie, Pennsylvania 1, 60
Escanaba 43
Escanaba Fire Department 3
Escanaba, Michgan v, 2-4, 72-73, 116
Estonia 156
Euclid, Ohio 40
Evanston, Illinois v, 130
Evergreen Inn 118
Everleigh Club 128
Expositor (Sturgeon Bay) 160
F
Fayette State Historic Park 109
Fayette, Michigan v, 108, 112
Federal Bureau of Investigation 62, 133
Feldman, Bonnie Ann 63
Felt Mansion 120
Felt, Agnes 120
Felt, Dorr 120
Ferris wheel 138
Ferrysburg, Michigan 58
Field, Marshall Jr. 128
Fillmore, Millard 70
Firestone, Harvey 158
Fischer, Marilyn 78, 85
Fisherman Shoal 53
Fleetwing 41
Flight 2501 64
Flying Dutchman 20
Flying Dutchmen 20, 22

Ford Center for the Performing Arts 130
Ford Island 158
Ford, Henry 116, 158
Fort William, Ontario 46
Fox Point 27
Fox Point Shoals 46
Francisco Morazon 145
Frankfort, Michigan 45, 51
French Revolution 134
Fresnel lens 71, 74, 81, 86, 96, 146, 152
Friends of Pottawatomie Light 95
G
Gable, Clark 133
Gallery, Daniel V. 16
Galloping Gertie 119
Garden Island 149
Garden Peninsula 70, 108
Gary, Indiana v, 139, 143
Gaynor House 116
George F. Whitney 37
George W. Wood 168
Gibraltar Town Park 68
Giddings Boardinghouse 124
Giddings, Mrs. William 124
Gills Rock, Wisconsin 22, 94
Gladstone, Michigan 120
Glen Haven, Michigan 51
Glenn, Michigan 64
Globe Iron Works 44
Gobel, George 116
Goetz, Fred 136
Gogebic Range 108
Good Hope 20
Goodrich Steamship Company 23
Graceland Cemetery 129
Graham and Morton Transportation Company 24
Grand Ballroom 139
Grand Banks 9
Grand Haven, Michigan 23, 26, 58
Grand Haven Theater 120
Grand Old Lady Lightkeeper 97
Grand Portage, Minnesota 50
Grand Rapids & Indiana Railroad 47
Grand Rapids, Michigan 62, 157
Grand Traverse Bay 158, 165
Grand Traverse Herald 47
Grand Traverse Lighthouse 70
Grant, U.S. 96
Gratiot County 114
Gray Lady 92, 131
Gray, Alice Marble 100
Gray's Reef Passage 33, 145
Great Chicago Fire 113, 126
Great Lakes Cruiser 81
Great Lakes Engineering Works 58
Great Lakes Naval & Maritime Museum 15
Great Peshtigo Fire 113
Green Bay 21, 45, 68, 94, 121, 160
Green Bay Lighthouse 177
Green Bay, Wisconsin v, 165, 179
Green Island 45

Griffon 20, 173
Grindstone City, Michigan 114
Groton, Connecticut 11
Guadalcanal 15
Gull Island 53
Gulliver Historical Society 75, 78, 80
Gulliver, Michigan v, 74
H
H.B. Tuttle 53
Hackley, Charles H. 120
Hackley Public Library 120
Hall, Frederick & Ann Eager 158
Hall, Marion 158
Halley (Mr.) 160
Hamilton, Polly 133
Hammerhill Paper Company 44
Harbin, Mike 15
Hargrove, Benjamin L. 1
Hargrove, W. H. 1
Harned, Virginia 115
Harpo Studios 131
Harriet B. 44
Harrisville, Michigan 55
Hartwell, Anna C. 96
Haunted Lakes 20
Hayes, Pat 117
Helfenstein 55
Hellenkoetter, Roscoe H. 174
Helling, Frederich 61
Henry W. Cort 42
Herman, John 86
High Island 41, 149, 156
Highway 16 54
hodag, black 165
hodag, cave 165
hodag, sidehill 165
Hoffa, Jimmy 66, 116
Hog Island 149, 158
Holland, Michigan v, 34, 59, 67, 113, 123, 175
Hollow Earth Society 172
Hollyhock 64
Homer, Michigan 174
Hooters 132
Hoover, J. Edgar 133
House of David 41
House of Ludington 116-118
Houston, Ralph Clark 11-12
Hudson's Bay 172
Huron City, Michigan 114
Huron County 114
Hutzler place 145
Hyde Park 168
I
Illini Indians 163
Illinois National Guard 131
Illinois River 163
Indiana 165
Indiana Sand Dunes v, 99, 172
Indiana Dunes State Park 100
Ingallston, Michigan 66
Ionia, Michigan 158
Ira H. Owen 1

Irish banshees 156
Irish fishermen 153
Iroquois Theater 129
Isle of the Dead 159
J
Jack the Ripper 114
Jackson Harbor 94
Jackson Iron Company 109
Jackson Mining Company 109
Java Sea 11
John Kelderhouse 2
Johnson, Reuben A. 54
Joliet, Louis 163
Jones Island 171
Joseph Paige 51, 53
Junction Asylum 121
Justice, Illinois 125
K
Kalamazoo 56
Karpis, Alvin 137
K-D-Bob 54
Kennedy, John 67
Kenosha, Wisconsin v, 106
Kentucky 165
Kewaunee, Wisconsin 44-45
Keweenaw Peninsula 121
Kimball, Charles 168
Kincardine, Ontario 33
King Strang 154
Kingston 42
L
L-39 Albatross jet 66
La Llorona 140
Lady Elgin 1, 38-41
Lady of the Lakes 38
Lake Delavan 167
Lake Elkhart 167
Lake Erie 20, 40, 42-43, 67
Lake Geneva 167
Lake Huron 54-55, 58, 114, 149
Lake Koshkonong 167
Lake Leelanau, Michigan 166
Lake Oconomowoc 167
Lake Ontario 41
Lake Pewaukee 167
Lake Superior 51, 53, 58, 121, 162, 172
Lakeside Anti-Horse Thief Association 114
Lakeside Hotel 114
Lakeside Inn 116
Lansing, Michigan 107, 114
Leatham D. Smith Company 58
Leelanau County 166
Leelanau Peninsula 70, 146
Leland, Michigan 51
Lewis, Gene 127
Lexington Hotel 128
Life-Saving Service 44, 52-53, 91, 144, 147
Lighthouse Board 91
Lighthouse Service 75, 87
Lima, Ohio 132
Lincoln Park 131
Lincoln Park Zoo 168

Lind, Robert C. 63
Lockheed 1011 Tristar 179
Lombardo, Guy 116
Lorient 19
Ludington (Michigan) High School 174
Ludington, Harrison 116
Ludington, Michigan v, 43, 54, 64, 166, 176
Ludington, Nelson 116
Luke the Dane 21, 173
lumber pirates 103
M
M.J. Cummings 46
Mackinac Bridge 119, 120
Mackinac Island 6, 34, 79, 93, 149, 153
Mackinaw 64
Mackinaw City 51, 149
Madam Emma Duvall's French Elm 128
Madame Guillotine 134
Malott, Nelse 38
"Manhattan Melodrama" 133
Manistee, Michigan v, 34, 102, 114
Manistique, Michigan 44
Manistique cemetery 79
Manitou Islands v, 52, 147, 171
Manitou Passage 6, 9, 32-33, 61, 70, 92, 142, 145-146, 148
Manitou Passage Long Point 36
Manitou Passage State Bottomland Preserve 146
Manitoulin Island 21
Manitowoc, Wisconsin v, 10-11, 15-16, 41, 43, 45, 51-53, 118, 179, 181
Mare Island Navy Yard, California 14
Marianas 15
Marine City, Michigan 23
Marion Island v, 158-159
Marion Island lodge 159
Marion Isle 158-159
Marquette mines 73
Marquette Range 108
Marquette, Jacques 163
Marquette, Michigan 55, 72, 79
Mary Celeste 27
Material Service 56
McCormick, Doug 70
McCormick, James 70
McDonnell, Karen 87
McGregor 168
McGurn, "Machine Gun" Jack 136
medicine man 162
Meldrum Bay 21
Mellencamp, John 62
Menominee, Michigan v, 66, 163
Menominee Range 108
Menominee Triangle 66
Mentor 167
Michigan Army National Guard 92
Michigan City Lighthouse 96-97
Michigan City, Indiana v, 28, 54, 96, 100, 131
Michigan Gazetteer and Business Directory 116
Michigan Legislature 151
Michigan Shipwreck Research Associates 65
Michigan State Ferries 45

Michigan State Police 119
Michigan State University 114
Michigan Street Bridge 171
Midland County 114
Midvale 42
Miller, Harold 3
Milwaukee v, 4, 6, 24-27, 34, 38-39, 41, 43-44,
    46-47, 51-52, 54-55, 62, 64, 91, 124, 143,
    165, 167, 171
Milwaukee Fire Department 63
Milwaukee Journal 26, 62
Milwaukee Police 63
Milwaukee River 125, 165
Milwaukee Sentinel 52
Minneapolis 64
Miranda 53-54
Mishegenabeg (great snake) 162, 171
Mississippi River 163-164
Missouri 13, 28, 165
Missouri River 164
Mojave 40
mooncussing 152
Moore, Verna 122
Mooresville, Indiana 132
Moran, George "Bugs" 136
Moroni (angel) 150
Mrs. O'Leary's cow 113
Mulke, Joseph 168
Municipal Pier Number Two 138
Museum of Science and Industry 16
Muskegon 23, 43
Muskegon Airport 176
Muskegon Harbor 54
Muskegon, Michigan 15, 42, 48, 55, 120, 176, 181
N
Nahant 3-4
Napier, Nelson W. 23
National Cherry Festival 66
National Historic Landmark 11, 15
National Park Service 146-147
National Register of Historic Places 11
National Underwater Maritime Agency 65
National Weather Service 176
Naval Air Station 58
Naval Reserve 15, 91
Navy Pier 15, 125, 138
Navy Pier Auditorium 139
Navy Pier Headhouse 139
Navy Vessel Register 11, 15
Neal, Patricia 116
Nelsen, Tom 121
Nelsen's Hall Bitters Pub and Restaurant 121
Nelson, Baby Face 116
New Jersey viii, 67
New London, Connecticut 15
New York 39, 49, 64, 91
Niagara 21
Ninth District 91
North Bluff Cemetery 120
North Manitou Island 6, 92, 143, 146
North Manitou Life-Saving Station 147
North Manitou Shoal Light 145

North Wind 63
Northern Michigan Line 51
Northport 51
Northwest Airlines Flight 2501 63
Nyack 26
Nymph of the Dunes 100
O
O. Henry Ballroom 126
O.M. McFarland 60
O'Boyle, Clyde 157
O'Brien, Sean 62
O'Rourke, Mick 157
Oceana County 178
Ogdensburg, New York 96
Old Arthur 114
Old Mission Peninsula 106, 158
Old Mormon Print Shop 154
Old Sparky 128
Omar Pasha 55
Oprah Winfrey Show 131
Oprah Winfrey Studio 31
Oregon 135
Oscar the ghost 99
Oscoda, Michigan 173
Oswego, Illinois 27, 38
Ottawa 149
Ottawa County Sheriff 176
Ouatoga 163
Outer Island 172
P
Paradise Bay 34, 149, 152
Park Place Hotel 158
Pearl Harbor 11, 13-14
Pearl, Joseph F. 26
Pearson, Loretta Bush 88
Pentwater, Michigan 46
Pere Marquette 16 43
Pere Marquette 54
Peshtigo Fire Museum 114
Peshtigo, Wisconsin v, 44, 113-114
Pet Milk Company 174
Petoskey, Michigan 107
Petosky 26
Pfister Hotel 124
Pfister, Charles 124
Piasa 163-164
Pictured Rocks 162, 172
Pine River 173
pirates 152
Pleasant Grove 114
Pleasanton, Stephen 95
Pluhar, Leslie Ann 119
Poe, Edgar Allan 127
Pogo 154
Point Au Barques 44
Point Betsie 27, 146
Port Austin Reef 54
Port Credit 40
Port Hope, Michigan 114
Port Sheldon, Michigan 59
Port Washington, Wisconsin 46, 60, 62
Porte des Morts 22, 94

Pottawatomie lighthouse 95
Power Island 159
Power, Glenn & Annette 159
Presidential Unit Citation 14
Prins Willem II 6
Prohibition 121
Project Blue Book 174
Protar, Feodar 155-157
Public Enemy Number One 133
Purvis, Melvin 133
Pyramid Point 146
Q
Quincy A. Shaw 44
R
Racine, Wisconsin 43
Ramsdell Theater 103
Ramsdell, Frederic 103
Ramsdell, Thomas Jefferson "T. J." 103-104
Ramsdell's Folly 103
Ravenna 40
Rawley Point 51, 176
Red Cedar Lake 167
Red Lion Pub 132
Reed, B. L. 48
Reid Murdock building 31
Resurrection Cemetery 126
Resurrection Mary 125, 139
Rhinelander, Wisconsin 165
Rhode Opera House 106
Richmond, Virginia 47
Riker, Ronald 145
The Rime of the Ancient Mariner 20
Robinson, Bill 181
Robinson, Sarah 88
Robinson, William 87
Rock Island 94
Rock Island Passage 45
"Romeo and Juliet" 159
Root (Mr.) 160
Rosa Belle 41
Rosebud 44
Rosie, Ronald 81
Roswell, New Mexico 48, 171
Royal Oak, Michigan 119
Russell Island 21
Russell, F. D. 49
Russell, Ives 49
Russell, Spenser 163
Russell, William J. 25
S
S.B. Pomeroy 52
Sacred Cow 63
Sage, Anna 133
Saginaw, Michigan 77
St. Brendan 153
St. Catherines 40
St. Cosmo 163
St. Ignace 51
St. James lighthouse 34, 151
St. James, Michigan 35, 51
St. John's, Newfoundland 72
St. Joseph, Michigan v, 24-26, 31-32, 63, 176

St. Joseph River 91
St. Joseph Yacht Club 92
St. Joseph, Michigan Lighthouse 90
St. Joseph-Chicago Line 28
St. Lawrence River 40
St. Martin Island, Michigan v, 70, 161
St. Valentine's Day Massacre 135
Salmon Point 42
Sand Point 3
Sand Point Lighthouse 72
Sanilac County 114
Saugatuck, Michigan v, 67, 101, 120
Sault Locks 172
Schetterly, Henry 70
Schwarz, Michael 123
sea lamprey 153
sea monster 171
Sea Shell Harbor 110
Second Regiment Armory 29, 131
Serius 61
Seul Choix Lighthouse 53, 74, 80, 84
Seul Choix Point 74, 76, 79, 82, 84
Shakespeare, William 159
Shamrock Bar 35
Shamrock Restaurant and Pub 157
Sheboygan, Wisconsin 52
Shenango No. 2 43
Shipwrecked Restaurant, Brew Pub and Inn 122
Shotgun George Ziegler 138
Shurtleff College 163
Sialia 158
Siegert, J. 122
Silver Lake 43, 178
Silversides 14-15, 181
Sinclair Chicago 6
Sinclair No. 12 6
Singapore, Michigan 101
Sky Lark 168-169
Sleeping Bear Dunes National Lakeshore
    6, 101, 146
Sleeping Bear Point 143, 146
Slyfield, Alonzo 145
SMC Cartage Company 135
Smith Dock Company 56
Smith, Emma 150
Smith, Joseph 150
Solomon Islands 15
Sommers, Jim 112
Soo Locks 73
Sousa, John Philip 116
South Beach 64
South Fox Island 147
South Haven, Michigan 28, 56, 64, 67, 176
South Manitou Island 6, 142-146
South Manitou Lighthouse 145
South Manitou station 147
Southern Illinois University 163
Soviet Air Force 66
Spanish-American War 158
sperm whale 172
Spiegel, Mary 124
Station Ludington 176-178

197

Station St. Joseph 177
Station Two-Rivers 176, 178
Steward, E. W. 160
Stewart, Jimmy 116
Stickney, Genevieve 106
Stickney, J. W. 106
Stines, Bennie 25
Stines, Edward G. 25
Stone, Axel 52
Straits of Mackinac 2, 6, 9, 32, 36, 45, 52, 74,
    91, 119, 149
Strang, James Jesse 34, 150, 160
Strang, James Jesse 34
Sturgeon Bay 34, 56-57, 177
Sturgeon Bay Canal 44
Sturgeon Bay, Wisconsin 56, 58, 176
Sugar Island 37
Sullivan, Paddy 157
Superior 51-53
Superior, Wisconsin 42
Sutton's Bay 51
Sylvan Beach 48-49
T
Tacoma Narrows Bridge 119
Task Group 22.3 16
Teamsters 67
Tennessee 165
Terry, John 72
Terry, Mary 72-73
Vernon 51
Theodore Roosevelt 28
Titanic 30
Tito 118
Toledo, Ohio 43
Townshend, Joseph Willy 79
Traverse City, Michigan 47, 62, 66, 106, 158, 166
Travis, Randy 116
Tuscarora 47-48
Tuscola County 114
Two Harbors, Minnesota 44
Two Rivers, Wisconsin v, 53, 176
U
United States Air Force 48, 171, 174
United States Army 13
United States Army Air Corps 63
United States Army Reserve 92
United States Coast Guard 31, 43, 45, 58, 61-
    66, 68, 70, 73, 75, 81, 146, 152, 175, 178
United States Coast Guard Auxiliary 63
United States Coast Guard stations 176
United States Lighthouse Service 90
United States Marines 13
United States Navy 16-17, 41, 47, 64, 91, 130, 171
United States Revenue-Marine 147
U-505 17-19, 181
Union Pier 114
United Airlines 63
University of Chicago 100
University of Illinois 140
Upper Peninsula 108, 120, 145
Urim and Thummin 150
V

Van Riper, Clement 152
Vanderbuilt, Cornelius Jr. 116
Vermilion 37, 53
Vernon 49-53
Virginia 165
Volstead Act 172
W
Wacondah 58
Waring, Fred 116
Washington Island v, 3, 71, 94, 121, 160
Waugoshance 86
Waugoshance Lighthouse 87
Waugoshance Shoal 86
Waukegan, Illinois 44
Weekly World News 171
Welland Canal 39, 58
West Bay 47
West Virginia 165
Western Electric Company 28
Western Navigation Company 46
Westmoreland 6
Whisky Point 149, 152, 154
White House 67
White Lady 105
White Lake 27, 87
White Lake Channel 27
White Lake Lighthouse 98
White Lake, Michigan 98, 181
White River Channel 87
White River Light Station Museum 87
White Shoal Light 86-87
Whitefish Bay, Wisconsin 62, 65
Whitehall, Michigan 176
William B. Davock 46
William Home 52-53
William Sanderson 27
Williams, Elizabeth Whitney 152
Williams, Lewis 69
Willy 8
Wilmette 30
Wilson, Paul 100
Wind Blown 110
Winnetka, Illionois v, 38
Wisconsin Maritime Museum 10, 16, 181
Wisconsin-Michigan Steamship Company 54
Wolfe, Verne F. 63
Wolff, Ludwig 129
Woodbine 64
Woodrush 64
World Columbian Exposition 138
Y
Young, Brigham 150-151
Yugo 118
Z
Zschech, Peter 18

About the Author

Frederick Stonehouse

Frederick Stonehouse holds a Master of Arts degree in history from Northern Michigan University, Marquette, Michigan, and has 16 authored books on Great Lakes maritime history. Among them are his first *Haunted Lakes, Haunted Lakes II* and *Shipwreck of the Mesquite: Death of a Coast Guard Cutter, Wreck Ashore, The U.S. Life-saving Service on the Great Lakes*, published by Lake Superior Port Cities Inc., and *The Wreck of the* Edmund Fitzgerald.

He has also been a consultant for both the U.S. National Park Service and Parks Canada.

His articles have been published in *Lake Superior Magazine, Skin Diver* and *Great Lakes Cruiser* magazines and *Wreck and Rescue Journal*. He is president of the board of directors of the Marquette Maritime Museum and the U.S. Life-Saving Service Heritage Association. He teaches Great Lakes Maritime History as adjunct faculty at Northern Michigan University and he has appeared as an on-air expert for the History Channel and National Geographic Channel, as well as numerous regional media productions. He resides in Marquette, Michigan, with his wife, Lois, and his son, Brandon. See www.frederickstonehouse.com for more details.

Also from Lake Superior Port Cities Inc.

Haunted Lakes (the original)
by Frederick Stonehouse
Softcover: ISBN 0-942235-30-4

Haunted Lakes II
by Frederick Stonehouse
Softcover: ISBN 0-942235-39-8

Wreck Ashore: United States Life-Saving Service, Legendary Heroes of the Great Lakes
by Frederick Stonehouse
Softcover: ISBN 0-942235-58-4

Shipwreck of the Mesquite
by Frederick Stonehouse
Softcover: ISBN 0-942235-10-X

Haunted Lake Michigan
by Frederick Stonehouse
Softcover: ISBN 0-942235-72-X

Julius F. Wolff Jr.'s Lake Superior Shipwrecks
by Julius F. Wolff Jr.
Hardcover: ISBN 0-942235-02-9
Softcover: ISBN 0-942235-01-0

Shipwrecks of Lake Superior, Second Edition
by James R. Marshall
Softcover: ISBN 0-942235-67-3

Lake Superior Journal: Views from the Bridge
by James R. Marshall
Softcover: ISBN 0-942235-40-1

The Night the Fitz *Went Down*
by Hugh E. Bishop
Softcover: ISBN 0-942235-37-1

By Water and Rail: A History of Lake County, Minnesota
by Hugh E. Bishop
Hardcover: ISBN 0-942235-48-7
Softcover: ISBN 0-942235-42-8

Haunted Lake Superior
by Hugh E. Bishop
Softcover: ISBN 0-942235-55-X

Lake Superior, The Ultimate Guide to the Region
by Hugh E. Bishop
Softcover: ISBN 0-942235-66-5

Haunted Minnesota
by Hugh E. Bishop
Softcover: ISBN 0-942235-71-1

Michigan Gold, Mining in the Upper Peninsula
by Daniel R. Fountain
Softcover: ISBN 0-942235-15-0

Minnesota's Iron Country
by Marvin G. Lamppa
Softcover: ISBN 0-942235-56-8

Betty's Pies Favorite Recipes
by Betty Lessard
Softcover: ISBN 0-942235-50-9

Shipwrecks of Isle Royale National Park
by Daniel Lenihan
Softcover: ISBN 0-942235-18-5

Schooners, Skiffs & Steamships: Stories along Lake Superior Water Trails
by Howard Sivertson
Hardcover: ISBN 0-942235-51-7

Tales of the Old North Shore
by Howard Sivertson
Hardcover: ISBN 0-942235-29-0

The Illustrated Voyageur
by Howard Sivertson
Hardcover: ISBN 0-942235-43-6

Once Upon an Isle: The Story of Fishing Families on Isle Royale
by Howard Sivertson
Hardcover: ISBN 0-9624369-3-3

Superior Way, Third Edition
by Bonnie Dahl
Softcover: ISBN 0-942235-49-5

Lake Superior Magazine (Bimonthly)

Lake Superior Travel Guide (Annual)

Lake Superior Wall Calendar (Annual)

Lake Superior Mini Wall Calendar (Annual)

Lake Superior Wall Map

Lake Superior Map Placemats

Lake Superior Puzzles

For a catalog of the entire Lake Superior Port Cities collection of books and merchandise, write or call:

Lake Superior Port Cities Inc.
P.O. Box 16417 • Duluth, MN 55816

1-888-BIG LAKE (888-244-5253)
218-722-5002
FAX 218-722-4096

E-mail: guide@lakesuperior.com
www.lakesuperior.com